TWO TUDOR
CONSPIRACIES

TWO TUDOR CONSPIRACIES

BY

D. M. LOADES

Lecturer in History in the University of Durham

CAMBRIDGE

AT THE UNIVERSITY PRESS

1965

PUBLISHED BY

THE SYNDICS OF THE CAMBRIDGE UNIVERSITY PRESS

Bentley House, 200 Euston Road, London, N.W. 1
American Branch: 32 East 57th Street, New York, N.Y. 10022
West African Office: P.O. Box 33, Ibadan, Nigeria

© CAMBRIDGE UNIVERSITY PRESS

1965

Library of Congress Catalogue Card Number: 65-11204

Printed in Great Britain by
Willmer Brothers & Haram Limited, Chester Street, Birkenhead

CONTENTS

TO THE MEMORY OF
MY FATHER

PREFACE

The opposition to Mary Tudor's government is a subject which has been more remarked upon than studied. With the exception of the invaluable work done before the war by E. Harris Harbison, there has been no scholarly treatment of the reign, as distinct from biographies of Mary and Elizabeth, since Professor A. F. Pollard wrote the sixth volume of *The Political History of England*. Any understanding of the period must begin with an understanding of the circumstances and motives relevant to the conflict which developed between Mary and a significant proportion of her subjects. Such an understanding can only be sought among the conspiracies and turmoils of the reign, and the government's reaction to them.

The first part of this book, dealing with the conspiracy and rebellion of Sir Thomas Wyatt, was awarded the Prince Consort Prize in the University of Cambridge in 1962; and it is in the first place to the Trustees of the Prince Consort Fund that I owe the opportunity of publishing it. My thanks are due to many for their help and co-operation at different times over the last five years: to the staffs of the Public Record Office, the British Museum and the Cambridge University Library; to my forbearing colleagues at Queen's College, Dundee, where the latter part was written; to Dr Gerald Harris for reading the proofs, and offering much helpful advice; and above all to Dr G. R. Elton, who presided over the beginnings of my research, and whose advice and encouragement have been invaluable. Portions of the Wyatt MSS are printed by kind permission of the Earl of Romney, and the portrait of Sir Thomas Wyatt is reproduced by courtesy of the National Portrait Gallery.

In quotations I have adhered to the form of the source used, except for the expansion of some abbreviations which might obscure the meaning. In dating I have used the modern system throughout.

University College, Durham,   D.M.L.
July 1964

of Fortescue—the *dominium politicum et regale*—but, by promulgating the Royal Supremacy, they rendered it inadequate as an exposition of the King's authority. That Supremacy may have made very little practical difference to ecclesiastical appointments and administration, but without it neither the dissolution of the monasteries nor the legislated Reformation of 1549 could have taken place. When the Crown absorbed the jurisdiction of the church, it inevitably became something different. The King was then ultimately responsible for both the spiritual and the temporal welfare of his subjects. To the modern mind the claim to sovereignty is logically inescapable, but no such claim was made at the time. It was merely recognized that the Crown had taken another long step away from feudal limitation; there could no longer be any equation made between the *dominium* of the King and the *dominium* of the feudal lord. There was nothing new in this distinction, i[t] had been growing clearer for centuries, but Henry's actio[n] implied a final break which even the most conservative we[re] forced to recognise. It could be, and was maintained that t[he] was in accordance with the ancient traditions of theocr[atic] kingship, but such an explanation raised serious difficultie[s of] its own. This was made clear by Christopher St Germa[n, a] lawyer and royal publicist who wrote a number of pam[phlets] in defence of the Royal Supremacy. St German was care[ful to] point out that the King was subject to the law in ter[poral] matters, and that he must therefore remain subject to lim[itation] in the exercise of his new authority.[1] Thomas Starkey m[ade the] same point in his 'Dialogue between Pole and Lupset':[2] [the] King may '. . . dispense with the common laws . . [. an] open gate to all tyranny . . .'.[2] No one would have [thought] least of all Henry himself, that he was free from th[e] bility to act in the interests of the common we[al. That this] responsibility was inherent in the whole concept o[f] ent law. What this meant in practice, howeve[r]

[1] Christopher St German, *An answer to a letter* (and other works)
S.T.C. 21559—21588.
[2] 'Dialogue', edited by K. M. Burton, London 1948, p. 101.

obscure. For St German the traditional supremacy of statute offered an answer of sorts. The extended authority of the Crown should be controlled by extending the competence of Parliament; the supreme authority of the realm should not be the proper person of the King, but the King-in-Parliament. Unfortunately St German never elaborated upon this proposition, nor explained what the relationship between the Crown and the Parliament ought to be. The medieval Parliament had an established legal function which did not appear to lend itself to the exercise of an effective control over public policy.

The extension of the royal authority which resulted from the crisis of the early 1530's thus removed a number of traditional landmarks, without immediately replacing them with new ones. At the same time social and administrative developments turned what might have been an abstract issue into one of great practical importance. The 'increase of governance' which characterized the whole century had already begun to make the country more aware of the royal power, when this awareness was suddenly and greatly increased by the dissolution of the monasteries. In 1549 this was followed by the introduction of the protestant faith by a group of noble councillors wielding the power of the state in the name of a boy king. The implications of Henry's revolution could not have been more clearly demonstrated, and the result was rebellion. However, the rebels, particularly the leaders of the Pilgrimage of Grace, rapidly found themselves in an impossible position. They accepted the King's authority over the church, but objected to the way in which he used it, taking refuge in the usual medieval scapegoat of 'evil counsel'. There was, of course, no traditional or customary law to appeal to in this matter, so when the King refused to be coerced the rebels were faced with the choice of fighting to a finish or giving up. This was precisely the situation which St German had feared; where the royal authority was not clearly limited by human law, it could be restrained only by a successful appeal to force. Force meant rebellion, and rebellion was a grievous moral and social evil. Kett's followers in 1549 showed that this problem could be carried into secular politics, and the more society and government changed, the more frequently would such issues arise.

By 1553 it was already becoming apparent that the relationship between the monarch and the 'Commonwealth', represented by an increasingly conscious political class, would have to be adjusted both in theory and practice to meet changing conditions. The reign of Mary forced this issue to a crisis of which the whole country became aware.

II

When the Queen came to the throne in the troubled summer of 1553, she was conscious of the revolutionary changes which had taken place in English government only to the extent of recognizing her father's usurpation of the ecclesiastical power. She was not aware that by that act he had diverted the royal authority onto a new path. The act itself could be undone, but the consequences could not. Mary, it is clear, was not aware of the uncertainty over the nature and extent of her authority which prevailed among politically conscious Englishmen. The ease and completeness of her triumph over Northumberland had confounded every prophet. Just after Edward's death, her cousin's ambassadors in London had assessed her chances gloomily.[1] The Duke held the Tower, the treasury and arsenal of the kingdom; the Council was at his command; he had men, ships and artillery. There was little chance, they wrote, that one woman could prevail against such power, however legitimate her claim. There were many who hated her for her adherence to Rome, and the preachers were busy in London proclaiming the dangers of an unmarried queen. Yet within two weeks Northumberland's power was broken without a blow being struck, and Mary entered London in triumph. Catholics all over western Europe proclaimed a miracle, and many, including the Queen, assumed with facile optimism that

---

[1] Ambassadors to the Emperor, 14 July 1553. *Cal. Span.* Vol. XI, p. 89.

England's better nature had at last rejected innovation in favour of the good old ways. Her victory certainly resulted from the will of the people, and as such it made a profound impression on all who witnessed it, but the uncomplicated symbolism by which it was interpreted bore little relation to the tangled circumstances which lay behind it.

The English wanted Mary as Queen rather than the protégé of the hated Northumberland. This preference was temporarily strong enough to subdue doubts as to how she would use her position, but certainly not strong enough to remove them. Her personal claim to the throne was enthusiastically endorsed, but it was soon apparent that this did not amount to a mandate for any particular policy. Mary regarded her triumph as acceptance, not only of herself, but of all she stood for. Her personal *dominium* and her public policy were therefore inseparable, and the fact that her subjects accepted one and rejected the other could only result in a crisis of great bitterness and confusion. Northumberland's position had been far less strong than was generally supposed. He had alienated the commons by his support of the enclosing gentry, and most of his associates by his extreme arrogance. The only group which expressed an unfeigned admiration for him was the extreme wing of the protestant party, to whose beliefs he professed allegiance for reasons of his own. He was also handicapped by the obvious nature of his manipulations. Not only had he proposed to divert the succession in his own interest, but into his own family. No amount of specious argument could disguise these pretensions, or conceal the fact that the legitimate heir was being defrauded. If Northumberland supposed that legitimacy could be overcome by an acceptable 'party platform', backed by vested interests, then he was a century and a half in advance of his time. The motives which were to replace the Stuarts with the house of Hanover had little force in 1553. The author of that doggerel epic 'The legende of Sir Nicholas Throgmorton' put into the mouth of his hero a sentiment which must have been typical of the attitude of those who had the most cause to distrust

Mary, the protestants,

> And though I lik'd nott the Religion
> Which all her life Queene Marye had profest,
> Yett in my mind that wicked Motion,
> Right heirs for to displace I didd detest.[1]

A similar sentiment, but showing more of the common man's hatred of the Duke, was expressed by the author of the pseudonymous letter of 'poore Pratte' to Gilbert Potter, published in London during the crisis.[2] Whatever Mary might herself have thought, the credit for her success was almost entirely due to the power of Tudor legitimacy, and the violent unpopularity of her opponents.

Two months after her accession the Imperial Ambassador, Simon Renard, described her as ' . . . good, easily influenced, inexpert in worldly matters, and a novice all round.'[3] She needed all the Divine protection in which she so firmly believed. The times demanded statesmanship of a high order. The social unrest which had produced the risings of 1548–9 was alleviated, but not cured, by the fall of Northumberland. A firm and independent policy would be required if the Crown was not to become again the pawn of a faction, and forfeit the confidence of those who looked to it for relief. Equally dangerous, and more immediately apparent, was the religious strife. Nobody knew how strong the respective parties were, but the ultra-protestants would not tamely surrender their positions of power, or willingly accept the overthrow of their achievements. Most of Mary's catholic supporters agreed that the kingdom was rotten with heresy, and no one who knew her doubted that the restoration of England to the church was closest to her heart.[4] The Queen's character, with its mixture of innocence

---

[1] Add. MS 5841, f. 272. There are several copies of this poem. The author is unknown. It is printed in an edition of 1874, edited by J. G. Nichols.

[2] *The copie of a pistel or letter sent to Gilbard Potter, in the tyme when he was in prison for speakinge on our most true quenes part, the Lady Mary.* Printed by H. Singleton. 20188 in the *S.T.C.*

[3] Simon Renard to the Bishop of Arras, 9 September 1553. *Cal. Span.* Vol. XI, p. 228.

[4] For instance, Renard wrote in the same letter: ' . . . and she has no thought but to restore the Mass and religion, which will also provoke attacks if God does not remedy it.'

and obstinacy, did not bode well for the peaceful solution of these problems.

Many also feared that they had not heard the last of the Suffolk succession. The remnants of the Dudley faction, reinforced by dispossessed reformers, might seek a favourable moment to reverse the decision of July. Foremost among these pessimists was Renard. He had no respect for the English, regarding the gentry as venal adventurers and the commons as 'capricious seekers after novelty'. They might, in his opinion, at any moment change their minds, and remove the Queen as easily as they had raised her. Nor did he have to look far for the possible inspirers of such a *volte face*. In August 1553 he wrote: ' . . . I have scented out that the French, their partisans and the Lutherans are doing their utmost to discover means of robbing the Queen of her subjects' affection, and brewing discord in the realm.'[1] The French distrusted Mary because of her Imperial connections, and for that reason had promised help to Northumberland which had never materialized. England's prestige was so low in Europe that both the major powers hoped to control the country through the person of its ruler, and it was quite clear where Mary's sympathies lay. However, fearing for the stability of her regime, Renard early recommended his master to build up his position by bribery and promises before the French should do the same.[2] Only a strong Imperial party, he considered, could keep the Queen upon her tottering throne.

The Ambassador was right in his suspicion of French intentions, but wrong in his estimate of the domestic situation. Mary's position was much less precarious than he supposed. Like many other observers, Renard fell into the error of measuring her security by the observable support for what she did, rather than for what she was. Many times during the reign both he and his French counterpart, Antoine de Noailles, looked at the mounting hostility towards the Queen's religious and dynastic policy, and assumed that her days were numbered.

[1] Renard to the Bishop of Arras, 15 August 1553. *Cal. Span.* Vol. XI, p. 166.

[2] Ibid. 'It must be remembered, my Lord, that it will be difficult to bring the Council and country to consent (to the marriage) unless the leading men are won over with offers, money, promises and the like. . . .'

On this assumption they both spent liberally, both money and energy, on bribery and the fostering of intrigue—only to reap frustration and anger. There was a bitter tension beneath the surface as Englishmen tried to decide how far, and in what matters, they were prepared to obey their Queen without calling her to account. The factions and interests upon which foreigners were wont to base their calculations were not irrelevant to this problem, but were transcended by it. In the event Mary survived; but to assume that this survival was inevitable, and the opposition to her of little significance, would be to make as great an error as Renard and Noailles. The crisis was genuine, and the issues important. By studying it in detail, and at its acutest phases, we can learn a good deal about its nature, and its relevance to the development of Tudor government and society.

III

Within a few days of her accession Mary demonstrated her incapacity by creating a large and heterogeneous Council, which was to cause trouble and discord for the remainder of her reign. The *ad hoc* Council which had gathered around her at Kenninghall and Framlingham consisted of loyal Catholic familiars whose services she could not ignore. They were for the most part men such as Sir Robert Rochester and Sir Edward Waldegrave,[1] of unimpeachable antecedents, but lacking the stature or ability to determine matters of high policy. To them was added a large proportion of Edward's Council, those such as the Earls of Arundel and Shrewsbury who had abandoned Northumberland at the eleventh hour, and demanded the price of their allegiance. The Queen did not trust these men, but she could not afford to alienate them, and their recent experience of affairs made them indispensable. In addition there were

---

[1] Both these men had been household servants of Mary for a number of years, and had suffered imprisonment in the Fleet in 1551 for conniving at her private Mass. Rochester's grandfather (also Robert) had been yeoman of the pantry to Henry VIII. Waldegrave was the second son of John Waldegrave of Borley, in Essex, and was Rochester's nephew (*DNB*).

others whose sufferings for the sake of religion demanded compensation: the old Duke of Norfolk; Thirlby, Tunstall,[1] and Stephen Gardiner. The last named, restored to his See of Winchester, sworn of the Council and appointed Lord Chancellor within a few days of his release from the Tower, was almost the only man of ability brought into a position of authority by the new regime. Many leaders of the defeated party, notably Northumberland himself, Cranmer, and the Marquis of Northampton,[2] lost their seats, but by September 1553 the Council had swollen to the monstrous size of nearly 50.[3] Although the great majority of this unwieldly body never attended its meetings, it was so composed that its active membership included the leaders of all the important factions which the disputes of the reign were to create. These factions began to make their appearance even before the Queen was crowned, and in spite of some kaleidoscopic changes, defied all attempts to eradicate them. In a letter to Philip dated 10 March 1558, Count Feria repeated the by then familiar lamentations:

They change everything they have decided, and it is impossible to make them see what a state they are in. . . . They do nothing but raise difficulties, whatever one proposes, and never find any remedy . . . numbers cause great confusion . . . Figueroa and I went to the Queen . . . to warn her of the danger to her person and kingdom caused by these incompetent Councillors.[4]

The councillors were not as incompetent as Feria believed, and much of his annoyance was caused by the fact that they had no desire to comply with his wishes. They were, however, beset with uncertainty and bitterly divided, so that the impotence of the English Council was common knowledge among European diplomats.

At such a difficult time, and under a ruler of such limited attainments, this situation was little short of disastrous. Mary

---

[1] Thomas Thirlby, Bishop of Norwich, and Cuthbert Tunstall, Bishop of Durham.
[2] William Parr, brother of Catherine, Henry's last Queen. He was pardoned, but lost his rank and the greater part of his estates.
[3] For a detailed account of the Council changes at this time see A. F. Pollard, *Political History of England*, Vol. VI, pp. 94–5.
[4] *Cal. Span.* Vol. XIII, p. 366.

inherited no strong minister, and lacked the discrimination to appoint one, so that her own limitations were ruthlessly exposed. She was permanently conscious of her inadequacy, and this consciousness added to the unhappiness of her singularly unfortunate life. A woman of exemplary piety and domestic instincts, who would have made an excellent housewife, she was compelled to wrestle with problems which would have baffled much wiser heads. She was frequently ill with worry, sometimes prostrate with grief and frustration, and ever and anon gave way to ill-considered bursts of rage. Naturally, one of her first preoccupations on coming to the throne was to find a husband who would share the burden of her responsibilities, and supply her lack of political acumen. In the forced seclusion of her upbringing, and the trials of her adult life, Mary had always been taught to look to her Imperial kinsfolk for aid and support; particularly to her cousin, the Emperor Charles V. At the climax of her life she instinctively looked in the same direction, to the only people in whom she had implicit trust. The result was her marriage to Philip of Spain, a personal failure and a political catastrophe.

Not only did the Queen derive small comfort and little support from her consort, but she found his position in England a more unavoidable and explosive issue than any which she had inherited. It raised in an emphatic form the vital problems of the succession and the alienability of the royal authority. This was the substance of the crisis which shook England between 1553 and 1558. The uncertainties which surrounded the royal power, legal and theoretical in their nature, were given form and identity by the threat of Spanish rule. Spanish soldiers in billets; Spanish officials in office; Spanish wars to be fought; at the command of an English Queen but recently raised to the throne on a wave of popular enthusiasm! The

---

[1] Frederick Dietz's work, *The Finances of Edward VI and Mary* (Smith College Studies in History, January 1918), is by no means complete, and has not been satisfactorily revised. Contemporaries were insistent that poverty greatly weakened the government, and that attempts to remedy it added to the opposition and discontent.

situation was aggravated and exploited by interested propaganda, confused by religious passion, and complicated by chronic poverty,[1] but to explore every aspect of such an all-embracing problem would require a far greater work than this. What I have endeavoured to do in the pages which follow, is to present two climactic and closely linked episodes which between them bring out the major implications of the crisis, and give some instructive glances at the grass roots of English politics.

I

THE MARRIAGE AND THE CONSPIRACY

I

Long and complicated negotiations were brought to an end on 12 January 1554 by the signing of the Anglo-Spanish marriage treaty. The initiative for this treaty had come from the Emperor, who had first intimated the possibility of such a match to his Commissioners in London at the end of July 1553, as soon as it was clear that Mary had defeated Northumberland's attempt to deprive her of the succession. It was by such means that the Habsburgs were wont to extend their power, and the strenuous opposition of the French was inevitable. For that reason, and because of the well-known touchiness of the English, the greatest secrecy was observed. Philip himself was not consulted until some time after the first moves had been made, and Charles carefully entrusted the negotiations to one of his Commissioners, Simon Renard. The remainder were withdrawn, together with the Ambassador previously resident.

Renard proceeded with caution and skill during September and October, gradually hardening his hints into proposals as the Queen responded. To persuade Mary, it was soon apparent, was the least of his tasks. On 29 October, after much prayer and distress, she yielded to her personal inclinations, and decided to accept Philip as her husband. To one of her pious and emotional nature such a decision was equivalent to an act of dedication, and thereafter Renard was able to proceed in his negotiations secure in the knowledge of her support. He had no illusions as to the difficulty of his task. Not only was the country as a whole hostile, but he was confronted with the determined opposition of the French Ambassador, Noailles, and of the powerful 'patriot' faction on the Council, led by Gardiner. French opposition was mainly negative, for Henri II had no alternative candidate to advance, but the Chancellor and his followers united in support of Edward Courtenay, the newly created Earl of Devon. Courtenay was of royal blood, being a great grandson of Edward IV through Margaret, Countess of Salisbury. His name had been connected with that of the Queen before the Emperor's proposal was known, even to Renard; but he had been in prison since his childhood, and was inexperienced, weak, and foolish. Gardiner's opposition was not altogether a loss to Renard, since he had enemies of his own, who were jealous of him, or feared his influence. These enemies naturally tended to support the Ambassador, and Renard gained a valuable ally within the Council in the person of Lord Paget,[1] whose ambitions he soon succeeded in identifying with his master's cause.

Outside the Council, and the inner circle of the court, Courtenay was very popular. He had had no opportunity to make himself disliked, and he seemed to those who did not know him well the ideal answer to the unprecedented problem of a ruling Queen. The doubts occasioned by Mary's unmarried state and her Habsburg affiliations, which had been suppressed during the succession crisis, burst out again as soon as it was over, and Renard knew well enough that the knowledge of his negotiations would be a confirmation of the worst to most Englishmen. Some news may have leaked out, or shrewd guesswork been responsible, but over a month before Mary finally made up her mind rumours were circulating that she would marry the Prince of Spain. Under these circumstances, breaking the news of her decision was an exceedingly difficult matter, and at first Mary proceeded with caution. On 8 November she gave a formal but secret audience to Renard, at which he proposed the conclusion of a marriage treaty, and she intimated her acceptance of the proposal. The interview was carefully managed. Only five councillors were present, and of those five only Gardiner was a known opponent of the match. Rather surprisingly, Renard seems to have regarded the silence

---

[1] Renard to the Emperor, 5 October 1553. *Cal. Span.* Vol. XI, p. 265.

of this selected audience as representing the consent of the Council.[1] Meanwhile, circumstantial rumours had reached Noailles, convincing him that his rival had won the Queen. He did not know of the secret audience, and was uncertain what to do. A hostile gesture might precipitate the very situation which he feared, but at the same time he wished to be in a position to encourage opposition to the marriage, in whatever form it should appear.[2]

The basis of this doubt was removed just over a week later, on 16 November, when the House of Commons presented a petition, begging the Queen to marry within the realm. This petition had been drawn up at the end of October, and a deputation had sought to present it before the Queen's audience to Renard. Indeed, awareness of the petition probably played a large part in bringing the audience about. Mary prevaricated, and pleaded illness, putting the Commons off until the ground had been cut from under their feet. When the Speaker and his fellow-representatives appeared before the Queen, they were not aware that their cause was already lost. Their intentions were serious, and they had behind them a weighty body of opinion, both official and popular. Mary's reaction was singularly unfortunate. Being devoid of both guile and tact, she interrupted the Speaker, Sir John Pollard, in the midst of his discourse. Rebuking the Commons sharply for their presumption, she added petulantly that

. . . to force her to take a husband who would not be to her liking would be to cause her death, for if she were married against her will she would not live three months, and would have no children.[3]

Baffled by this display of femininity, the deputation retired discomfited, and Gardiner was roughly handled by the Queen for his supposed complicity in the framing of the petition. Thereafter it was clear to all that the Chancellor and his party

---

[1] The other councillors present were Paget, Arundel, Petre and Thirlby (later Ambassador to the Emperor). Renard to the Emperor, 8 November 1553. *Cal. Span.* Vol. XI, p. 349.

[2] E.g. his letter to the King, 9 November 1553. Vertot, Vol. II, p. 239.

[3] Renard to the Emperor, 17 November 1553. *Cal. Span.* Vol. XI, p. 364. Gardiner seems to have accepted the decision loyally, but with a bad grace.

had been defeated, and that the Queen's heart was set on the
Spanish marriage.

II

The opponents of the match were left in great difficulty. Mary's
decision was a personal one to which she was totally committed;
deaf to arguments of expediency and public policy. Both
Gardiner and Noailles continued to hope, down to the middle
of December, that diplomacy and constant representations
might deter her,[1] but they were deceived. By then it was
apparent that the only alternatives were to accept the situation
and make the best of it, or to resist by force. There had been
talk of a rising even before the petition was presented, but it was
probably the Queen's behaviour on that occasion which led to
the formation of a definite conspiracy. Of all the great many
who disliked the Spanish connection, only a few were prepared
to carry their opposition to such an extremity. The catholic
supporters of Gardiner, such as Waldegrave and Rochester,
realised that any assault upon Mary would play into the hands
of that small faction of the protestant party which favoured
violent measures, and would inevitably lead to attacks upon
the priesthood and the religious settlement. Those nobles, such
as Northampton, Pembroke and Arundel, who had followed
Northumberland, and whose star was their own interest, had
suffered a very narrow escape, and were not in the mood for
further adventures. Consequently the leadership of the extremists devolved upon a group of lesser men with more resolution,
and more to gain.

This group met together in London on 26 November to
discuss plans for a rising. Those present, according to the indictment later found,[2] were Sir Peter Carew, Sir James Croftes,
Sir Nicholas Arnold, Sir William Pickering, William Winter,
Sir Edward Rogers, Sir Thomas Wyatt, Sir George Harper and

---

[1] Noailles was at one stage of the opinion that the storm of opposition which the
proposed treaty had aroused would force the Queen to abandon the marriage.
E.g. his letter to the King of 24 November 1553. Vertot, Vol. II, p. 271.

[2] KB27/1174 Rex V.

William Thomas. They were all men of substance and influence, and most of them had held office in the previous reign. Winter had been appointed Surveyor of the Navy in 1549, a post which he still held; Rogers was a Principal Gentleman of the Privy Chamber in the same year; and Thomas had been Clerk to the Privy Council. Pickering had been Northumberland's Ambassador in France, and Croftes had held, among other posts, that of Lord Deputy of Ireland from 1551 to 1552. A different version of the indictment[1] also includes the names of Sir Edward Warner, who had held the Tower for Northumberland in July 1553, and Sir Nicholas Throgmorton, who had dallied with both sides during that dangerous period.[2] Although Carew and Wyatt, who had been adherents of Somerset, were among the first to declare for Mary, all the conspirators had been prominent supporters of one or other of the Edwardian regimes. Apart from Thomas, who was a well-known and enthusiastic protestant,[3] their religious affiliations were shadowy. All had conformed without protest under Edward, and those still alive were to do so again under Elizabeth, but throughout the period of the conspiracy, and of the rebellion and trials which followed it, all protested their loyalty to the Catholic Church. Other evidence is suggestive, but by no means conclusive. Carew had been specially recalled by the Protector from his wife's estates in Lincolnshire to help put down the Catholic rising in his native Devon in 1549, but he was a skilled soldier and his own interests were at stake.[4] John Proctor, the author of the *Historie of Wyate's rebellion*, declared that Sir Thomas was a protestant, but Proctor was consciously attempting to prove that heresy was the root of all treason. Sir Thomas's son George also recorded that his father had been a staunch protestant, but he was writing in the 1580's,

---

[1] KB8/29.

[2] It was supposedly Throgmorton who warned Mary of her brother's death, and so enabled her to escape. Otherwise he is known as an adherent of Northumberland. See *DNB*.

[3] See his several tracts written for King Edward's guidance, printed in Strype, Vol. II, (2), pp. 21-9, 59-78.

[4] See Frances Rose-Troup, *The Western Rebellion of 1549*, London, 1913.

and had been only three years old at the time to which he was referring.[1] In view of his father's association with Cromwell and the Boleyns it is unlikely that Wyatt was brought up in the conservative tradition, but more than that cannot be said.

At some unspecified time before Christmas, this group was joined by the Duke of Suffolk. Unlike Northumberland, he had made no pretence of conversion to the Catholic faith, and on 1 November Renard had reported that the Queen was angry with him for 'bad work in connection with religion'.[2] He was probably a sincere protestant, but of all those who had taken advantage of the Queen's clemency the previous summer, his escape had been the least justifiable, and since then he had lived in an understandably acute state of insecurity. It seems that, when approached, he threw in his lot with the mal-contents, partly in a desperate bid to repair his fortunes, and partly out of genuine antipathy to the catholic reaction.

As a group, however, the conspirators seem to have been as indifferent to doctrinal issues as to the blasts which churchmen of both persuasions directed against the evils of rebellion. To that extent their claim to orthodoxy was justified. On the other hand most of them probably believed that the Pope's authority was usurped and evil, not doubting that if it was again acknow-ledged many uncomfortable questions would be asked about the doings of the previous twenty years. The background of the conspiracy was thus secular and anti-clerical rather than protestant. The conspirators main concern, however, was with the threat of Spanish domination. The Council might try to temper the effects of the Queen's obstinacy by extracting a favourable treaty, but the fear in every mind was expressed by an anonymous member of the House of Commons at the end of November:

In case . . . the Bands should be broken between the Husband and

---

[1] Wyatt MSS, no. 10, ff. 3–8, a vindication of Wyatt, by his son, in the course of which he says that his father was known by the Queen to be a protestant but was not molested, because of his good services against Northumberland. George also states that at the time of the rising Sir Thomas had a royal licence to go abroad (f. 7), but I can find no evidence to support this.

[2] Renard to the Emperor. *Cal. Span.* Vol. XI, p. 332.

the Wife, either of them being Princes in their own Country, who shall sue the Bands? Who shall take the Forfeit? Who shall be their Judges? And what shall be the Advantage?[1]

No treaty reservations could remove the suspicion that once the Spaniards arrived in England they would take the government into their own hands and do as pleased themselves. Not only was this prospect abhorrent on patriotic grounds, but it would also mean that the profits of office and the fruits of patronage would be engrossed by the foreigners and their creatures instead of being distributed among the deserving English gentry. It would be unfair to dismiss these suspicions as groundless, for Philip's reaction on receiving the final draft of the treaty on 4 January was to sign a secret clause absolving himself from the necessity of observing its provisions.[2]

When Parliament was dissolved on 6 December the conspirators' plans were still nebulous. Their main strength lay in having a large circle of influential friends and contacts, but for fear of premature disclosures they do not seem to have made any attempt to build up a party among the members, and the dissolution deprived them of the opportunity. Consequently they were thrown back upon their own resources. Croftes, Carew, Wyatt, and Arnold were all men of standing in their own counties, and the last three had been Sheriffs of Devon, Kent and Gloucestershire respectively. Rogers was in the confidence of Courtenay, and seems to have been associated with the Earl of Arundel.[3] Croftes and Throgmorton had access to Princess Elizabeth, and seem to have been welcome visitors.[4] They were connected by marriage with each other, and with men in the confidence of the government such as Lord Cobham and Dr Nicholas Wotton, the Ambassador in France. At the beginning of December there were two possible courses open to them. Either they could use their contacts in and around

---

[1] Strype, Vol. III, p. 55.

[2] A writing 'ad cautelam' to this effect is enclosed with the copy of the marriage treaty preserved at Simancas. *Cal. Span.*, Vol. XII, p. 4.

[3] *DNB*. He was sufficiently intimate with the Earl to have been involved in his misdemeanours in January 1550.

[4] Harbison, p. 112.

the Court to try and bring about a palace revolution, or else they could rely upon their local influence to stimulate a popular rising. The main obstacle to either was the uncertainty of their objectives. It was futile to imagine that Mary could be coerced into changing her policy and left in possession of her throne. The conspirators were early agreed that she must be removed, but as to how, and in whose favour, there was no agreement. From the evidence which later emerged at their trials we can piece together something of the debates which were held during November and December. William Thomas, who was probably the initial ringleader by virtue of being the most radical and determined, proposed that the Queen should be assassinated,

. . . who brake the matter to master John Fytzwilliams, that he sholde have done the dede; this Fytzwilliams denyed the same; at last he was half determyned to shewe the same to sir Nicholas Arnolde, and dyd, who moche dyscomended the facte, and tolde yt to maister Croftes, who also tolde it to maister Wyat; and they bothe detest(ed) the horryblenes of the cryme. . . .[1]

Whether or not his colleagues reacted as violently as they later pretended, his proposal was rejected and the leadership seems to have passed to Sir James Croftes. If, as was now inevitable, they should aim to depose Mary, the only practicable substitute was Elizabeth. However, as the conspiracy had grown out of the attempt to persuade the Queen to marry Courtenay, and he was at least aware of its existence, a place had to be found for him. Consequently the policy which was eventually agreed upon was to marry Courtenay to Elizabeth and place them on the throne together.[2] When the time for action came, as we shall see later, this 'platform' was freely subordinated to the immediate needs of the situation, and the real foundation of the conspiracy remained negative rather than positive. At first it had been hoped that Clinton, Pembroke, and perhaps some

---

[1] *Q.J*, p. 69.
[2] The way in which this agreement was reached is nowhere specifically described, but it was during the discussions which took place before Christmas. The idea of a match between Courtenay and Elizabeth had been broached at least as early as the previous August.

other members of Gardiner's faction would co-operate,[1] but by the middle of December this hope was gone. The Duke of Suffolk, supported by his two brothers, Thomas and John, was the only member of the nobility to join the conspirators, and he was not an unqualified asset. This fact, combined with the rejection of Thomas's proposal, led them to abandon the idea of a *coup d'état* and concentrate upon plans for a popular rising.

The implications of any movement directed against Mary made the participation of the French inevitable. As early as the middle of November, before any plans had been made, Noailles was receiving oblique enquiries about the availability of French warships.[2] Thereafter he was in constant touch with the malcontents, but they were forced to approach him with great caution. The French were hardly more popular than the Spaniards, and when Carew suggested that Henri should be asked to supply munitions and money, he was warned to '... beware that he brought any Frenchmen into the realm forcibly, inasmuch as he could as evil abide the Frenchmen after that sort as the Spaniards.'[3] The part played by Noailles in the conspirators' deliberations, and by the expectation of French aid in their plans, has been thoroughly investigated by E. Harris Harbison,[4] and his conclusions need only be briefly summarized. Although Henri very much wished to prevent the Anglo-Spanish alliance, he was sceptical of the power which the English malcontents could raise, and unwilling to weaken his continental position by detaching forces to support them. He was also torn between the conflicting advice of the Constable, Montmorency, who was anxious for an accommodation with the English government, and the Guises who were anxious to overthrow it. Consequently the instructions which Noailles received blew alternately hot and cold, and it was not

---

[1] Mémoir de ce que la Marque aura à dire au roi; 9 November 1553; Vertot, Vol. II, p. 246.

[2] Ibid.

[3] Testimony at the trial of Sir Nicholas Throgmorton. William Cobbett *et al.*, *A Complete collection of State Trials*, London 1816–98, Vol. I, p. 883.

[4] *Rival Ambassadors*, Chapters IV and V, from which the following information is taken.

until 22 January, when it was already too late, that Henri decided to support the coming rebellion unreservedly. The conspirators were unaware of these complications, and seem to have had no doubt that when the time came the French would, out of self-interest, give them whatever support they required. They were therefore in no hurry to take Noailles into their confidence before their plans were complete.

It was not until 22 December that the outline of these plans was agreed upon:[1] a fourfold popular rising, converging upon London. Croftes was to raise his friends and neighbours in Herefordshire; Wyatt in Kent; Carew and Courtenay in Devon, and the Duke of Suffolk in Leicestershire. Palm Sunday, 18 March, was named as the day for action. At this stage Devon seems to have been thought of as the key to the situation. The influence of Courtenay, the strategic importance of the county for the exercise of sea-power in the Channel, and the probability that Philip would make his landfall there, all contributed to that assumption. On 23 December news reached Noailles that the town of Plymouth was actively preparing to resist a Spanish landing,[2] and at about the same time an unnamed Englishman, probably one of the piratical Killigrew brothers, arrived at Fontainebleau offering to bring eight or nine warships into the French service by the end of January.[3] Noailles was keenly alive to the value of sea-power, and believed that it would be possible for the rebels' ships, with French support, to hold the Channel against the Spaniards. Henri, however, was in a cautious mood at the end of December, and ordered his Ambassador to scrutinize Croftes' plans with care.

By this time news of the impending rising had already begun to leak out. Renard and Paget had been on the alert for such an intrigue since the middle of November. The Ambassador's despatches were full of rumours and suspicions. On 11 Decem-

---

[1] Arnold's testimony at Throgmorton's trial, Cobbett, loc. cit.
[2] This news reached Noailles through one of his regular agents, probably Jean de Fontenay, Sieur de Bretville, a naturalized Englishman. It was accompanied by a request for naval assistance to which the Ambassador sent a non-committal reply. Vertot, Vol. II, p. 342.
[3] Harbison, p. 117.

ber he had written ' . . . before Easter . . . there shall be such a
turmoil in England as never was seen', and on the 29th he
reported ' . . . the Queen will not be surprised (through any) lack
of warning from me, for I am doing my utmost in my sphere,
and Paget, who has good spies, is equally active in his'.[1] By
early January Renard knew that there was a plot, woven
with the assistance of the French Ambassador, and centring on
Courtenay and Elizabeth. He did not know the identity of the
conspirators, or any details, and he did not inform the Queen
for fear of alarming her with inadequate information, but he
was on the alert, and his knowledge was dangerous. Much was
likely to depend upon the element of surprise. A swift and
successful blow, bringing promise of a decisive victory, would
encourage the French diplomats and English waverers to show
their hands, setting the seal of Divine approval upon the enterprise. For this reason it was essential for the conspirators to
retain the initiative, and Renard's suspicions threatened them
at their weakest point. Courtenay was a liability rather than
an asset, his impetuosity and instability ill fitting him for the
perils of intrigue. Before the end of November he had been upon
the point of throwing up the game and fleeing overseas; only
Noailles' persuasions had kept him to his purpose.[2] How much
he knew of his friends' plans is obscure, but they were certainly
relying on him to raise his friends and family adherents in
the South West. For that purpose he was in close touch with
Carew, and had begun to collect arms and equipment at his
London home. None of the conspirators had much confidence
in his courage, however, and Noailles several times alluded to
the possibility of his betraying them, and warned them not to
let him know too much. Elizabeth was a very different proposition, but equally a source of danger. Cautious by nature, the
circumstances of her position made her closer still, so that
although Croftes was liberal with promises on her behalf there
has never been any direct evidence that she was associated with
the conspiracy. They used her name freely, because she was

---

[1] Renard to the Emperor. *Cal. Span.* Vol. XI, p. 472.
[2] Noailles to the King, 14 November 1553. Vertot, Vol. II, pp. 253-4, 255-6.

very popular, and she must have been aware of the fact. They wrote to her, but she never replied in writing, and when the crisis was over even her bitterest enemies were forced to admit that nothing could be proved against her. There was talk of her fleeing from Court and riding to the West with Courtenay, but this seems to have been wishful thinking, designed by Croftes to convince Noailles that the plot had that 'foundation' which so much concerned him.[1] There was no risk of Elizabeth losing her nerve, but she would not move until success was assured, and in the face of premature revelations would deny all knowledge of the affair.

On 2 January occurred the first of the three incidents which were to force the conspirators' hands. On that day Sir Peter Carew was summoned to appear before the Council.[2] Carew had gone down to Devon as soon as the necessary decisions had been taken in London, about 23 December. This action was not in itself suspicious, and although he had spoken against the marriage in the recent Parliament, he had supported Mary earlier, and was not a marked man. There is no evidence to show why this summons was issued. It may have been for some quite irrelevant reason, but probably the Council had discovered something of what was afoot. No other summons was issued, so the intelligence must have referred to Carew alone, but it was enough to provoke a crisis. If Sir Peter appeared, there was every chance that the whole story would come out. If he refused to come suspicions might be confirmed, and the rebels forced to act before they were ready, but at least they would not face the prospect of being arrested before any action could be taken at all. Relying upon the slowness of official reactions to give him a breathing space, Carew ignored the summons, and made such preparations as the time allowed. When his defiance was surely known in London, Renard was convinced that he was implicated in the general conspiracy, and feared an immediate outburst. When, on 18 January, news reached him

[1] Harbison, p. 113 et seq.
[2] APC, Vol. IV, p. 382. The entry suggests that this was a repetition of an earlier summons, but there is no trace of such.

that a French fleet was assembling on the Normandy coast, he dared delay no longer. The same day he took the second decisive step by laying all his information before the Queen, and urging her to take immediate steps to protect herself.[1] When the news of this audience reached the conspirators in London, already warned by events in the West, they resolved to act at once. The following day Wyatt and Pickering rode down into Kent, while Croftes remained behind to watch events in the capital.[2] The rising had therefore already begun when Gardiner took the third step. On 21 January he sent for Courtenay, and wormed out of him all that he knew of the affair. How much he learned we do not know, but it was enough to make his position exceedingly difficult. Opposition to the marriage had already cost the Chancellor much of his influence on the Council. If the confessions of his friend and protégé became public property he would not only lose what was left, but might find himself accused of complicity. He therefore suppressed as much as he could of the embarrassing interview, and set out to achieve a settlement by negotiation.

[1] Renard to the Emperor, 18 January 1554. *Cal. Span.* Vol. XII, p. 34.

[2] Noailles to Montmorency, 21 January 1554, Archives du ministère des affaires étrangères (Correspondance Politique, Angleterre), Paris [Ab. Etr.], Vol. IX, f. 120, quoted Harbison, p. 126.

THE ABORTIVE RISINGS: LEICESTERSHIRE AND DEVON

I

When the news of these untimely developments reached the Duke of Suffolk he was at Sheen, apparently quite unprepared for action. How much had been disclosed he did not know, but his own participation was bound to be discovered because it would be at once suspected. Less than two months previously he had been pardoned for his earlier treasons,[1] and this impending disclosure would certainly be fatal to him. Understandably he lost his nerve, and so precipitated his own downfall. It seems that the Council had it in mind to put him to the test by offering him a command in the field against his accomplices; when, however, a messenger arrived on 25 January, summoning him to Court, he interpreted the gesture very differently, and assumed that the axe was already sharpened for him. The Tower chronicler wrote:

Yt is said that the same morning that he was going ther came a messenger to him from the quene, that he shulde come to the court. Marye, quoth he, I was comyng to her grace. Ye may see I am booted and spurred redy to ryde, and I will but breke my fast and go. So he gave the messenger a rewarde, and caused hym to be made to drink, and so thence departed himself, no man knoweth whither.[2]

His friends already knew, and it did not take his enemies long to find out, that his destination was Bradgate, his principal seat in Leicestershire. 'The Duke of Suffolk is on Frydaye also stollen from his howse at Shene, and roone awaye with his ii

---

[1] *Cal. Pat.* Vol. I, p. 194, 27 November 1553.
[2] *Q J*, p. 37.

brethren into Lesystershere, for he was mett at Stony Stratt-
ford.'[1]

Three weeks later, at his trial, the Duke recalled that his
brother Thomas had persuaded him to that course of action,
saying that ' . . . yt was to be feared that he shoulde be put
agayn into the Tower; where, being in his own countrey, and
emongst his frendes and tenauntes, who durst fetch hime?[2]
Leicestershire was his home country, and there, if anywhere,
he could expect to find support, but Thomas must have been
extraordinarily stupid if he really believed that a Tudor government could be defied by such simple means. Renard, always
suspicious of French machinations, believed that it was Noailles
who had persuaded Suffolk.[3] Probably the Ambassador had
added his voice to Thomas's, because it was clearly in his
interest that the Duke should be committed. The Council was
not slow to grasp the significance of his sudden departure. On
the following day, the 26th, the Earl of Huntingdon was despatched to the Midlands with orders to apprehend the fugitives,
and on the same day they were proclaimed traitors.

Here the government displayed none of that timidity and
hesitancy which Renard so much deplored in its dealings with
Wyatt. Some of the circular letters sent into the shires denoun-
cing Suffolk's treason bear the same date as the proclamation,
and on the following day Gardiner wrote to Sir William Petre;

In the mornyng I thought good to serch the mynoresse and
medle's lodging there for letters and among others found a letter
lately wrytten by Harryngton, which Harryngton cam to me this
nyght, and after examination I have taken him tardy by occasion
of that letter, and kepe him with me as a prisoner this nyght,
entending in the mornyng to send him to the towre.[4]

The content of these letters is not disclosed, but clearly

[1] Letter from the Earl of Shrewsbury to the Earl of Arundel. Printed by Edmund
Lodge in *Illustrations of British History*, London 1791, Vol. I, p. 189.
[2] *Q J*, p. 61.
[3] Report of the Imperial Ambassadors, 29 January 1554. *Cal. Span.* Vol. XII,
p. 54.
[4] SP, Vol. II, no. 20. This Harrington was John, father of the author of the
Nugae Antiquae, wherein some of his sufferings at this time are related.

Gardiner's action was not merely the result of a lucky guess. The Council had some knowledge of what was afoot which enabled it to act swiftly at the first overt sign.

Meanwhile the Duke went on his way. His two brothers did not accompany him from Sheen because they were not with him on the 25th, but he sent a message by John Bowyer, one of his secretaries, requesting them to join him at St Albans.[1] This they attempted to do, but apparently lost the way, since in his letter already quoted Gardiner declared that Harrington told him

. . . howe upon fridaye at nyght the Lord John Gray cam to Cheston, where master Wroth and he was, and spake with Master Wroth and him to get a gyde to leade him the waye to Saincte Albons, bicause he was commanded by the quene, he said, to levye men in his countrie in al hast.[2]

As a result they missed the Duke at St Albans, and did not come up with him until they reached Lutterworth. At Lutterworth they stopped 'two nights and a day', presumably to do some recruiting, but without much success. Bishop Cooper asserted some years later that ' . . . in divers places as he went (he) again proclaimed his daughter; but ye people did not greatly incline onto him'.[3] The second part of this statement was certainly true, but the first, as well as being directly denied by Holinshed, is intrinsically improbable. Lady Jane was in the hands of the government, her cause was tainted by its association with the odious Northumberland, and a much better rallying cry was to be found in resistance to the Spaniard. Bowyer, who was with the lords throughout the journey, and later confessed their intention to 'go upon the Spaniard with all their power', made no mention of Jane, and the Duke's later behaviour confirms the absence of any such intention. Cooper recorded the official attitude, which was naturally not going to admit that the malcontents might possess a genuine grievance.

---

[1] Second deposition of John Bowyer, SP, Vol. XIII, no. 26.

[2] SP, Vol. II, no. 20. 'Mr Wroth' was almost certainly Sir Thomas Wrothe, who escaped into exile shortly after this letter was written. Garrett, p. 344.

[3] Thomas Cooper, Bishop of Winchester, *Chronicle*, London 1565, p. 363.

A letter sent to the Sheriff and Justices of Gloucestershire on 28 January expressed this attitude more fully.

The Duke of Suffolk forgetting his duty to God . . . and mercy showed . . . has, with John Gray and Thomas Gray his brethren, and Carews, and Wyatt of Kent, and others, conspired to stir our subjects to rebellion, pretending upon false promises that the Prince of Spain and the Spaniards should come over to conquer this said realm, while indeed they traytorously purpose to advance Lady Jane his daughter, and Guildford Dudley her husband. . . . [1]

The Justices were instructed to disabuse the people by proclaiming the terms of the marriage treaty, and to raise 500 men against the rebels. The Duke's association with an unpopular cause was thus exploited to prevent him from taking advantage of one which might turn out to be more dangerous.

The only man of any substance to join Suffolk in the course of his journey seems to have been his kinsman George Medley, whose residence was at Tilty in Essex. This was the same 'medle' whose lodgings Gardiner had seen fit to search, and his action was clearly not spontaneous. Consequently when he reached Bradgate on the 29th, the Duke had only a handful of followers and the 100 marks cash that Bowyer had hastily collected from a debtor before they left London. Both these deficiencies were tackled immediately. The ubiquitous Bowyer was employed to write proclamations on the Duke's behalf with covering letters to the cities of Leicester and Northampton, and to write to Robert Palmer, the Bailiff of Kegworth, who was already in their confidence, for money and advice. [2] After some hasty consultations, which included drafting a letter of justification to the Queen, Suffolk rode the same night to Leicester. He entered without opposition, and his command that the City gates should be closed was obeyed.

The following morning, by his order, the proclamation

---

[1] From a letter in the Fitzhardinge MSS, calendared in the *Fourth Report of the Historical Manuscripts Commission*, Appendix, p. 365.

[2] Robert Palmer was made bailiff of Kegworth by William, Lord Parre, afterwards Marquis of Northampton, on 10 November 1540, and afterwards was the General Receiver and supervisor of the Marquis's estates. John Nichols, *History and Antiquities of the county of Leicester*, London 1795–1815, Vol. III, p. 851.

against the Spanish marriage was read in his presence; whereupon

. . . master Damport, then maior of that towne, said to him, My
lord, I trust your grace meaneth no hurt to the queenes majestie.
No, saith he, master maior, laieing hand on his sword, he that would
hir anie hurt, I would this sword were through his hart, for she
is the mercifullest prince, as I have trulie found hir, that ever
reigned, in whose defence I am, and will be, readie to die at hir
foot.[1]

He may even have believed it; his capacity for self-deception
was considerable. His audience, however, was unimpressed, and
we are told that ' . . . few there were that would willingly
hearken' to his exhortation. Only about 140 horsemen, most
of whom must have been his own retainers, accompained the
Duke when he rode to Coventry the same afternoon. The only
comfort that he took away from Leicester was the news that
Palmer had subscribed £500, but in a fit of optimism he sent
a letter by Berridge, the Leicester carrier, to his servants at
Sheen to send up his plate.[2] How he thought it was likely to
reach him is not recorded.

Coventry was the key to the success of his enterprise, and
Suffolk had high hopes of being well received there. In
Coventry, by contrast with Leicester, he had been at pains to
prepare the ground. Before he left London a secretary, Thomas
Rampton, had been sent down to spy out the situation and
create a party in his master's interest; and Rampton had not
been idle. Upon his arrival he had talked with one Anthony
Corbet, 'an old familiar' in whom, as he later confessed, he had
'no great truste',[3] and with various other malcontents who
responded more favourably. A group of these quickly gathered
round him; Richard Astlyn, a haberdasher, William Glover, a
draper, 'on Francis' (presumably the Francis Symcockes later
mentioned), and Clerk, whom Rampton noted to be an out-

[1] Raphael Holinshed, *Chronicle,* edition by Henry Ellis, London 1807–8,
Vol. IV, p. 24.
[2] First deposition of John Bowyer, SP, Vol. XIII, no. 19.
[3] Deposition of Thomas Rampton, SP, Vol. III, no. 20.

spoken protestant.[1] These men had been full of enthusiasm and optimism. 'My lords quarrel is Gods quarrel', Glover had declared, 'let him come without delay.' They talked eagerly of the importance of seizing Warwick and Kenilworth castles, with their supplies of ordnance. They blithely assured Rampton that 'the whole of this town is my lordes, and at his commandment,' only later adding 'unless it be certain of the counsayle of the town'. If the secretary took these assurances at their face value, he was much to blame. Glover and Clerk had only just arrived from London, and Astlyn was already known both to the local authorities and to the Council as a trouble-maker, having been in the Marshalsea only a few months before.[2] They were all humble men, and there was not the slightest justification in their claiming to speak for the City. None of them filled any borough office, either then or at any other time.

Acting upon their urgent advice, Rampton despatched a messenger to a friend of his in Warwick, a man named Hudson, and sent his servant William Burdet to hasten the Duke's approach. Burdet, however, refused to lose a night's sleep, and did not leave until the morning of Tuesday, 30 January. If an opportunity had ever existed, it was lost by that delay. The effects of the proximity of the Earl of Huntingdon were already evident. Proclamations of the Duke's treason had been read in the neighbouring towns, and when Rampton's messenger reached Warwick, Hudson was already in custody. In Coventry itself ' . . . the citizens, through comfort of the erle of Hunting-don . . . had put themselves in armor, and made all provision they could to defend the citie against the said duke.'[3] Seeing the hopelessness of the situation, Rampton quietly slipped away.

Suffolk himself was curiously confident in face of the Earl's approach. While at Leicester on the Monday evening he let it

[1] Ibid.
[2] *APC*, Vol. IV, p. 368, 20 November 1553. The Clerk mentioned may, or may not, have been the same.
[3] Holinshed, Vol. IV, p. 14.

be known that Huntingdon would take his part, and had sent him word to that effect.[1] The loyalty of the Hastings was not above suspicion, and it seems possible that Suffolk had construed the news of the Earl's departure from London to suit himself. He later claimed that he was ignorant of Huntingdon's Commission as royal lieutenant,[2] but there is no evidence that he was the victim of a deliberate deception. Although he did not realize it, the Duke's fate was sealed before he left Leicester. When his emissary, that same Burdet who had carried the last message, reached Coventry on the afternoon of 30 January, he found the gates closed, ' . . . whether through the misliking which the citizens had of the matter, or through negligence of some that were sent to sollicit them in the cause, or chieflie, as should seeme to be most true, for that God would not have it so . . . ,'[3] as Holinshed piously commented.

Burdet returned to the Duke, who was following with his band of horsemen about a quarter of a mile behind, and delivered the fatal news. Suffolk gave up without a struggle. He turned aside to his manor of Astley 'half dismaied', and directed his mind to flight. There he divided his remaining money among his followers, and bade them shift for themselves.

II

The Leicestershire 'rebellion' lasted only five days, and not a blow was struck. It was ineptly executed, and unrealistically conceived. This was no doubt partly the result of the precipitancy with which the conspirators were forced to act, but even if their plans had been given full leisure to mature it would have been a desperate venture. At that stage in the Midlands the Spaniards were a distant threat, but the Greys were well known and disliked. It did not need the Council's denunciations to

[1] First deposition of John Bowyer, SP, Vol. III, no. 19. There is no corroboration of this from any other source.
[2] At his trial. See below, p. 103.
[3] Holinshed, Vol. IV, p. 14.

remind the people that Suffolk had attempted to place his daughter on the throne only a few months before. There was no reason to suppose that he had changed either his nature or his ambitions. Even if the Greys had been the only great family in Leicestershire it is doubtful whether they could have raised much popular support. The presence of the Hastings reduced their chances still further. Francis Hastings, second Earl of Huntingdon, was a man as ambitious and unscrupulous as themselves, and more realistic. A firm adherent of Northumberland, he had been employed by him in 1549 to suppress disturbances in the Midlands, and had been imprisoned in the Tower for his part in the conspiracy of July 1553.[1] Suffolk's attempted rising gave him an excellent opportunity to ingratiate himself with the new regime, and assume the undisputed leadership of his own county. There may well have been truth in Renard's assertion that he requested the mission.[2] In acceding to his request the Council showed courage and shrewdness. They gambled on Huntingdon's self-interest outweighing his sympathy with the Queen's enemies, and were fully justified.

A survey of those few individuals who are known to have joined the Duke, or to have worked for him, reinforces the impression that his attempt was little more than a private foray. Out of a total of sixteen indicted, seven are known to have been his kinsmen or members of his household, and three more probably were. Apart from his two brothers, there was George Medley, his half-brother;[3] Thomas Rampton and John Bowyer, his secretaries; William Burdet, Rampton's servant; and John Wullocke, his chaplain. All these ranked as gentlemen, but only Wullocke was a personality of any interest. By birth he was a Scot, a native of Ayrshire, and had at one time been a friar. Having imbibed reforming doctrines, he abandoned his habit and came south to London, where he was quickly noticed as an advanced protestant. In London he

[1] *DNB.*

[2] According to Renard, the two men were mortal enemies. Letter to the Emperor, 29 January 1554. *Cal. Span.* Vol. XII, p. 55.

[3] *Q J*, p. 66 note (a). The Duke of Suffolk's mother was Margaret, daughter of Sir Robert Wootton of Boughton Malherbe, and widow of William Medley.

established contact with such prominent divines as Bullinger. He also suffered a period of imprisonment in the Fleet, and came to the notice of the Duke of Suffolk, who made him his chaplain and obtained his appointment to the Rectory of Loughborough. His share in the rising is obscure, and may have been negligible, but he lost no time in making his escape, and prudently remained abroad for the remainder of the reign.[1] His real importance belongs to the Scottish reformation, in which he played a leading part, but he returned to his restored rectory at Loughborough in 1562, and continued to officiate there intermittently until his death in 1585. Bartholomew Wullocke, presumably his kinsman, was also involved in the rising in some unspecified way, but nothing is known about him.[2] Probably he was a gentleman of the Duke's household. Similar uncertainty surrounds two of the other names which appear: John Foster of Loughborough and Leonard Dannet of Bradgate. The latter was a member of the Middle Temple, having been admitted in 1551, and can probably be identified with the Leonard Dannet 'of Dannettes Hall, co. Leicester', who appeared in the General Pardon Roll of I Elizabeth, and sat in the Parliament of 1562–3, but this is not certain.[3]

Only one of the indicted gentlemen appears to have been a figure of any independent significance. This was Thomas Dannet, second son of Sir Gerrard Dannet. He had been at St John's College, Cambridge, where he matriculated sizar in 1548, and was married to Anne, daughter of Sir Mathew Browne of Surrey. His diplomatic career had begun in 1550 when he was associated with Sir William Pickering in the latter's Embassy to France, and he had advanced his fortune further by following Northumberland against the Protector,

---

[1] His place of refuge was Emden, where he practised as a doctor, and undertook several diplomatic missions to Scotland on behalf of the Duchess of Friesland. He returned to Scotland in 1558, and after 1562 led a double life, being normally resident at Loughborough but continuing to hold the office of Superintendent of Glasgow and the West. He was Moderator of the General Assembly of the Kirk in 1564, 1565 and 1568. Garrett, p. 336. *DNB.*

[2] He appears on the general indictment. See below p. 101.

[3] For details of proceedings against these men, see below pp. 101–3. Return of Members of Parliament, Vol. I, p. 406. *Cal. Pat.* Elizabeth, Vol. I, p. 150.

and picking up some useful pieces of Somerset's land.[1] Although certainly a minor figure, he has some right to be considered as an associate of the Duke, and not merely a servant or functionary.

However, one gentleman does not make a rebellion, and his isolation is emphasized by the fact that only five others, four of them humble townsmen, were similarly in trouble for supporting the rising. Of these, one, William Grene, tailor of Leicester, is a mere name.[2] The other three are those who featured in Rampton's testimony—Symcockes, Glover and Astlyn. These were almost certainly religious malcontents. Astlyn's earlier offence had been 'lewde and sediciouse behaviour on All Hallowe Daye',[3] and Glover is mentioned by Foxe as a brother of that Robert Glover of Coventry who suffered for his faith in 1556.[4] The fifth man, John Aylmer, was Rector of Bosworth, and like Wullocke, was a clerical dependant of the Duke.[5]

In its scale, and the threat which it presented, Suffolk's attempt may not unfairly be compared with Stafford's abortive raid on Scarborough, three years later. Only the Duke's private resources gave it a greater semblance of success. With the exception of the projected Herefordshire rising, which never materialized at all, this was the weakest stroke of the conspiracy. It caused the government anxiety because of its coincidence with the other attempts, and because its weakness was not at first apparent, but it never carried a real threat to the security of the Midlands. The moment may have been propitious, but both the place and the man were wrong. Alone among the would-be rebel leaders Suffolk was an uncompromising protestant, and a man with a 'record' for treason. Neither the country gentry nor the commons would follow him.

---

[1] Garrett, pp. 139–40. He was later to be in favour under Elizabeth, and received an annuity of £150 in 1561. *Cal. Pat.* Eliz. Vol. IV, p. 396.

[2] See below, p. 101.

[3] *APC*, Vol. IV, p. 368. 20 November 1553.

[4] Foxe, Vol. VII, p. 386.

[5] He had been under the patronage of the Duke from an early age, and had been tutor to his children. Subsequently he became Archdeacon of Lincoln (1562) and Bishop of London (1577).

III

When Carew decided to defy the Council's summons, he knew that he must act swiftly, but unlike Suffolk he refused to be panicked into showing his hand at once. Just before Epiphany the most alarming rumours began to circulate in Devon. The Prince of Spain was coming with a great navy to subdue the kingdom, and his landing place would be Devon.[1] Before many weeks were out, if they did not prepare to resist, many good Englishmen would be murdered in their beds, and their wives and daughters ravished by the Spanish soldiers. These rumours caused alarm and confusion, but hardly the spontaneous re-action which their originators must have hoped. Either before or immediately after the arrival of the Council's letter, Sir Peter seems to have taken into his confidence his uncle, Sir Gawain Carew, and William Gibbes of Sulferstone.[2] Pressed by the urgency of the situation, these three made every effort to build up a party among the gentry before Sir Peter should be publicly denounced. Losing no opportunity of declaring, and emphasizing the danger, they even took the perilous step of sending their servants to sound out friends and neighbours. Their zeal outran their discretion, for when the gentry of the county assembled at Exeter for the Assizes on the Monday after Epiphany, which was 8 January, their association with the rapidly spreading alarm was a matter of general dis-cussion.[3] The Assizes themselves soon developed into a contest between those who wished to take the rumours seriously, and those who regarded them as treasonable and malicious.

Unfortunately for Carew the Sheriff, Sir Thomas Dennis, took the latter view, and determined to safeguard the county against any tumult. On the same evening that he arrived in Exeter, while he and John Priedeux were supping with one of

---

[1] Declaration of John Priedeux, 24 January 1554, SP, Vol. II, no. 15.

[2] Sulferstone appears from the context to have been his parish of residence, but he is officially described as 'of Rewe'.

[3] Priedeux.

the Canons of the cathedral, he was told by another cleric
' . . . that Sir Gawen Carewe shuld cause harnes to be made in
the Crismas tyme yn the Deans house there. & that yt was to be
feared that yt was rather (prepared) agenst a tumulte than otherwise.'[1] Further information only served to confirm Sir Thomas's
suspicions that there were sinister intentions behind the apparently patriotic concern. Sir Thomas Parry, 'a symple gent.', had
been visited by one Thomas House of Exeter 'to know whyther
(he) wuld assent to the landing of the Kynge of Spayne in
Devon.' Parry, like a wise man, declared that 'he would not
meddell (with it)',[2] but his news determined Dennis to find out
how far this sort of canvassing had proceeded, and what lay
behind it. The following day he tackled Sir John Christopher,
one of the county's leading landowners, and charged him upon
his allegiance ' . . . to declare if he or anye other had determyned
to make anye resistens ageynst the Kinge of Spayne . . .'[3] Sir
John replied that he knew nothing of the matter, and positive
information was naturally hard to obtain, but two further
reports which reached Dennis on the Monday evening helped
him to focus his suspicions, and gave him an excuse for action.
The parishioners of Sulferstone came with a complaint that
church ornaments had been stolen and defaced, but they were
unable to locate the culprit ' . . . for fear of Mr Gybbes and his
servaunts'.[4] At the same time the Canons told him that the
Carews were suspected of being in league with Giles Strangeways, the pirate, and of conspiring to seize Exeter.[5]

Exeter was a key position, and the city which had held out
so stoutly for the protestant government in 1549 might well be
suspected of housing protestant rebels in 1554. After a hasty
consultation with Priedeux and the others at Canon Holwill's
lodging it was agreed ' . . . that fore as muche as the Mayor of
Exeter and his bretheren were of serverall religions, that Mr.
Blackballer the Mayers deputie and Mr. Hurste, being knowen

[1] Ibid.   [2] Ibid.   [3] Ibid.   [4] Ibid.
[5] Ibid. This is the only mention of Strangeways in connection with the rising,
and probably resulted from a rumour. It was noted by Priedeux, however, that the
mayor was 'the more suspected' as a result of it.

to be of a good catholik faythe, should give good respect to the keping of the same Cytie.'[1] Deprived of the connivance of the city authorities by this high-handed action, the attempts of the conspirators to infiltrate were effectively checked. There was an element of shadow boxing in the events of the next few days. Dennis was reasonably certain that the Carews were attempting to raise an insurrection amongst the protestant gentry of the county, but he had neither sufficient evidence nor sufficient authority to order their arrest. Carew, who knew that it was only a matter of time before the Council acted against him, tried hard to place himself at the head of a strong county faction. On the Tuesday, which was the first day of the Sessions, Sir Peter, Sir Gawain, Sir Arthur Champernowne, and one or two others went to Dennis and blandly assured him that there was a general rumour in all parts of the shire that ' . . . yf the King of Spain should land, there would be a great destruction to the country.' Sir Thomas replied that if it was the Queen's will that the Prince should land ' . . . yt were no subjects part to let yt,'[2] and that consequently any attempt to do so would be treason and not patriotism, but he was prepared to discuss the situation with them. After due consultation, on Wednesday, which was 10 January, a letter was drafted by John Ridgeway and despatched to the Council. Since it did not satisfy the Carews' wishes, this presumably marked a further victory for the Sheriff.[3] Events were not working out well for the malcontents, and one afternoon after the Session, in St Peter's church, Exeter, William Gibbes gave indiscreet voice to their frustration.

. . . yf any man woold not stande to defende the Kynge of Spayne for his entri ynto thys realme, because they woold ravyshe ther wyves and daughters and robbe and spoile the commons, that then theyr throtte shold be cutte. And yf Sir Thomas Denys and

---

[1] Ibid. There is no record of the city's reaction.
[2] Ibid.
[3] Ibid. By that time the rumours of the Prince's coming had crystallized. 'Upon Wednesday night it was understode that the King should land at Portsmouth', and that Bedford, Paget and Bonner were appointed to wait on him. Therefore there was felt to be less cause for alarm.

John Prydaux dyd work to the contrary therein that then bothe theyr throttes shold be cutte.[1]

There is no record in the Privy Council Register of the arrival of Ridgeway's letter, but on 16 January the Council at last sent instructions to Dennis to arrest Carew and send him up under safe escort.[2] When these arrived, on or about the 19th, the situation in Devon was already upon the verge of crisis. Rumours were current in Exeter that certain of the gentry of the county were about to descend on the city and turn out the mayor and council; it was reported that armour was being made there, and that the Earl of Devon was living secretly at Carew's house, awaiting the time to act.[3] Point was given to these rumours by the suspicious behaviour of some of Carew's servants, one of whom seems to have paraded a waggon-load of armour through Exeter in broad daylight. A war of nerves was in progress, with the allegiance of the county as the fruit of victory.

The tension which this generated was altogether dispropor-tionate to the material strength of the conspirators, for doubt and confusion worked strongly in their favour. As long as the will of the government was not clearly known both sides could pose as loyal and patriotic citizens. The issue was essentially one of confidence. Carew's only chance of success was to usurp the leadership from Dennis and persuade the local gentry to arm at his instigation, irrespective of the pretext. As a clever opportunist, he might then be able to take advantage of the misunderstanding to commit them against their real intention. There was no question of Sir Peter being able to 'carry' the county, or even a substantial part of it, by the force of his personality and the use of local influence. Although he was a native of Devon, and the bearer of an old Devon name, his estates in the county were not extensive by comparison with those of Dennis or the Earl of Bedford, and he had in a sense cut him-

[1] Sir Thomas Dennis to the Lord Chancellor (Enclosure), 2 February 1554. SP, Vol. III, no. 10 (2).

[2] APC, Vol. IV, p. 385.

[3] Priedeux. This news was picked up by one of Priedeux's servants, and gossip embellished the supposed event with dramatic details.

self off from the west by his marriage with Lady Talboys, and residence upon her estates in Lincolnshire.[1] In addition, his part in the suppression of the 1549 rising had made his name hated among the catholic rural population.[2] Although both Sir Peter and Sir Gawain later alleged their loyalty to the catholic church, there is no reason to doubt that Dennis was right in supposing that they would rely upon receiving the support of the protestants, even though their enterprise might not be religious in its inspiration. The protestants and a certain section of the gentry seem to have been their chief hopes—these gentry, who, like Carew himself, conformed to the established religion of the time but had no desire to see Erastianism overthrown, or Spaniards in positions of influence. The potential strength of a rising on that basis was unpredictable because these views were held, more or less, by a majority of the gentry and there was no certain means of telling how many would be prepared to act on them under given circumstances.

In the event so few adhered to the Carews that we may be tempted to underestimate the seriousness with which the threat was taken. Apart from Gibbes, who seems to have been a brainless chatterer, and was in any case a comparatively humble man, only Sir John Christopher and Sir Arthur Champernowne are known to have been involved. The former was an irresolute man, whose role was purely passive,[3] and the presence of the latter may be accounted for by the fact that he was a nephew of Sir Gawain, and married to the widow of Sir Peter's elder brother, George.[4] Sir Arthur was almost the only one of the Carews' many kinsmen in Devon to be involved in the enterprise, and he does not seem to have been in their confi-

---

[1] Lady Talboys was the daughter of Sir William Skipwith, and a considerable heiress. She was later to prove a tireless advocate for her husband. Her title was derived from her first husband, Lord Talboys de Kyme.

[2] Rose-Troup, *The Western Rebellion of 1549* (London, 1913).

[3] His fault seems to have been that he did not show sufficient resolution in rebuffing the conspirators' advances. When Sir Gawain escaped from Exeter he visited him unbidden in the middle of the night. SP, Vol. III, no. 10 (2).

[4] Sir Arthur's mother, Catherine, was daughter to Edmund Carew of Mohun's Ottery, and sister to Sir Gawain. Sir George Carew died in 1545, and his widow, Mary, daughter to Sir Henry Norris, remarried Sir Arthur. John Tuckett, *Devon Pedigrees*, London n.d., pp. 123, 131.

dence.[1] The men who did support the conspirators in full awareness of what was afoot were hardly a moral asset. The connivance of Strangeways is pure supposition, but the Killigrews were certainly in the plot, and seem to have acted as agents between Carew and the French. Their reputation for piracy went back to the previous reign, and was not connected with religious or patriotic motives.[2] The other group which might have been expected to play a leading part, the friends and kinsmen of the Earl of Devon, hardly appeared at all. Edward Courtenay, the son of that Sir Peter who had featured prominently on the royalist side in 1549; John Courtenay, the second son of Sir William of Powderham; Andrew Tremayne, later a servant of the Earl, and James Kirkham of Blagdon all went into exile when the rising collapsed, but there is no evidence to show what part they played before that.[3] The same is true of John Bodley, the Exeter merchant who had financed the loyalist party in 1549, although it is reasonable to assume that he had underwritten the purchase of armaments.[4] The strength of Carew's following at the time of the crisis is hard to estimate because he failed to seize the initiative from the watchful Dennis, and was never therefore drawn into the open. Despite many rumours the Earl never declared himself, and the government seems to have made no great effort to pursue suspects.

So great was the alarm in the county by 17 January that Dennis decided to garrison Exeter against a surprise attack.[5] This move convinced the Carews that their apprehension was imminent, but in London it was rumoured that the Sheriff had taken the rebels' part, and seized the city on their behalf. The

---

[1] Most of their closest kinsmen carefully dissociated themselves from the enterprise, notably Sir William Courtenay the younger. St Leger wrote on 29 January that he had found him 'a good servant to the Queen' (SP, Vol. II, no. 26). His brother John was involved, and fled with Carew to France.

[2] Thomas and Peter, the sons of John Killigrew of Arwenack, whose piracies off the Irish coast had caused trouble in Edward's reign. Garrett, pp. 206–7. *APC*, Vol. IV, p. 245. They were captured by government ships in 1556. See below, p. 164.

[3] See the entries relating to these men in Garrett.

[4] Ibid.

[5] The decision to take this step seems to have been inspired by a rumour of Courtenay's arrival (Priedeux).

conspirators were placed in a severe dilemma, for they had not the power to fight, and dared not risk a show-down. On the 10th they wrote to Dennis with an air of injured innocence, protesting their loyalty to the Queen and to the catholic church.[1] If the Sheriff had sufficient commission to proceed against them, they would come to him wherever he might appoint; but if not, they would resist him to the utmost of their power. Under cover of this righteous indignation, Sir Peter then made a final attempt to gather his friends and servants around him at Mohun's Ottery. On Sunday the 21st he was visited by Sir Arthur Champernowne, who was clearly alarmed by the progress of events, and the interview resulted in a rupture.[2] Sir Arthur then made immediate attempts to restore his position by spreading it abroad ' . . . that the Prince sholde be well received because . . . yt was the Queenes pleasure'. On the night of the 22nd Gibbes arrived with about a dozen armed horsemen, and with the arrival of Sir Gawain, probably the following night, the garrison of Mohun's Ottery reached about 70.[3] Sir Peter was a soldier, not a fanatic, and he realized that he had failed. On the 23rd he wrote to Dennis ' . . . whereas I promysed by yor messenger to repayer this daye to Exeter unto you . . . I am this daye departed hence towards London.'[4] But he did not leave his house until the 25th, and then his destination was not London, but France.

Meanwhile the Council slowly responded to the situation. On 7 January Renard reported that there was a plot among 'certain heretics . . . to induce Courtenay or the Lady Elizabeth to act as their leader,'[5] and a few days later Noailles declared:

. . . the Queen and the lords of her Council are working to break

---

[1] SP, Vol. II, no. 3.

[2] John Ridgeway to Sir Thomas Dennis, 24 January. SP, Vol. II, no. 13. Sir Arthur's alarm led him to make two attempts to see Ridgeway, and eventually he wrote saying that he had been to Mohun's Ottery, and that he 'could not agree upon the enterprise' with Sir Peter.

[3] 'lxx men or thereabouts' being the words of Sir Gawain's deposition. SP, Vol. III, no. 10 (2). The indictment later said 40.

[4] SP, Vol. II, no. 11.

[5] Renard to Granvelle, 7 January 1554. Cal. Span. Vol. XII, p. 16.

up the plot . . . and thus those who are in the plot will have to take up arms sooner than they think.[1]

He may have overestimated the Council's vigilance, but his conclusion was sound, and was soon shared by Croftes, who redoubled his efforts to secure French aid. The news which reached London was not altogether reliable, for although it was known that Carew was the centre of a conspiracy in the south-west, it was not known who adhered to him, or what progress had been made. The only official communication which had been received was the Justices letter of the 10th, which does not seem to have been very explicit, and which aroused suspicions that the whole county was disaffected. About the 20th it was rumoured in the capital ' . . . that sir Peter Carowe, sir Gawen Carowe, sir Thomas Dey(nis) . . . with dyverse others, wer uppe in Devonshire resysting of the king of Spaynes comyng, and that they had taken the city of Exeter and castell ther into their custodye,'[2] Not only were the efforts of the Sheriff thus misrepresented, but it was generally believed that the gentry of Devon had signed a solemn obligation to resist Philip's landing. Such rumours were very probably the work of the conspirators' allies in London, and while there is nothing particularly surprising in their being spread, it is surprising that the Council should have been so short of reliable intelligence that it believed them. There is, however, no other explanation for the fact that Dennis was studiously ignored after the 16th, and his authority virtually superseded by that of Sir John St Leger who was sent down about the 23rd with a special Commission to safeguard the peace and order of the shire.[3] At the beginning of February Dennis wrote to Gardiner strenuously defending his conduct, and pointing out that if it

---

[1] Noailles to Montmorency, 12 January 1554. Archives du ministère des affaires étrangères [Aff. Etr.], IX, f. 118 (Harbison, p. 119).

[2] *Q.J*, p. 35.

[3] I have not been able to find this Commission, but the tone of St Leger's letters, and the lead which he took in rounding up the conspirators imply that special responsibilities had been given him.

had not been for his action at Exeter the position might have been very much worse.[1]

Not until 22 January did the Council take any official notice of the agitation produced by the marriage treaty, and then evinced only minor concern over Devon. On that day circulars were sent to the Justices of all shires, with copies of the treaty provisions and orders to proclaim them, lest malcontents should be inspired '. . . under the pretence of misliking this marriage, to rebelle against the catholique religion and divine service restored within this our realme.'[2] Separate letters were sent in the Queen's name to the President and Council of Wales and the Bishops of Exeter and Salisbury, but their purport was the same. The only distinction about the letter sent into Devon was that it was addressed to Sir Hugh Pollard (not Dennis), and that it mentioned 'some lewd practices of late unnaturally attempted'.[3] The Council must in this case have displayed a confidence which it did not altogether feel, for the situation was then believed to be worse than it really was, and even in reality the danger was not quite over. It could not have been until many days later that St Leger's first report (dated the 26th) arrived with the comforting news that the commons of Exeter and Devon as a whole were loyal, and the great majority of the county well affected.[4]

By the time St Leger arrived in the west the crisis was over, although neither he nor Dennis realized it. On the 24th Sir Peter Carew sent for a fresh supply of harness from Dartmouth, as though it was his intention to stand siege at Mohun's Ottery.[5] The following night, however, he slipped down to Weymouth accompanied by Andrew Tremayne, John Courtenay and James Kirkham. There they were taken off by one of the Killigrews' boats, and shortly after landed in Normandy. It is a mystery why such obscure men as Tremayne and Kirkham

---

[1] SP, Vol. III, no. 10. [2] SP, Vol. II, no. 8.
[3] Ibid. no. 5. [4] Ibid. no. 18.
[5] Dennis took these warlike preparations seriously, and wrote anxiously to the Council on 25 January that the Queen's subjects had no adequate armour or siege weapons to attack the house, because everything was concentrated in Exeter. SP, Vol. II, no. 16.

should have fled, while Sir Gawain and Gibbes remained
behind to face almost certain trial and punishment. Perhaps
they stayed to cover Sir Peter's flight, but it seems more likely
that they were unaware of it. On the 24th Sir Gawain wrote to
Dennis from his house at Tiverton, expressing wonder at the
warlike preparations in Exeter, which were the sole reason for
his going to Mohun's Ottery: ' . . . you have chayned the gate,
layd ordonance upon the walls, kepe watche and wards . . . and
also blowne abroade that the gentlemen should pracitise to take
the Queenes highness.'[1] He went on to express his undying
loyalty, and it seems probable from this letter that he had
already parted company with Sir Peter. Most probably when
he had reached Mohun's Ottery a hasty conference decided
that their resources were inadequate to continue the enterprise,
and thereafter it was every man for himself.

IV

The Devon rising, upon which the conspirators had pinned so
many hopes, thus also perished without a sword being drawn,
and again we are bound to ask whether it ever stood any real
chance of success. It seems clear that the commons of the county
had no desire to stir. They may have been smarting under the
punishments of five years before, but could expect no revenge
by rising in support of the very man who had inflicted them.
Here we find the distinction between the 'gentlemen' and the
commons more explicitly drawn than in any other area. The
feeling that the gentry were a class apart, independent in their
actions and motives rather than natural leaders, seems to have
been strongest in Devon. This was a relic of the earlier rebellion,
rather than a reflection of purely agrarian or social divisions,
and its basis was partly at least religious. Although the leaders
of the 1549 rising had been gentlemen, the great majority of
the county gentry had taken the government side, and were
consequently associated with the protestant governments of

[1] Ibid. no. 12.

Somerset and Northumberland.[1] This association remained, even though the malcontents had no desire to make an issue of religion in 1554. It would not be true to say that the gentry were protestant and the commons catholic, but rather that the gentry were not much influenced by religious considerations, and the commons were. This applied as much to the small minority of the commons who were convinced protestants as to the majority who were catholics, or, more correctly, Henricians,[2] No doubt in Devon, as elsewhere, indifference was widespread among the ordinary people, but antipathy to the gentry and their supposed protestantism did service for catholic zeal, and can hardly, at this range, be distinguished.

Carew's real failure lay in the fact that he did not succeed in identifying himself with a cause which any sizeable party in the county would take to heart. His anti-Spanish propaganda caused alarm but did not convince; so that, unlike Wyatt, he did not succeed in winning the support of catholic patriots from any social class. Consequently his only adherents apart from his own servants were an unpromising mixture of extreme protestants, and anti-social elements such as the Killigrews. On 24 January John Ridgeway wrote from Totnes to Sir Thomas Dennis that '... the people be in good quiet ... except some few that do much malign.'[3] Remarks like this, and the suspicions cast upon the mayor of Exeter, suggest that the material for a 'tumult' did exist in Devon; but, because of the shortness of the time at his disposal, and the vigilance of Dennis, Carew could not create sufficient confidence to make his party 'snowball'. The failure of the Earl of Devon to declare himself also contributed to this. He was known to be a catholic, was popular, and had a considerable personal following in the county; all the qualities which Carew lacked, and which were vitally important to give the movement 'foundation'. The

[1] Northumberland's party in Devon appears to have been very small. Most of the gentry seem to have supported Somerset, and, perhaps, as a result, were at first enthusiastic for Mary. The same tendency can be seen in Kent. See below, p. 51.

[2] Rose-Troup, *The Western Rebellion of 1549* (London, 1913). It was the protestant services, not the Royal Supremacy, to which they objected.

[3] SP, Vol. II, no. 13.

persistent rumours of his coming indicate the importance which was attached to his attitude, and it was probably the final certainty of his defection which decided Carew to abandon the attempt. If everything had been in their favour, it seems probable that the conspirators could have raised a party among the gentry, which, backed by their retainers and a determined minority of the commons, could have seized Exeter and harassed the government in co-operation with the French. They were not upon a hopeless quest, but they overestimated the amount of disaffection upon which they could rely, and were roundly defeated by the diligence of the authorities.

3

THE REBELLION IN KENT

I

Although Noailles wrote bitterly that 'that young fool' Courtenay had given away the whole plot, his revelations really made very little difference to the conspirators. The real consequences of his defection were confined to Devon, because the decision to act had already been taken, and because Gardiner's anxiety to save him from himself meant that very little beyond the fact of his breakdown was known. The necessity for premature action, however, removed any chance of persuading Elizabeth to show her hand. Wyatt wrote to her '. . . that she shoulde gett hir asfar from the cyty as she coulde the rather for hir saftye from strangers . . . ',[1] but she was not to be drawn, ' . . . and she sent him worde agayn, but not in wryting, by sir William Seyntlowe, that she dyd thanke him moche for his goodwill, and she would do as she sholde se cause.' Thus although their rapid reaction to events had for the time being retained the initiative for the conspirators, their chances of achieving anything more than a demonstration of discontent were heavily reduced. Of the fourfold stroke which had been planned, only that of Sir Thomas Wyatt in Kent succeeded in putting a force into the field, and therefore the whole burden of sustaining the operation fell upon what had been intended as a subsidiary thrust. Wyatt later claimed that he was 'but the iii or iv man' in the conspiracy, but when it came to the point he alone had the qualities and resources which the situation demanded. Several accounts of his rising exist, but none gives a satisfactory explanation of its development, or attempts a

[1] *Q.J*, p. 69.

detailed analysis.[1] Consequently it tends to be forgotten that this was the only popular insurrection upon an appreciable scale to emerge from a period of intense disturbance and agitation, and therefore it is of unique importance for an understanding of the crisis as a whole.

Kent in this period was a county without any very clear structure in its local politics. Because of its proximity to London, and strategic importance in relation to the channel coast, the Crown had a clear interest in preventing the rise of powerful families there, or the clash of powerful interests. Partly from convenience, and partly for reasons of security, the Tudors tended to reward their faithful servants and administrators with lands in Kent whenever the demise of an existing family produced a suitable escheat. It was by such means that the Wyatts had become powerful in the county, and for this reason that Sir Robert Southwell, Sir John Baker, Sir David Broke and others featured prominently upon the Commissions of the Peace. There were thus a great many small interests, and a fluid land market. Many of the county gentry were full-time diplomats or lawyers, and there was consequently nothing like the same intensity of feeling over local issues as was to be found in contemporary Norfolk or Gloucestershire. No big cases in Chancery or Star Chamber indicate family feuds, or suggest that there were deep factional divisions waiting to find expression in the field of national politics. The commons of Kent had a bad reputation for turbulence. There had been agrarian riots in the county in 1543, and in 1548 the town authorities of Canterbury had sent to the Council for artillery to use against 'the rebellyous' that lay beside the city.[2] In the following century Godwin rather surprisingly called Kent 'the fountain of general uproar' in the period 1548–9,[3] but the riots then were directed against men who were to feature on both sides in 1554, and there is no evidence of agrarian motives

[1] For instance, H. F. M. Prescott, *Mary Tudor*, New York 1953, pp. 232–47.
[2] E. F. Gay, 'The Midland Revolt and Inquisitions of Depopulation, 1607,' in *The Transactions of the Royal Historical Socity*, Second Series xviii, 1904, p. 202.
[3] *Annals of England*, London 1630, p. 229.

behind the latter disturbances. Protestant influence was strong, and 48 Kentish men and women were to go to the stake or die in prison during the ensuing persecution.[1]

Although Sir Thomas Wyatt had earned some unpopularity as an encloser, he was in a strong position to act as a local leader. The grandson of one of Henry VII's favourite servants, and the son of a man prominent in the royal service and favour, he had inherited a position of wealth and influence. His father's active life at Court had been rewarded with many grants of land, and although when he died in 1542 he had left his estates encumbered with debt, he was probably the largest landowner in the county. The younger Sir Thomas had been able to clear the debt in November 1543 by selling lands to the Crown to the value of £3669, and still remain in the front rank of the county gentry. He had been about twenty-one when his father died, and was apparently a wild and impetuous young man.

He ran into some danger for taking part with the Earl of Surrey in his famous window-breaking escapade, but, not being a regular member of the Norfolk faction, was released after a short period of imprisonment.

From about 1540 to 1549 his main interests had lain outside the county. He took part with distinction in a number of foreign campaigns, and earned the reputation of being a skilful and fearless soldier. After Henry's death he adhered to Somerset, and began to take a leading part in the affairs of the county. Like many other prominent gentlemen he had been greatly alarmed by the disorders of 1548–9, and had sought to devise a means of protecting the government against such outbursts in future. A description of his scheme survives among the Wyatt MSS in the British Museum, in the handwriting of his son George, who wrote

. . . my father, and divers of good sort (for yt concerned ye nobillitee and Gentlemen manie waise) concidering hereupon conceavid that the most suer and prop. remedie for this headstrong mischife would be to strengthen the Kings part wt a power of the choise of his most able and trusty subjects, which might be upon a very short

[1] Foxe, Vol. VIII, Index of Martyrs.

warninge in a reddiness, wel armed and ordered against all sudden attemptes, either at home or abrode, and whereby he might not doubt to use without danger his other subjects armed and trained ... against any mightie prince that shold make invation upon this realme.[1]

This last statement makes it clear that the militia which he envisaged was to be a highly selective affair, for its main purpose was the defence of the Edwardian establishment, and 'the greater number were evel effected to ye religion then professed'. Sir Thomas's religion never seems to have been more than conformist but this clearly provided a useful test of political reliability at the time. The Council accepted his scheme, but the Protector's government fell almost immediately after, and it was never officially put into effect.

Whereupon, (continues George) my Father, notwithstandinge, partly for his private exercise and partly yt he might have sum thinges reddy for this purpose when a better opertunitie might serve ye first waye not taking place, conceived that he wt sum of his familiars and companions at many martial bankets, men yt had seene and experienced muche in their travels and servese abrode and at home, might doe suwhat that should not be unworthy their travel . . . but his own hand and travel therein was most, as I have yet wel to show, and as he had in a manner in his travel in Italy, Germany and France, and spatialy amongst ye Switzers, made observations of althings yt might be of use and servise for this his particular intencion and longe prepared purpose. Thus for the better accomplishinge of his millitary exercise did distribute amongst themselves the sundry parts of this business to those yt were best acquainted with the same. Wch after was by ye rest so used and perfected by one and mo consent and opinion in such sort as yt grew to a large volume. . . .[2]

As to those who were associated with Sir Thomas in this attempt to make England safe for gentlemen, George names

. . . Sir William Pickering, Sir James Acraftes, Sir James Willfordas I suppose, for they were alise and neighbours companions in the same profession of armes, Mr Edward Randolf, Mr Cotton, Mr Lenard Digs, Mr Robert Rudstone, and divers such others.[3]

---

[1] Wyatt MSS, no. 17, f. 1.   [2] Ibid. f. 3.
[3] All those named except Sir James Willford and Mr. Cotton took part in the conspiracy or rising.

Although he was writing years after, so that he may have exaggerated and introduced some names anachronistically, there is no reason to doubt the substance of George's testimony. Sir Thomas was certainly interested in military problems, and a formal treatise on the militia in his own hand exists side by side with his son's record.[1] His leadership of such an organization, however rudimentary, goes some way towards explaining his success in an enterprise which defeated his colleagues. His association with Somerset had not been sufficiently close to bring him into danger or disgrace, but it led to a partial retirement which threw him more into contact with local affairs. He was pricked as Sheriff in 4 Edward VI, and played a prominent part in the proclamation of Mary at Rochester in July 1553.[2] Through his mother, who was a sister of George, Lord Cobham, he was connected with the powerful influence of the Brookes, and as early as 1537 he had married Jane, the daughter of Sir William Hawte of Bishopsbourne. By January 1554 he was the father of three daughters and two sons, the younger of whom was George.

Wyatt's first action when he reached Allington Castle on Friday, 19 January, was to summon such of his friends and familiars as were within reach to a council of war. For the next two or three days there were hasty and furtive arrivals at Allington, as a plan of campaign was evolved. There were some departures, too, as not all those whom Sir Thomas tried to arouse had stomach for his confidence. There survives among the State Papers the testimony of Sir Anthony Norton, describing his visit to Wyatt at this time.[3] Norton alleged that he knew nothing of what was afoot, but it is unlikely that his presence was accidental. Apparently he lost his nerve, for after his hasty departure he made no attempt to alert the authorities, but disappeared and played no part on either side. It must have been during this weekend that the plans were laid which resulted in the almost simultaneous publication of the rebels'

[1] Wyatt MSS, no. 23.
[2] In common with many other gentlemen, he received a letter of thanks for his good service in that crisis.
[3] SP, Vol. III, no. 18 (i).

proclamations in different parts of the county on the following Thursday, but we have no direct evidence of who was present or what was decided.

The early reactions which these preparations provoked are interesting. The Sheriff, Sir Robert Southwell, does not seem to have been aware of the assembly at Allington, but he knew that trouble was brewing. On the evening of the 23rd he wrote to the Council

. . . this present Tewsday (the same day) abought thre of the cloke in the after none came unto me tow persons, the one cawled Benet, the other . . . Cotman, & sent unto me by Richard Clarke gent, being a justice of peace, for woords opened by Cotman unto the sayd Clark (which words be written on a paper herin Inclosed). . . .[1]

The paper contained a statement that William Isley had ridden into Ightham near Maidstone the previous day, and had declared ' . . . that the Spanyards was commynge into the realme wt harnes and handgonnes, and would make us Inglish men wondrous . . . vile. . . .' He had urged them to rise in self-defence, and when the villagers replied 'these be wondrous words and we shall be hanged if we stir', he had told them that the people were 'alredy upp in Devonshire'. Southwell realized that this was not just an ordinary rumour, and he reacted swiftly. 'I dyd imediately sent to maydstone to enquire for the sayd Isley, and sent also to such gentilmen as dwelleth abought me to be in a rediness yf case should so require. . . . ' The response from the neighbouring gentry was not overwhelming, as many of them were absent on mysterious errands.

In London and Westminster there was already complete confusion. The Queen, Gardiner, Paget and Renard were all aware in differing degrees that serious trouble was imminent, but their eyes were on the south-west rather than Kent. Mary had already ordered the raising of troops; there had been several arrests in London, and a special oath of loyalty had been administered to the Royal Household.[2] Beyond this the Queen's

---

[1] SP, Vol. II, no. 10.

[2] Renard to the Emperor, 18 January, *Cal. Span.* Vol. XII, p. 31. This oath involved a promise of loyalty to Philip as King.

three advisers were completely at odds. Renard urged an appeal to the Emperor for military aid, a proposal which both Paget and Gardiner rightly regarded with horror;[1] Gardiner, for reasons which we have already noticed, was in favour of conciliation, while Paget wished to rely on such English troops as could be raised, under the command of Clinton and Pembroke. Mutual suspicions meant that there were long delays in the circulation of news. Renard did not learn of Gardiner's interview with Courtenay until the 23rd or of the assembly at Allington until the 24th. The pro-Spanish party claimed that the rising was religious, and blamed the Chancellor for pressing the reaction too fast. The catholic patriots feared lest the Queen might use an army to punish them for their earlier opposition to the marriage, and so made no effort to raise their powers. The Earls of Arundel and Shrewsbury feigned sickness and withdrew from the Court. Under these circumstances Gardiner's was the only feasible policy, so when the first news of the trouble in Kent reached the Council, which must have been about the 21st or 22nd, the response was in accordance with his wishes.

On the 22nd Mary wrote to Sir Edward Hastings and Sir Thomas Cornwallis 'we doo understand that they pretend to be ... our trew subjects and that they have assembled our people only for thimpeachment of the marriage. . . .'[2] They were instructed to send to Wyatt and find out the truth of the matter, pointing out, if it was indeed a question of the marriage, that it was the duty of true subjects to sue by petition and not with arms in their hands. If a favourable answer was forthcoming

---

[1] Paget was severely rebuked by the Queen for concealing information from Renard, which he undoubtedly did on account of this fear, although he did not say so (Harbison, p. 128). Mary by this time mistrusted all her English Councillors, and leaned more and more on Renard. See especially Cardinal Pole to Cardinal di Monte, 8 February 1554. *Cal. Ven.* Vol. V, p. 461.

[2] SP, Vol. II, no. 9. This letter would seem from its contents to refer to the mission sent to Wyatt on 31 January, and was understood by Harbison in that sense (*Rival Ambassadors*, p. 132, n. 66). On the other hand George Wyatt describes the herald's approach to his father as being made before he left Allington; that is, before the 25th. I have accepted the date tentatively ascribed to it in the SP on the assumption that Cornwallis and Hastings undertook two missions, but the point is by no means settled.

they were to offer negotiations, provided that the malcontents laid down their arms. 'We will be content', the royal letter concluded, 'to appoint such personages as shalbe fyt for the purpose to commun with them uppon theyr devise and meaning.' A herald, presumably sent by Cornwallis and Hastings, visited Allington some time on the 23rd or 24th, but Wyatt dismissed him contemptuously, and would not allow his message to be proclaimed.[1]

This was clearly a tactical manoeuvre. Even if we assume that the Chancellor was sincere in wishing to negotiate, there was no real chance that the Queen would meet the rebels' grievance. The offer was not exactly insincere, for it promised nothing positive. It was exploratory. The Council did not know at this stage whether there was any connection between the assembly at Allington and the general conspiracy which exercised them. If Wyatt was really a misguided loyalist, then there was no reason why he should not agree to talk; if he was a determined rebel, then it would force him into the open. Paget clearly regarded it as a device to gain time, and agreed to it only for that reason. To Wyatt such an overture was a serious threat. Sensing the temper of the county he had decided to take his stand upon a patriotic call to reject the Spaniards and all their works. Very few of his Kentish followers were in his confidence as to the professed aims of the conspiracy, or even its existence.[2] He deliberately encouraged them to believe that they were taking part in a spontaneous and nation-wide outburst to rescue the Queen from the consequences of evil advice and her own folly. A lack of defined aims was a source of strength to him since his main concern was to raise a force, which could only be done by uniting moderates and extremists. The extent to which he succeeded can be illustrated by some incidents which occurred

[1] Wyatt MSS, no. 29 f. 38.

[2] John Proctor, the Tonbridge schoolmaster who wrote the only detailed account of the rising, recorded that in a moment of misplaced elation after his victory at Rochester bridge Wyatt revealed his true intentions to those of his Captains who were not already in his confidence, and some of them ' . . . understanding by that talk the end of their purpose, whereof before they were ignorant, wished themselves under the earth for being so unhappy as to be so much as acquainted with so damnable an enterprise' (Proctor, p. 72).

later in the rising. After he had raised his standard several doubters came to him and said ' . . . Sir, is your quarrel only to defend us from overrunning by Strangers, and to advance Liberty, and not against the Queen?'[1] To which he replied 'we mind nothing less than any wise to touch her Grace', and received assurances of their strenuous support. A few days later another ardent follower declared to his neighbours that the rebels' victory was certain, and when asked what should happen to the Queen in that event, he replied 'her hed shall bee chopped off'.[2] At another juncture 'one of good wealth' came to Wyatt saying that he 'trusted to see the right religion restored again'. Sir Thomas did not rebuff him, but replied, 'you may not so much as name religion, for that will withdraw from us the hearts of many'.[3] If he were to allow the herald to proclaim the royal offer, and then reject it, it would be tantamount to an admission that his real aims were not the ones which he professed. He solved the problem on this occasion by making light of the matter, and forcing the disgruntled messenger to retire with his mission unaccomplished. This situation was to recur several times during the next three weeks.[4]

The dividing line between loyalty and disloyalty over the question of Spanish intervention was very fine indeed, and Wyatt's repeated emphasis upon the 'avoidaunce of Straungers' awakened a response in all classes. Even more important than the numbers which it attracted to his standard was the paralysing effect which it had upon the forces of authority. One of the most significant facts about the rebellion is the paucity and hesitancy of the armed opposition which it encountered, right up to the last moment. This was particularly true in Kent itself. Only about thirty gentlemen are known to have joined Wyatt at any time, but that is more than twice the number

---

[1] Proctor, p. 48; cf. Damport's reaction at Leicester, above p. 29
[2] KB9/587, f. 77.
[3] Proctor, p. 48.
[4] Wyatt was very anxious that his soldiers should not be subject to the tempting lure of a royal pardon. Proctor wrote that he ' . . . would not suffer his soldiers in anywise to hear . . . any proclamation coming from the Queen'. Even if the offers were sincere at least half their purpose was to weaken his position.

that can be shown to have fought against him. The great majority lay low until there should be some indication of the outcome. The attitude of the commons was the same. When Southwell and Lord Abergavenny, realizing the seriousness of the situation, first attempted to raise a force on 24 January, they had little success: 'Sundry of (their) neighbours' . . . , as Proctor later wrote, 'and towns most populous, which should have been (their) chief aid, being contrary bent'.[1] It was the same throughout the campaign; the soldiers raised for the Queen in Kent were few and unreliable. For this reason Wyatt was able to retain the initiative, and move more or less as he pleased. This was of great importance as time was against him. A quick victory was necessary if he was to achieve that nation-wide support to which he pretended. If he should allow himself to be contained, the disillusionment of inaction and the bitter January weather would defeat him without a blow being struck.

Wyatt raised his standard at Maidstone on Thursday, 25 January, and caused a proclamation to be read, declaring that the realm was in imminent danger, and appealing to the townsmen

. . . because you be our friends and because you be Englishmen that you will join with us, as we will with you unto death, in this behalf; protesting unto you before GOD . . . we seek no harm to the Queen, but better counsel and Councillors. . . .[2]

Almost simultaneously identical proclamations were issued in Rochester by Sir George Harper, in Tonbridge by Sir Henry Isley, and in Malling, Milton, and various other places within the county. There was virtually no opposition. Christopher Roper of Milton, George Darrell of Calehill, and 'Master Tucke', 'being Gentlemen of good worship, and Justices of the Peace' spoke out against the proclamations and were carried off as prisoners by the rebels 'without any manner of rescue'.[3] No one else seems to have stirred. That evening Southwell wrote to the Council that his recruiting had made some head-way, but that the rebels' proclamations had gone as far abroad

---

[1] Proctor, p. 52.   [2] Ibid. p. 50.   [3] Ibid. p. 49.

as Sussex and Essex, and he urged that the Queen should withdraw to a place of safety until the trouble was over.[1]

London, as usual, was full of rumours. A contemporary
chronicler wrote

... the xxvth of Ianuary the counsell was certyfyed that ther was
uppe in Kent sir Thomas Wyat, mr. Cullpepper, the lord Cobham,
... the lord warden, ... sir Henry Isley, ... sir James Crofts,
mr. Harper, mr. Newton, mr. Knevett (etc.) ... [2]

As we have seen, the situation in Devon was similarly misrepresented, and it was also generally supposed that there were
big risings in Cornwall, Wales and elsewhere, though whether
this resulted from the rebels' propaganda or independent
sources is not apparent. Renard, Noailles and Soranzo all
reported these rumours as the truth, and the news spread
rapidly across Europe. In the face of this situation the Council
made a belated attempt to appear resolute. The Lord Treasurer
went in person to the Guildhall to ask the City for a force of
200,[3] and warrants were sent to such Lords as were considered
trustworthy commanding them to raise their dependants.
William Howard, the Lord Admiral, was placed in overall
command, and letters were sent to Southwell, the Sheriffs of
Surrey and Sussex, 'and all faithful lieges' to aid and obey him.
The following day the Marquis of Northampton and Sir
Edward Warner were committed to the Tower, where they
were joined on the 27th by Sir Thomas Cawarden whose large
armoury at Bletchingley was confiscated to the Queen's use.[4]
On Saturday also a further attempt was made to persuade the
rebels to negotiate, with the same result as before. Arguments

---

[1] SP, Vol. II, no. 17.

[2] Q.J, p. 36. Croftes was by this time in Herefordshire, and Cobham and the
Lord Warden (Sir Thomas Cheney) later declared for the Queen.

[3] Q.J, p. 37, says 2000, but the City records state clearly that 200 were asked for
(Guildhall Repertories, 27 January 1554). These probably remained behind for
the defence of the City, as the band sent with Norfolk on the 28th had been mustered
on the 26th.

[4] Q.J, p. 36, and Molyneux MSS, Calendared in *The Seventh Report of the
Historical Manuscripts Commission*, Appendix, p. 611. Cawarden complained
bitterly that when arrested on the 27th he had already been questioned and released by Gardiner on the 25th.

raged at Court as Paget and Renard accused the Chancellor of trying to sabotage the military preparations, and hinted that he was in league with the rebels. Noailles scarcely troubled to conceal his satisfaction, and expected many defections among the nobility. However, some time on the 26th or 27th it was decided that immediate action must be taken to prevent the spread of the rebellion. A force of about 800, mainly Londoners, was hastily scraped together[1] and placed under the command of the Duke of Norfolk for the purpose of linking up with, and encouraging, the Kentish loyalists. To resolve any lingering doubts that might remain, Sir Thomas Wyatt and all his associates were proclaimed traitors.

As soon as his business in Maidstone was done, Wyatt had removed to Rochester, and there set up his headquarters while his associates came in to join him, or spread his propaganda around the countryside. Such a one was Thomas Culpepper who posted down from London to Tonbridge to join the Isleys, and cheerfully declared that ' . . . all Ingland was upp, and that betwene London and tunbridge every towne was upp to drive away Spanyards'.[2] On Saturday, probably in response to the news of his proscription, Wyatt caused a proclamation of his own to be read, declaring that Southwell, Abergavenny and all who adhered to them were traitors to the Queen and Commonwealth.[3] By the 27th he probably had had about 2000 men in Rochester, as many as all the scattered royalist forces, put together, in addition to the forces under Thomas Isley at Tonbridge, and Henry Isley at Sevenoaks.

In an endeavour to prevent the rebels from joining forces, Southwell and Abergavenny, with about 600 men, stationed themselves at Malling, blocking the road from Tonbridge to Rochester. There, on the 27th, the Sheriff harangued the towns-men, urging them to take up arms like true subjects for the

---

[1] Q.J, p. 37, ' . . . ther was made redy by vi of the clock at nyght about Vc harnessed men, and came together at Leadenhall; and the sonday following they went towardes Gravesend against the Kentyshe men . . . '. The remaining 300 or so were raised in North Kent.

[2] SP, Vol. III, no. 32.

[3] Proctor, pp. 53–4.

Queen's defence, but the response was meagre and Southwell did not feel strong enough to risk an engagement with the Isleys. Further north Lord Cobham and Sir Henry Jerningham, with one or two other loyal gentlemen, lay at Gravesend with about 400 men waiting for reinforcements from London. On Sunday, the 28th, Sir Henry Isley suddenly quitted Sevenoaks and marched his force, about 500 strong, towards Rochester. Southwell was faced with a tricky decision: if he let Isley pass it would be a confession of weakness and his followers would lose what little heart they had. On the other hand he was desperately anxious to keep his force in being, and could not risk a defeat. Eventually, taking his courage in both hands, he intercepted the rebels at Wrotham. After a sharp engagement Isley's men scattered, leaving a few dead and about 60 prisoners in the Sheriff's hands. Sir Henry himself escaped into Hampshire.[1] The news of this victory somewhat reduced the rebels' prestige, and there are signs that by Sunday evening the rising was being contained. The city of Canterbury[2] on that day sent a messenger 'to Maidstone, to know the state of the commocyon begun there by Wyat', and from what they learned determined to place the city in a state of defence against him.[3] The same day Lord Abergavenny wrote to Sir Henry Jerningham: 'last nyght the Mayor of Rochester stole from them and came to us, also sundry of (Thomas) Isleys men'.[4] The east of the county, and the Channel coast, were almost unaffected and there was no sign of the support which Wyatt hoped for from the neighbouring counties.

It was also on Sunday that the Duke of Norfolk set out from London, and the news of his coming must have been an added discouragement to further trouble. Only the leaders on both

---

[1] For a full description of this incident, see Proctor, pp. 61–4.

[2] The Mayor of Canterbury at this time was John Twyne, the author of *De rebus Albionicis* (*S.T.C.* 24407). Twyne was a well-known anti-protestant, which no doubt partly accounts for the rebels' lack of success in the area.

[3] Records of the City of Canterbury, Borough Accounts, Calendared in *The Ninth Report of the Historical Manuscripts Commission*, Appendix, p.154.

[4] SP, Vol. II, no. 22 (1).

sides seem to have been aware how feeble the government's demonstration really was. Only his unimpeachable loyalty to the Queen and the catholic faith can explain the Duke's selection for this particular task, unless he was being deliberately sacrificed. He was an old man, and his military reputation belonged to the middle years of Henry VIII's reign, since when his faculties had been impaired by long years of imprisonment.[1] Worse still the 500 Londoners who formed the core of his force were already sold out to Wyatt. A Scottish agent of Noailles called Broughton had successfully approached Sir William Pelham, and no doubt the other Captains also were in the secret.[2] Certainly this was true of Alexander Brett, who had been a business associate of Carew's for a number of years in the marketing of Cornish lead.[3] The Captains probably had little difficulty in persuading their men where the course of duty lay. Wyatt knew well enough that the Londoners were already his friends, and some time late on Sunday or early on Monday Lord Cobham also discovered their incipient treachery. Cobham's steward apparently caught a rebel agent trying to rouse his master's tenants. He questioned the fellow closely, and extracted from him the information that Wyatt expected the Londoners 'to take such part as he did'. On Monday morning Cobham passed this information on to the Duke, with an urgent warning not to advance further.[4] He also warned him not to trust Sir George Harper, who had ostensibly deserted from the rebels the day before with many professions of penitence. Norfolk, however, not altogether unreasonably, decided not to trust Cobham, who was Wyatt's uncle and at least one of whose sons was in the rebel camp. He ignored the warn-

---

[1] He had been imprisoned in December 1546 for suspected implication in his son's treason. Saved from the axe by the death of Henry, he remained in prison until Mary's accession. Proctor describes him (p. 67) as ' . . . an ancient and worthy captain . . . by long imprisonment diswonted from the knowledge of our malicious World'.

[2] E. H. Harbison, 'French intrigues at Queen Mary's Court', in the *American Historical Review*, xlv, April 1940, p. 548. The remainder of Norfolk's men were little better, having been ' . . . prest and taken up at greenwych and other places'.

[3] E159/334 Recognisances of the Michaelmas Term, r4.

[4] SP. Vol. II, no. 23 (i).

ing, and wrote to the Council the same morning that he would make a frontal attack on Rochester bridge. Cobham's letter he enclosed with his own, and let the Council make what they would of it.[1]

The Duke's boldness would have been foolish even if his men had been altogether reliable. Even when reinforced by the band which Cobham, Jerningham and Sir John Fogg had brought to Gravesend his strength was only about 1200; little more than half the force of Wyatt, who held the stronger position. Nor did he trouble to inform Southwell and Abergavenny of his intention to advance, so that they could neither join him nor support his attack by a co-ordinated move.[2] Apart from the effects of senility, the only feasible explanation of his conduct lies in the blandishments of Harper. Sir George seems to have painted him a dramatic picture of despondency within the rebel camp, and continual desertions, so that the Duke believed his enemy to be already beaten. There were, as we have seen, some genuine desertions, which would serve to confirm an impression already received.

The sequel was the dramatic desertion of the Whitecoats as they advanced upon the bridge. There is no need to dwell upon the incident, which has been often enough described,[3] except to mention that Wyatt's knowledge does not seem to have been shared by all his followers. Since it is clear that it was not a spontaneous move, probably the method as well as the fact was prearranged. Although Harper's stories were deliberately exaggerated, the rebels certainly stood in need of some signal success, both to hearten those who had already joined and to encourage others to do so. If he could not widen his basis of support the temporary strength of Wyatt's position would not avail. Proctor recorded exactly the impression which the rebel leader wished to create:

The traitors and their friends were grown as men revived from

---

[1] Ibid. no. 23.
[2] Abergavenny to the Council, 31 January. SP, Vol. II, no. 30.
[3] See Proctor, pp. 67–8, Q.J. pp. 37–9. The shout 'we are all Englishmen!' was clearly a prearranged signal given by Brett.

death to life, flattering themselves that a thing so far above men's expectation could not have happened to them so fortunately but by GOD'S miraculous provision. . . .[1]

To the Kentish loyalists it seemed that they had been over-whelmed by disaster, but the advantage which the insurgents gained was more apparent than real. Norfolk, accompanied by the Earl of Ormonde, Sir Henry Jerningham, and the remnant of their forces, retreated precipitately upon London, where a contemporary wrote

Ye shoulde have sene some of the garde com home, ther cotes tourned, all ruyned, without arowes or stringe in their bowe, or sworde, in very strange wyse; which dyscomfiture, lyke as yt was hart-sore and very dyspleasing to the quene and counsayll, even so yt was almoste no lesse joyous to the Londoners, and the most parte of all others . . . .[2]

Lord Cobham disbanded his force and retired to Cooling Castle, whence he wrote gloomily the following day, saying that he could not hold out if attacked, and enclosing an overture which he had received from Wyatt in earnest of his continued loyalty.[3] The rumour of what had happened did not reach Lord Abergavenny until midnight of the 30th. '. . . with the whiche bruit', he later wrote bitterly, 'my souldiors, some repayred to Wyat, some to ther habittations . . . the resydue, being not many besyde my household . . . accompanyd me to my cosyn Southwell's.' He was now, he complained, worse off than before, without men, arms or money, thanks to the Duke's irresponsibility.[4] When the news 'blew abroad', Proctor confirmed, 'as well by wind as by writing; the more part of the people being ready to believe it, as the case, in the heads of the multitude was wonderfully changed both for strength and opinion'.[5] Yet in spite of all this, and true as it may be, there was no great explosion, or even any very appreciable increase in the rebels' strength. Neither the general insurrection nor the French intervention which Renard feared materialized, and although there was no force in existence

[1] Proctor, p. 70.   [2] Q.J, p. 39.   [3] SP, Vol. II, no. 24.
[4] Ibid. no. 30.   [5] Proctor, p. 70.

capable of taking the field against him, the army which Wyatt led to Southwark on 3 February was no more than 3000 strong, including the Londoners. When the Northern rebels had advanced to Doncaster in 1536 they had had more than ten times that number.

The government had, by its ineptitude, presented Wyatt with a magnificent opportunity, but he was too weak to take advantage of it. Renard was later to write that of his 3000 followers not more than 400 were properly equipped fighting men, and although this was certainly an underestimate, it correctly emphasized the limited nature of the rising.[1] Although the men of Kent and their neighbours might be unwilling to fight against Wyatt, they were equally reluctant to fight for him. There were symptoms of disaffection everywhere, and yet the rebel leader could not raise sufficient force to press his advantage. It seems that most men were in standing water between loyalty to the Queen and dislike of her policies, so that their actions were effectively determined by the desire to keep their necks from the hangman, and their property from sequestration or plunder. Proctor was later to launch a violent invective against such 'vultures', but their dilemma is understandable, and there is no evidence that he was anything else himself until after the event. Many no doubt hoped that Wyatt would succeed without their help, and the lack of a resolute lead from the Council discouraged all but the most enthusiastic loyalists. It was not until Wyatt had departed towards London that Southwell and Abergavenny began to make headway again, and Sir Thomas Cheney first made his appearance as a defender of authority.

On 1 February the Lord Warden wrote to the Council, complaining that he had received no reply to his former communications. If he ever wrote such letters they have not survived, and probably his suspicion that they had been intercepted by the rebels was correct.[2] He was full of loyal protesta-

---

[1] Renard to the Emperor, 8 February. *Cal. Span.*, Vol. XII, pp. 86 and 90 (two letters).
[2] SP, Vol. III, no. 2.

tions, but claimed that the people around him in Sheppey were so bent upon their 'devilisshe enterprise' that he could not trust ten of his own men. However, the next day he wrote to Abergavenny, appointing to meet him with such men as he could raise at Rochester on the 4th.[1] When 4 February came he was still at Sheppey, writing to the Council to excuse his delay, and claiming in mitigation that he had busied himself about publishing the royal proclamations. Meanwhile Southwell and Abergavenny had pressed on to Greenwich with such 'worthy gentlemen and honest faithful yeomen' as had summoned up the courage to join them. Their strength was rumoured in London to be 3000 men, but there is no evidence as to their actual numbers.[2] As late as 7 February Cheney was still writing to the Council expressing his intention of joining them, but it is not certain that he ever did.[3] By this time events in Kent were irrelevant. Wyatt expected no further reinforcements, and no retreat was possible. The Kentish forces stayed south of the river and played no part in the final engagement.

At Westminster Norfolk's defeat had increased the tension, and bitter wrangles continued. Mary, bewildered by the apparent changes which had transformed her loyal subjects since the previous October, turned as usual to Renard, and wished to accept his suggestion of an appeal to the Emperor.[4] However, the chronic divisions of the Council, and the Queen's lack of control over it, had at least the good effect of preventing that disastrous expedient. The most that could be agreed upon was that Renard should ask for an Imperial fleet to patrol the Channel in case the French should try to intervene.[5] Despite the fact that summonses had been sent out with renewed urgency, and the Lord Treasurer had set an example

---

[1] Ibid., no. 3 (i).   [2] *Q.J*, p. 45.

[3] Proctor states that Cheney joined the others on about 5 February, but as his letter proves, he had not done so two days later. Nor is there any confirmation of Proctor's statement that at this time Cheney 'went in post' to the Queen for instructions (Proctor, p. 83).

[4] Renard had already written a cautious request that such assistance should be prepared. Renard to the Emperor, 29 January. *Cal. Span.*, Vol. XII, p. 55. Charles, despite his previous misgivings, was ready to comply (Harbison, p. 131).

[5] Ambassadors to the Emperor, 31 January. *Cal. Span.*, Vol. XII, p. 64.

by raising 500 foot and 100 horse,[1] at the end of January the Queen still had no field army. Consequently, although nobody now trusted Gardiner, there was no alternative to his policy, and on the 31st another approach was made to the rebel leader. Basically it was the same as before: an offer to appoint a committee to discuss grievances arising out of the marriage settlement, accompanied by a pardon to all those who should return to their homes within twenty-four hours. On this occasion, however, Wyatt was asked to name what securities he would accept for the performance of the articles.[2]

Probably most people on both sides hoped that he would accept these fair-seeming terms, and reunite opinion against the marriage. Unfortunately for this hope neither side was really sincere. The Queen and Renard had only agreed to the offer being made on the grounds that it would give them more time to prepare their defences, and might trap the rebel leader into an admission of his true purpose. The royal proclamations which had been made since the 26th had claimed that the rising was heretical and seditious, unconnected with any legitimate patriotic grievance. If Wyatt refused to negotiate on such generous terms, his prestige would be severely damaged. He, of course, could no more afford to accept such an offer than before, but his attempt to evade the issue was clumsy, and in the event probably more damaging than an outright refusal. He demanded as securities the custody of the Tower, and the Queen's person as a hostage.[3] This reply aroused all Mary's pride and obstinacy, and left the Council no further excuse for procrastination: the rebellion could only be ended by military defeat. Strangely enough Wyatt's stand had very little effect on

---

[1] Marquis of Winchester to Petre, 31 January 1554. *Calendar of State Papers, Domestic*, Vol. I, p. 58.

[2] Harbison, pp. 131–2, gives an account of this embassy, and the reasons for it, drawn from several sources.

[3] Harbison (loc. cit.) also mentions 'a return to the religion of her brother's reign', without comment. This is on the authority of Renard's report of 5 Feb. (*Cal. Span.*, Vol. XII, 79). If such a demand had really been made. it is incredible that neither Proctor (who was so much concerned with heresy) nor the Tower Chronicler should have noticed it. In view of Wyatt's frequently emphasized reticence about religion it is intrinsically improbable.

his own supporters. Their numbers did not increase, but neither did they greatly diminish.[1] Perhaps they allowed themselves to believe that Mary secretly sympathized with them; perhaps they still trusted in a widespread rising to bring them victory, or perhaps they felt too far committed to withdraw.

Gardiner's policy was now finally discredited, and he emphasized the fact by making the grave mistake of advising the Queen to withdraw to Windsor. Renard warned her that if she fled she would lose her crown, and her instinct accorded with his advice.[2] On Wednesday, the 31st, a further proclamation was issued ' . . . both in London and in Southwark that Wyatt and all his company were rank traitors', and on 1 February Mary took the initiative in person. Now that the confusion of conflicting advice was temporarily removed, she acted resolutely and wisely ' . . . abowt iii of the cloke at afternon the Quenes grace cam rydying from Westmynster unto yeld-hall with mony lordes . . . and all the gard in harnes. . . . ' There she read Wyatt's reply to the Council's last overture, and made a passionate appeal to the assembled citizens for their loyalty and support.[3]

Then she declared . . . her mind concerning her marriage that she never intended to marry out of the realm but by her council's consent and advice; and that she would never marry but that all her true sogettes shall be content. . . . But that her grace will call a parlement as shorteley as may be and (act) as they shall fynd. . . .

In this speech Mary showed herself to be her father's daughter. Both the manner and the matter of it were well calculated to arouse loyal enthusiasm at a crucial moment, on a basis of dishonest protestations. She had already assured Renard that 'She considered herself his Highnesses wife, that she would never take another husband, and would rather lose her crown,

---

[1] Such desertions as there were seem to have been made good in Southwark.

[2] Renard to the Emperor, 5 February. *Cal. Span.*, Vol. XII, p. 78. Some of Gardiner's friends were urging refuges as far away as Calais, and Renard was convinced that they were in league with the rebels. It was at about this time that the Emperor's special envoys, whose coming in January had helped to worsen the situation, fled to Flushing.

[3] There are several reports of this speech, which agree in all essentials: Proctor, p. 77; Machyn, p. 53; Foxe, Vol. VI, pp. 414–15.

her realm, her life'.[1] She never told him, or gave any serious indication, that she intended to leave the matter to the arbitration of a parliament whose interference she had previously repudiated. However, her resolution produced the desired effect. She was loudly cheered and there were loyal demonstrations in the city.[2] At the same time Paget and his military followers gained control of the Council. In her new mood the Queen would hear no talk of parley or compromise, and determined to trust herself to the prowess of the Earl of Pembroke and his fellow captains. Pembroke was appointed 'chief captain and generall agaynst ser Thomas Wyatt and ys felous in the field', while William Howard, whose previous command against Wyatt never seems to have been operative, was to be 'sosyatt with the [lord mayor] to kepe the cete from all commors thereto'[3]

The allegiance of London would determine the success or failure of the rebellion. If the city's loyalty had been beyond doubt there would have been nothing in Wyatt's rising to have threatened the safety of the crown. The defection of the Whitecoats had been far more serious for its implications in that respect than for the temporary accretion of strength which it brought to the rebels. It seemed on 1 February that the Queen had struck a decisive blow, but probably she had done no more than restore the balance. Well-informed sources still regarded the issue as open, and the insurgents made no secret of their confidence that the city would open its gates to them. Noailles let it be known in France that his friends had intelligence

---

[1] Renard to the Emperor, 5 February. *Cal. Span.*, Vol. XII, p. 79. Mary deliberately deceived Renard over her offer to refer the matter to Parliament. She told him that 'if the people had not understood the causes and occasions (of her marriage), she would repeat them to a parliament'. Foxe's version of her offer is confirmed in MSS Rawlinson B.102, ff. 83–5, in the Bodleian Library, reported in *The English Historical Review*, Vol. XXXVIII (1923), pp. 252–8.

[2] There were also a few bold dissidents, one of whom ' . . . most impudent of all others, stepped forward, saying, Your Grace may do well to make your Foreward in battle of your Bishops and Priests; for they be trusty, and will not deceive you'. For this he was commanded to Newgate 'who deserved to be hanged on the next bough'. (Proctor, p. 78).

[3] Machyn, p. 53.

within the walls,[1] and when one of his letters was intercepted his confidence was communicated to the government. Much would clearly depend on how quickly Wyatt could challenge admission, and give his friends an opportunity to act. The Whitecoat captains urged him to a speedy advance as soon as they joined him.

For London, they said longed sore for their coming, which they could by no means protract without breeding great peril and weakness to themselves. And having London at their commandment, whereof they were in no manner of doubt . . . their revenge . . . [of] their enemies . . . would easily follow.[2]

In response to their appeal he quitted Rochester on 30 January, but instead of making all haste to Southwark, a distance of some 35 miles, he turned aside to Cooling Castle and did not reach the south bank of the Thames until Saturday, 3 February. The explanation of his diversion to Cooling must be political rather than military.[3] No threat could have come from thence, for the place was almost undefended and capitulated after a few hours to a siege that was no more than a gesture. Wyatt gained the person of Lord Cobham, and lost a day in his advance. The Council clearly regarded the siege as a mere blind to cover Cobham's defection, but he wrote secretly from the rebel camp defending his action and protesting his continued loyalty. Two days later he escaped from Wyatt, only to find himself imprisoned in the Tower.[4]

While Wyatt was again delayed on the 31st by the Council's offer to negotiate, preparations for the defence of London were pressed ahead as though no doubts existed about the City's loyalty.

[1] See Summary of advices received from France, 1 February 1554, abstracted in *Cal. Span.*, Vol. XII, p. 68.

[2] Proctor, p. 73.

[3] Major Brian Cope, 'Wyatt's Assault on Cooling Castle' in *Archaeologia Cantiana*, Vol. 39, p. 167.

[4] Cobham to the Queen, 30 January, SP, Vol. II, no. 28. The Tower Chronicler described Cobham's desertion as follows, ' . . . this same fryday, being the seconde of Februarye, the lorde Cobham (leaving his ii sons with Mr. Wyat) at midenyght cam to the gates of the bridge, and ther was lett in at midenight, and the next morrowe was brought to the counsell . . . and was then brought to the Tower as prysonner. . . .'

The furst day of Feybruary cam nuw tydyngs that all craftes should fynd the dobull,[1] non but hossholders unto the bryge and the gattes and the draebryge, and there lay gret gones; and the bryge was broken down after; . . . and so every gatt (was guarded) with men in harnes nyght and day.

When the rebels entered Southwark on Saturday morning they thus found their main purpose frustrated, for the bridge was held against them and the city authorities stood to arms 'every one at his dore'.[2] Nevertheless there were some compensations to be had within Southwark, especially after the disappointments and desertions of the last few days.

. . . they were sufferyd peceably to enter . . . without repulse or eny stroke stryken either by the inhabitours or by eny other; yit was ther many men of the contry in the innes, raysed and brought thether by the lord William (Howard) and other . . . agaynst the said Wyatt . . . but they all joyned themselves to the said Kentyshe rebelles, taking their partes; and the said inhabitantes most willinglye with their best entertayned them.[3]

This reception was probably caused by fear of plunder and lack of resolute leadership rather than by active disloyalty, but it seemed at the time to show that the rebel cause was still attractive, and consequently dangerous. Except for an incursion into the palace of the Bishop of Winchester, which resulted in the destruction of his library, Wyatt's men behaved with excellent discipline, and he himself with tact and discretion.[4] However, as no sign came from across the river, consultations between the rebel leaders became ever more anxious. Some wished to cross into Essex, hoping to find fresh forces there, others to return into Kent and challenge the loyalists who were again making headway, but the key to the situation remained in London, and nothing was to be gained by abandoning the attack. After satisfying himself that the bridge was too strong to be assaulted, Wyatt determined to make a final attempt at forcing an entry by a surprise attack along the north bank. If he could approach undetected his friends might

---

[1] i.e. twice as many as had been previously commanded. Those of less substance than householders were apparently not trusted in positions of responsibility.

[2] *Q.J*, p. 43.   [3] Ibid.   [4] Ibid. p. 45.

still be persuaded to open the gates. On 6 February he suddenly quitted Southwark, which was becoming restive under the threat of the Tower guns,[1] and marched at great speed to Kingston. There he crossed the river almost unopposed, and advanced through the night in an attempt to reach the city before dawn.

The government forces seem to have expected an immediate attack when the rebels arrived in Southwark. There was a temporary panic, and all river craft were commanded to remain upon the north shore 'under pain of death'.[2] The same day there were musters of horse and foot in St James' Field and Finsbury Fields, and the citizens went about their business in armour. No doubt Wyatt's strength was grossly over-estimated, but the tension seems rather to have been caused by mutual suspicion within the city than by the threat from without. No one knew how strong the rebel sympathizers were, and indeed many citizens did not know quite where their sympathies lay. There was probably a good deal of truth in Cardinal Pole's statement that Wyatt was ultimately repulsed rather through fear of a sack than from any antipathy to his cause.[3] The royal proclamation of 31 January had revealed the Council's fear of what might happen when it had offered a free passage to any of Wyatt's adherents who wished to go out and join him! At the same time, although the Court of Common Council suspended its sittings, and the lawyers were forced to plead with armour under their robes, the Courts at Westminster were deliberately kept open to avoid creating a 'state of war'.[4] On the morning of the 3rd the encouraging news arrived from

[1] Ibid. p. 46. The Queen had commanded that the guns were not to fire on Southwark, but the townsmen did not know that.
[2] Ibid. p. 44.
[3] Cardinal Pole to Cardinal di Monte, 9 February 1554. *Cal. Ven.* Vol. V, p. 463.
[4] One of the many strange things about this rising is the fact that martial law was neither proclaimed (as it had been in 1549), nor, apparently, exercised without proclamation (which lay in the power of the Crown; see W. S. Holdsworth, 'Martial Law', in *Law Quarterly Review*, no. 18, April 1902). There is a gap in the records of the London Court of Aldermen from 25 January to 17 February (Journal of the Court of Aldermen, 1553/4, p. 289) and in the records of the Court of Common Council from 1 to 8 February (Guildhall Repertory). Despite all difficulties, however, the Courts at Westminster remained open.

the Earl of Huntingdon that Suffolk's force was scattered and himself taken. This was at once proclaimed to reduce the dangers of defection, and a further offer of pardon was made to the insurgents, excepting Rudstone, Harper, Isley, and Wyatt himself upon whose head the price of £100 was laid.[1] That day passed, however, and the next, with no sign of hostility on either side, and some more ardent loyalists began to wonder ' . . . that they be sufferyd all this while', and spoke openly of treachery in high places.[2]

The climax came speedily in the early hours of Wednesday morning, 7 February, when a startled city was awakened at four o'clock by the news that Wyatt was almost upon them. The musters which had originally been commanded for six were summoned immediately, and another panic commenced. ' . . . moche noyse and tumult was every where; so terryble and fearfull at the fyrst was Wyat and his armyes comyng to the most part of the cytezens, who wer seldom or nere wont before to have or here any suche invasions to their cyty'.[3] At the Court a hasty Council assembled at the Queen's bedside. Once again flight was urged, and once again, strengthened by Renard, Mary refused to listen to counsels of despair. Messages were sent to Pembroke and Clinton, and they begged her to trust herself to them. Overcoming her suspicions, the Queen '. . . sende worde (that) she would tarry ther (Westminster) to se the uttermost'. So great was her resolution that 'mayny thought she wolde have ben in the felde in person'.[4]

Despite the effect which it produced, Wyatt's advance had not proved to be a successful manoeuvre. From the moment that he left Southwark he had sent out messengers and manifestos, declaring to the people that he had 'spente (his) bloode in that theire cause and quarrell', and urging them to join him lest 'the myserable tyrannye of straundgers shalle oppresse theym', but few or none had done so.[5] Kingston bridge had presented no great difficulties, but when his artillery

[1] Q.J, p. 42.
[2] Ibid. p. 44. The words are attributed to Sir John a Bridges.
[3] Ibid. p. 43.   [4] Ibid. p. 48.   [5] Ibid. p. 46.

became bogged, he wasted precious hours before deciding to abandon it, with the result that when he came in sight of London he found the Earl of Pembroke and his men already in the field. He therefore decided to remain ' . . . at Knightes-bridge untyll daye, wher his men being very wery with travel of that night and the daye before, and also partely feble and faynte, having receyved small sustenance since ther comyng out of Southwarke, rested:'[1] and some of the less stout-hearted slipped away. The forced marches had been unavailing, and had only resulted in his bringing his force to battle weary and depleted.

The battle itself, as recorded in various chronicles, has an air of unreality about it that makes very strange reading. Proctor makes it appear that the royal commanders deliber-ately held back and let the rebels march into a trap, in order to force them to surrender and so prevent unnecessary blood-shed.[2] It seems more probable, however, that they had no control over their men, and that a mass desertion was a distinct possibility. Panic was only narrowly averted when Courtenay disputed the Earl of Pembroke's command and threatened to withdraw. His presence among the royalist leaders is a strange enough circumstance in itself. A contemporary described the development of events as follows:

The quenes hole battayle of footemen standing stille Wyat passed along . . . towards Charing Crosse. . . . At Charynge cross there stoode the lord chamberlayne withe the garde and a number of other, almost a thousande persons, the whiche upon Wyatts comyng shott at his company, and at last fledd to the court gates . . . . In this repulse the said lord chamberlayn and others were so amased that men cryed Treason Treason in the court[3] . . . . It is saide that in

---

[1] Ibid. p. 48. Rawlinson adds that Pembroke sent Chester Herald to Wyatt first thing on the 7th, to bid him yield ' . . . and stand unto the Queenes highness mercy unto whom he would be a mean for this pardon. In whom as was supposed lay in him for to obteyn by reason of a ring and letter wch was sent unto hym from the Queenes majesty by Secretary bourne. . . . ' I know of no other reference to this curious episode, but it fits well into the general pattern of uncertainty.

[2] e.g. ' . . . for policy he was suffered, and a great part of his men to pass so far quietly and without resistance'. Proctor, p. 87.

[3] The confusion within the court was, if anything, greater than that in London. For a full account of these eventful hours at Westminster, see Underhill's narrative (Harleian MS 425, p. 94) published as Appendix VIII to *Q.J.*

Fleet Street certayn of the lorde treasurers band, to the nomber of CCC men mett theym, and so going on the one syde passyd by theym coming on the other syde without eny whit saying to theym. Also this is more strandge; the said Wyatt and his company passyd along by a great company of harnessyd men, which stoode on bothe sydes without eny withstandinge them.[1]

The Kentish men, 'not going in any good order', followed their leader to Ludgate, crying that the Queen had granted their requests and pardoned them. As they approached the gate, '. . . one John Harres . . . sayd I know that theys be Wyettes ancienttes, but some were very anggre wyth hym because he sayd soo, but at hys worddes the gattes ware shutte'.[2] So near, it seems, did the rebels come to gaining entry to the city. When Wyatt reached the gate he found it held against him by Lord William Howard, and turned back with the significant words 'I have kept towche'.

Neither within the city nor at the Court was there any certainty as to what was happening. It was rumoured that Wyatt was victorious, 'whereat many holow hartes rejoyced'; that Pembroke had defected to him; that the rebels had surrendered. By five o'clock it was certain that the last news was true. Wyatt's repulse from Ludgate broke the spell. As he retreated towards Charing Cross the royal soldiers, sensing the situation, attacked him vigorously at Temple Bar. Once a battle developed the defeat of the weary and outnumbered rebels was certain. Their whole hope had lain in repeating the exploit of Rochester bridge, and when that hope was disappointed there was little purpose in continuing the struggle. Therefore when a herald appeared and called upon Wyatt to surrender rather than be guilty of unnecessary bloodshed, he complied, and Sir Maurice Berkeley brought him as a prisoner to the Court.[3] With their leader gone, the humbler rebels soon

---

[1] *Q J*, p. 49. Rawlinson states that as Wyatt's men approached Ludgate they cried 'God save the Queen we are her frendes', and the *householders* stood on either side in harness (as they had been commanded), watching them.

[2] *Grey Friars*, p. 87.

[3] *Q J*, p. 50. It was later alleged by some of Wyatt's followers that a pardon was offered by the herald.

followed the same course, and 'then was taking of men on all sides'. Within a few moments the rising was over, at a cost of about 40 dead and an uncounted number of injured.[1] The last band to yield was a small detachment under Cuthbert Vaughn, which had been sent to make a diversion at Westminster. When the news of Wyatt's surrender reached him Vaughn tried to cut his way out, but was overpowered.[2]

II

There had been remarkably little blood shed. The rebels had been in arms for eighteen days, yet only three small skirmishes had occurred, costing on both sides about sixty or seventy lives. Clearly the military parade was largely a sham. The royal forces in and around London on 7 February cannot have numbered less than twice Wyatt's band, and may have been three times as numerous. They were fresh and he was weary; they had artillery and he had none, and yet he was defeated more by chance than by armed opposition. Many years later George Wyatt wrote that there were men still alive who could testify how narrowly Pembroke had avoided the fate of Norfolk.[3] His testimony may be suspect, but he is supported by facts which are not in dispute. No one could accuse the Tower chronicler, who wrote the account quoted above, of being unduly favourable to the rebels. The real crisis was one of authority, to which the size of the insurgent army was largely irrelevant. Renard had realized months before that such a crisis would come, when he had written that the most difficult part of his mission would be to persuade the English people to accept the marriage. Even without the action of Wyatt there would have been a period of extreme tension after the conclusion of the treaty was made public. The decision of the

---

[1] Rawlinson states that the days fighting scost 'vii core' casualties altogether, but this figure is unsupported.

[2] Add. MS 34176, f. 24. When 'newes was brought that captayne Wyatt was taken, he cried out On, styll we are inough. . . .'

[3] Wyatt MSS, no. 10, f. 4.

conspirators to act when and as they did brought the situation
to a head. If the issue had been confined to Kent Wyatt would
have won a decisive, if not overwhelming, victory. He raised two
men to the Sheriff's one, and had a clear advantage in both
spirit and organization. However, he was fighting on a national
issue, and local resources were not enough. Even within Kent
his active supporters were only a minority of the able men,
numbered in 1575 at 8960.[1] Outside the county, where his
personality and influence counted less, he could not hope to
do so well. To have succeeded in his real purpose without
support from Leicester or Devon, Wyatt would have had to do
one of two things: either rely upon being able to raise a big
enough revolt in South-East England to defeat any army that
the government might be able to send against him, or use his
local support in Kent for a rapid stroke that would be a virtual
coup d'état. Geographical circumstances favoured the latter, and
it was soon apparent that large-scale active support from the
neighbouring counties would not be forthcoming. Wyatt never
ceased his efforts to recruit more active followers, but once the
Kentish phase was over his real strength lay in the passive
support of those who made no effort to oppose him. His stated
purpose, although dishonest, was peculiarly representative, and
under the circumstances the fact that he was at the head of an
army, however small, made him as great a menace to the
Queen's authority as the leader of a horde. Consequently the
real crisis during the first week of February was not how Wyatt
would act, but how others would react. Once he had raised his
band of Kentishmen the issue passed out of his hands because
his force was too small to control it. Clearly he could not hope
to take London by force if it was resolutely defended. The result
therefore depended upon two things: whether or not the Queen
could raise an army to take the field against him, and whether
London would open its gates. The result proved how delicate a
balance had been reached. The Queen's authority sufficed to
raise an army, but not to control its actions. The rebellion was

[1] Edward Hasted, *History and Topographical Survey of the County of Kent,* Canterbury 1778–99. Vol. 1, p. cxxxvii.

not defeated, but simply collapsed as soon as its unopposed progress ceased.

III

Although circumstances deprived the Kentishmen of control over the consequences of their action, it is nevertheless in Kent that an understanding of the situation must be sought. If it had not been for the rising which he stimulated there Wyatt would have succeeded no better than Suffolk or Carew, and no crisis would have developed.

The records have preserved the identities of some 750 individuals who were involved. Of these, 560 came from Kent, and the bulk of the remainder from London and Southwark.[1] How large a proportion this represents of the total number implicated it is very hard to say. As we have already seen, the number 3000 occurs repeatedly in contemporary estimates, and may be accepted, with some reservations. Renard's statement that only 400 of the 3000 who originally assembled at Rochester were fighting men need not be taken too seriously, as when he wrote he was concerned to minimize the danger. If we accept the normal estimate of two camp-followers to every soldier, and arrive at a figure of about 1000, that is probably as near as we can get. After Wyatt's departure from Rochester there was a moderate turnover, caused by desertions, the arrival of the Londoners, and some recruiting in Southwark. The total number of those who were at one time or another active members of his force can hardly have been less than 2000. Some guidance can be gained by a comparison with the position of the Londoners. 500 of them deserted to Wyatt at Rochester bridge, and about 80 appear in the records: a proportion of one in six. If we apply a similar calculation to the figures for Kent, we reach a total approaching 3500. Considering, however, that there was a particularly intensive round-up in Kent after the rising collapsed, as well as the arrests made in London, this figure is probably rather high. The most satisfactory estimate

[1] 76 from London and 37 from Southwark. See Appendix I.

that can be made is that those recorded represent about 20 per cent of the total, and between 40 and 50 per cent of the hard core. If any valid conclusions are to be reached from the study of these individuals, it must be assumed that they are representative, and there is no evidence to contradict that assumption.

In addition to his name, an indictment or pardon invariably included the status or trade of the accused, and the parish where he was normally resident.[1] We are thus in possession of a good deal of information concerning the social and geographical distribution of the rebels. They came from 124 parishes, of which 103 can be easily identified upon the modern map. When these parishes are plotted, with some indication of the numbers from each, it can be seen that the great majority of them fell into three or four distinct groups around the residences of the principal gentry involved.[2] The biggest group is around Maidstone, which supplied by far the largest single contingent (80), stretching roughly from Aylesford in the north-west to Lenham in the south-east. Within this area lived Sir George Harper at Chart Sutton, Thomas Culpepper at Aylesford and Wyatt himself at Allington. A second group, almost continuous with the first, includes Smarden (32), Pluckley (21), Bethersden (24) and the Charts (25); within this area lived Cuthbert Vaughn and John Goldwell at Chart, Robert Rudstone at Boughton Monchelsea, and George Moore at Pluckley. In the far west of the county a third group centred on the Isleys' residence at Sundridge, while the influence of William and Thomas Brooke, Lord Cobham's sons, can probably be traced in the scattered villages along the London-Canterbury road from Gravesend to Milton. The parishes in the extreme north-west must have been strongly under the influence of London, but it is interesting to notice that this was not the most disaffected area. Despite its importance, only

---

[1] This may not, of course, be the place where he was actually working at the time of the offence. It is clear from the form of many pardons that the same man might be described as coming from more than one place. Probably many of those described as coming from various Kentish parishes were in fact working (or begging) in London.

[2] See Map at end of volume.

five citizens of Canterbury joined Wyatt; the coastal towns were entirely unaffected, and east of Ashford the insurgents can practically be counted on the fingers of one hand. The concentration around the residences of the gentry is too consistent to be accidental, and this is emphasized by the fact that the most active royalist leaders, Abergavenny, Southwell and Cheney, all lived in the east of the county, which was largely unaffected.

If the rising had been basically an upsurge of the commons, inspired by economic and social motives, this pattern would have been almost reversed, but any attempt to impose an economic explanation breaks down. Over 30 different trades are represented among the known rebels; town tradesmen from Rochester and Maidstone appear with the labourers, husbandmen and yeomen of the surrounding villages, with no significant preponderance of any one group.[1] We may assume, following W. K. Jordan, that a general increase in population had led to a labour surplus, and consequently to spare hands ripe for mischief,[2] but there is no evidence that this particularly affected one area or group of trades. Aylesford Lath, the centre of the disturbance, is bordered on one side by the Medway, but the affected area lay across rather than along the river, and some of the most disturbed villages were many miles from its banks. Although social and economic discontent may have played some part, clearly the pattern of the rebellion was determined by causes more tangible and immediate. A gentleman of the standing of Wyatt, Isley or Abergavenny dominated the surroundings of his home, even if he was not a commanding personality, or particularly popular. His household absorbed a considerable number of the local inhabitants in one capacity or another, and many others would be his tenants or the servants of his familiars. It was not so much where he owned or held land that determined the boundaries of a gentlemen's influence, but where he normally lived and the scale of his housekeeping.

---

[1] Over the whole number there is a ratio of about three rural workers to two urban workers, but this is rather an arbitrary division.

[2] W. K. Jordan, *The History of Philanthropy in England*, Cambridge, Mass. 1959, Vol. I, pp. 26–8.

If he was an official resident at Court, or spent much of his time on diplomatic service, his influence would be seriously impaired, unless he enjoyed an ancient family position or his interests were exceptionally well cared for. Wyatt and his associates had, as we have seen, some coherence as a group, and it now seems clear that their leadership was real and not merely apparent.

There are several indications in indentures and other documents that the Isleys, Harper and Culpepper were closely associated with each other and with the Edwardian Council. Harper, Culpepper, Wyatt and Henry Isley followed each other in succession as Sheriffs of Kent between 1548 and 1552. The Isleys and the Culpeppers were old established Kentish families, but Harper was a newcomer to the county.[1] The only son of Richard Harper of Staffordshire, he had married, in about 1545, Mildred Clifford, heiress of the Clifford estates in Kent, who conveyed to him among other places Chart Sutton, where he took up residence. He had quickly come into favour after Henry's death, and had been dubbed a Knight of the Carpet at Edward's coronation. He played a considerable part in the spoliation of the Kentish churches, some of whose goods he still held in 1557,[2] but had no pronounced religious convictions. From his conduct during the rising, when he twice deserted Wyatt, he seems to have been a man of few principles and small courage.[3] As a parvenu among the county gentry his influence was not commensurate with his wealth. John Harper of Cobham, also involved in the rising, was his second cousin, being the grandson of his uncle.

By contrast, the Culpeppers had been domiciled in Kent since the twelfth century, and although their wealth was no more

---

[1] The following biographical details are taken mainly from the *DNB*, Hasted, the *Archaeologia Cantiana*, the Visitation of Kent by Garter King of Arms in 1563, published by the Harleian Society, and the *Calendar of the Patent Rolls*. Where other sources have been used, I have indicated them.

[2] *Archdeacon Harpesfield's Canterbury Visitations 1556–8*, Catholic Record Society 1950, 1951, (Harpesfield) p. 202.

[3] His first desertion was on the eve of Norfolk's coming, and may well have been a subterfuge. He rejoined the rebels when the Londoners deserted, only to leave them again on 6 February, when he surrendered to the Council.

than moderate, they had a network of family connections spreading all over the county. John, Robert and Thomas of that name appeared on the Commission of the Peace in 1547. Only the last named was an associate of Wyatt, but no member was listed on the Commission of 1554. Thomas had succeeded his uncle, Sir Alexander, as head of the clan in about 1543, and perhaps his example was sufficient to render the whole family suspect to Mary's government. The position of the Isleys was somewhat similar. Although their wealth was not equal to that of Wyatt or Harper, they held considerable lands around Sundridge in the west of the county, and were more truly a local family than their courtier neighbours. They had played a part in county politics since the middle of the previous century, and had grown in influence during the latter part of Henry's reign. Sir Henry had been Sheriff in 1543 and 1552, and was one of those supposedly associated with Wyatt in the militia plan of 1549. He was connected by marriage with Sir John Mason and the Rogers family.

Of the 560 Kentishmen recorded (p. 77 above), 30 are styled 'knight', 'esquire' or 'gentleman', and these certainly represent more than 20 per cent, and more than 50 per cent of the gentry involved in the rising. Some of those recorded were not apprehended,[1] but it seems likely that virtually all the gentry concerned were either arrested or proceeded against 'in absentia'. Some of them are mere names. We know next to nothing about John Warcoppe, Reginald Highgate, George Moore and Thomas Milles, and it is unlikely that their influence amounted to much. The Walter Mantells, senior and junior, were minor gentry whose only notable possession was Horton Priory, which they had acquired in 1547. Anthony Knevett appears to have been hereditary bailiff of Tonbridge, and William Browning was a member of the family which owned Hinxhill. John Goldwell was a son of William Goldwell of Great Chart, and brother of that Thomas who, in 1555, became Bishop of St Asaph, but the family does not appear to have been particularly

---

[1] For instance, William Pickering and Brian Fitzwilliam, who fled to the Continent (Garrett, pp. 154, 249).

influential. Robert Rudstone, who was another of Wyatt's militia colleagues, and was particularly active during the rising, was the son of Sir John Rudstone of London, and was married to Anne, daughter of Sir Edward Wotton and sister of the English Ambassador in France. He had appeared on the Commission of 1547, and was to be restored in blood on the accession of Elizabeth in 1559, but nothing certain is known about his antecedents, or his position in the county. William Cromer was a slightly more distinguished figure. His father was James Cromer of Tunstall who had died in 1541 when William was ten years of age. From the list of his estates given by Hasted he seems to have been a man of some wealth, but first because of his youth, and then on account of his attainder, he did not appear on the Commission of the Peace until 1562, in which year he was restored in blood. He was connected by marriage with the Kemps and the Isleys, and was to be Sheriff of Kent in 1567. Thomas Fane was the elder son of George Fane of Bodsell, and was presumably related in some degree to Sir Ralph Fane, but how closely is not apparent. His fortune seems to have been modest, but he married as his first wife Elizabeth, daughter and heir of Sir Thomas Culpepper of Begbury, and in 1574 he was to marry Mary Neville, daughter of Henry, Lord Abergavenny.

The two most interesting of the minor gentry, however, are Leonard Digges and Cuthbert Vaughn. The former is better known to posterity as a mathematician than as a rebel, and his part in the rising is altogether overlooked by the *DNB*. He was the second son of James Digges of Digges Court, Barham, and thus a member of an ancient Kentish family. He appears rather improbably amongst George Wyatt's militiamen, for despite his considerable fortune he played little part in the affairs of the county, spending most of his time and resources upon his mathematical studies. There is no trace of him on the Commission of the Peace in 1547 or 1562. By contrast Vaughn was an active adventurer. Apparently a younger son of William Vaughn of Dartford, himself a man of no very great wealth, Cuthbert was by profession a soldier, and bore himself throughout the rising with conspicuous gallantry.[1] At some time un-specified, but apparently before 1554, he had married a 'Lady Golding', the relict of one Twisden. This can only have been Elizabeth Roydon, heiress of Roydon Hall and widow of William Twisden. By her marriage with Twisden she had conveyed to him the extensive Roydon estates at East Peckham, which descended to her son Roger, the grandfather of the antiquary. By this marriage Vaughn became closely linked with an ancient and wealthy family, and although his fortunes were marred by his attainder, it was probably through this connection that he was to receive the manor of Eastridge from the Crown in 1563[2].

The extent and vigour of the rising was determined by the leadership and example of this group, and the ineffectiveness of the opposition seems largely to have resulted from the irresolution of the remaining county gentry. George, Lord Cobham, is the most outstanding example. He was one of the two or three most important men between London and the coast; wealthy, well connected and powerful; and yet his influence was virtually in abeyance during the rebellion. As we have seen, he raised a small force for the Queen at the begin-ning, and warned Norfolk of his approaching peril, but all his three sons were at one time or another in the rebel camp, and he was strongly suspected of trading Cooling Castle to Wyatt. He was Sir Thomas's uncle, and an old man, so it is possible that much of his influence had fallen to his eldest son, Sir William Brooke, who was to succeed him two years later. The active opponents of the rebels were very few. A list of gentlemen 'that were with hir Ma'ties power', preserved in the P.R.O.,[3] contains the names of only three Kentishmen. This list is not complete, for it contains only 25 names altogether, but it is

---

[1] Add. MS 34176, f. 24.

[2] In 1560 Vaughn was one of those appointed under Lord Grey of Wilton to command troops on the Scottish border. His name appears in significant proximity to those of Robert Cornwall and Edward Randall. Stow, *Annals* (London, 1605), p. 1085.

[3] SP, Vol. III, no. 36. A further 15 are listed as 'My lorde Stewards men', 'My lorde Pagets men' etc; none of whom appear to be Kentishmen.

indicative. Sir Robert Southwell and Henry, Lord Abergavenny, were the outstanding royalists, followed by Sir
Thomas Cheney, Sir Thomas Moyle, Sir John Fogg and
George Clarke of Wrotham.[1] The unfortunate Justices, Darrell
and Roper, can hardly be counted for this purpose. Fogg and
Clarke can be briefly dismissed, the former because he disappeared from the scene after the rout at Rochester Bridge, and
the latter because little is known about him, except that he
appeared on the Commission of the Peace for the first time in
1554, and received several grants of land in reward for his
services. Sir Thomas Moyle was typical of the official gentry
whom we have already had occasion to notice. The third son
of Sir John Moyle of Cornwall, he had made a career for himself
in law, and gained his first preferment in 1537 when he was
appointed a receiver of the newly erected Court of Augmentations. Thereafter he had served Henry zealously in several
offices, and had been rewarded with considerable grants of
monastic land in Kent. He took up residence at Eastwell Court,
and in 1542 was returned as knight of the shire. Elected
Speaker, he seems to have displayed a somewhat extravagant
loyalty to the Crown, and he survived all the changes of the
ensuing years, continuing to sit for Rochester until the second
parliament of Mary. There is no reason to doubt that his official
conscience was stronger than his private feelings, and that his
apparent lack of energy was due more to a lack of influence in
his adopted county than to any tendency to disaffection.

Sir Thomas Cheney, Lord Warden of the Cinque Ports and
Treasurer of the Household, had also pursued an active
diplomatic career under Henry and Edward, but his position
differed from that of Moyle in that he came of an established
Kentish family. His seat was at Shurland in the Isle of Sheppey,
and his estates mostly in the north and east of the county. Like
Moyle, he seems to have had no particular religious views, but
to have conformed to the practices established in the interest

---

[1] A few others, such as John Dodge and Richard Cavert, appear as signatories
of Abergavenny's letter to the Council on 28 January (SP, Vol. II, no. 22 (1)),
but they remain names and nothing is known of their actions.

of his career. By virtue of his office as Lord Warden he was the most important resident gentleman in East Kent at the time of the rising. His influence lay in that part of the county where the insurgents were weakest, but he was handicapped by lack of support for a different reason. The men of the coast had no intention of turning their backs upon the sea when a French invasion was imminent. Coastal politics were dominated by the fear of the French, and national events had not disturbed that orientation. In the same month that the rising broke out the townsmen of Hythe had attacked a French vessel in defence of an Imperial merchantman. Wyatt was a minor consideration to the men of Dover and Ramsgate. They might sympathize with some of his aims, but his association with the enemy made them unwilling to support him. They rightly considered it their main duty to guard their homes, and the danger came from the sea, not inland, so that Cheney was faced with great difficulties in raising a force, and aspersions were cast upon his loyalty.

Sir Robert Southwell and Lord Abergavenny were almost the only significant gentlemen in the county whose loyalty was never in doubt. So resolute was Southwell's opposition to Wyatt that it is tempting to regard them as personal enemies, but apart from an unverified statement by Proctor that they had quarrelled in the recent past, there is no evidence for this.[1] Sir Robert was the younger brother of Sir Richard, and came of a wealthy Norfolk family. Like Moyle, he had made his career in law, and gained his first promotion through the Court of Augmentations. Having gained considerable wealth by speculating in monastic lands, he had joined with his brother in his attack upon the Howards, and secured on their fall their valuable property at Badlesmere in Kent. This he sold, but he had retained as his principal residence Jotes Place at Mereworth, and was active in the affairs of the county. Although Master of the Rolls from 1543 to 1550, he seems to have been normally resident in Kent, and had gained some influence through his marriage with Margaret Neville, daughter of Sir Thomas Neville, and niece of Lord Abergavenny. However the

[1] Proctor, p. 50.

childlessness of this marriage greatly restricted the range of his connections, and his office as Sheriff could not compensate for his lack of status in the county.

It is unlikely that he would have made any head against the Wyatt group if it had not been for the support of Lord Abergavenny. The Nevilles were, with the exception of the Brookes, the oldest and most powerful family in Kent, and if there had been any anti-Wyatt faction they might have been expected to lead it. There were no marriage connections between the Nevilles and the Wyatts as there were between the Brookes and the Wyatts. However, there is no evidence that this was the case, and before 1554 the political affiliations of Sir Thomas Wyatt and Henry Neville appear to have been identical. The latter had been one of the 26 peers who signed the Letters Patent of July 1553, settling the crown on Lady Jane, but he had executed an extraordinarily rapid *volte-face*, and joined Wyatt in proclaiming Mary before the end of the month. He was rewarded with her favour, and served as Larderer at the coronation. The Nevilles had acquired the barony of Abergavenny by the marriage of Edward Neville, a cadet of the house of Westmorland, with the heiress Elizabeth Beauchamp in about 1424. The grandson of that marriage, George Neville, father of Henry, had served Henry VII as Constable of Dover Castle and Lord Warden. As a reward for his services his lands in Kent had been substantially increased, but not, it seems, sufficiently for his needs, as before his death in 1535 he was complaining to the King of his poverty. Perhaps after his unfortunate association with the Duke of Buckingham such pleas had fallen on deaf ears, and Henry, like the younger Wyatt, succeeded to an embarrassed estate. At the time of the rising Lord Abergavenny was unmarried, but through his numerous brothers and sisters had many personal connections both in and out of the county. His Kentish lands were not as extensive as those of Wyatt, and were for the most part in the east of the county.

There is very little in the history of these gentlemen to explain their choice of sides in 1554. It cannot be pretended that Wyatt and his friends had been dispossessed in favour of men who had been excluded by the Protector and Northumberland. They had been no more closely associated with the Edwardian regimes than Moyle and Abergavenny, and, with the possible exception of Harper, had not conspicuously failed to make their peace with the Queen.[1] All had equally conformed to changes in the established religion, and there was nothing to choose between Wyatt and Southwell in respect of secularized monastic lands. Both Wyatt and Cheney had been objects of popular hatred during the enclosure riots of the 1540's, and all alike seem to have taken what they could get out of the Commissions for Church goods. There were no clearly defined parties or factions in Kent over national, any more than over local, issues. The significant gentry, without exception, were opportunist and secular. There is consequently no reason to doubt that as far as they were concerned the issue of loyalty or disloyalty was determined by the matter of the moment, that is to say the Spanish marriage, and such political principles as they possessed. Since no one liked the marriage, and almost no one doubted that rebellion was normally immoral, the division was a question of degree rather than choice, which explains why so many attempted to evade the issue, and why the antecedents of both sides were so similar.

The attitude of the commons is, if anything, easier to assess. On this occasion there were none of those attacks upon the houses of the gentry which had characterized the Pilgrimage of Grace, or Kett's rebellion. Nor were there the same hints of class divisions that we have noticed with reference to Carew's attempt in Devon.[2] Taken in conjunction with the significant distribution of the rebels which we have already noticed, these facts indicate very strongly that the commons took no initiative in the rising. They followed, or did not follow, the gentry according to whether or not the appeal of their ostensible cause

---

[1] Harper, Culpepper and Isley had all been under arrest during July of the previous summer. They had then been dismissed, but Harper had been in trouble again. *APC*, Vol. IV, p. 306.

[2] See above, pp. 44–5.

could overcome the inertia of loyalty and fear. The government assumed at the time, and it has often been assumed since, that one of the significant factors in overcoming that inertia was religious discontent. It would be simple to explain the limited success of the agitation in these terms, but the evidence is all against it. Even Proctor, who believed that Wyatt was inspired by devotion to the reformed church, was bound to admit that he repudiated such a motive in public. With the possible exception of the elder Mantell there is no evidence that any of the gentry involved did not profess conformity to the established faith.[1] None of them was indicted (as Carew was) 'impie et erronie religionis',[2] and there were no ecclesiastical proceedings against them. Such positive evidence as we have all points in the same direction. Not one of the 560 recorded rebels appears in Foxe's list of the Kentish martyrs (48 in number). Only one features among the considerable number presented for various irregularities during Harpesfield's extensive visitation of Canterbury diocese in 1557. On the other hand no fewer than 43 appear in the records of the same visitation as Church-wardens and 'parochiani'. Since only men of some substance occupied these positions, such a figure is strikingly large. Significantly, too, the protestant divine John Bradford wrote to his friends Royden and Elsing about the middle of February 1554: 'Do not we see before our eyes men to die shamefully—I mean as rebels and other malefactors—which refuse to die for God's cause. . . . '[3] He was writing in the midst of the executions which followed Wyatt's rising, and it is hard to believe that he did not have them in mind. There were, of course, some protestants in the rebel ranks. Kent was a county where their influence was strong, and their complete absence could only

---

[1] Foxe, Vol. VI, p. 546.
[2] KB27/1174 Rex V.
[3] *Writings of John Bradford*, Parker Society 1853, Letter xxv. Another Divine, Thomas Mowntaine, declared in his autobiographical notes that Wyatt sent to the Marshalsea while he was in Southwark, offering to release the religious prisoners, but they declined his offer with thanks (*Narratives of the Days of the Reformation*, edited by J. G. Nichols, Camden Society, 1859, p. 185). If his assertion is true it complicates Wyatt's own position, but emphasizes his estrangement from the protestant leaders.

have resulted from deliberate exclusion. The nine clergy who appear on the records were probably of that persuasion, although the only one who was obviously so was William Allbright, the Vicar of Kingston, who preached a last-minute sermon to the rebels at Charing Cross.[1] Most of the remainder do not seem to have been beneficed, and one, surprisingly enough, retained his benefice until 28 January 1556, when he was deprived as 'clericus coniugatus'![2]

For Wyatt it was clearly expedient to be all things to all men, but if there had been any substantial religious element in the rising it would have shown among his followers. Nothing that we can learn either about the gentry or the commons suggests that they were inspired by such a motive. The Queen wished to believe the religious explanation, because religion was the one fixed point on her political horizon, and because she was deeply committed to the marriage. To Gardiner it offered an escape from suspicion of complicity, and to Renard a hope that Philip might be acceptable to the English people. For all these reasons the complicity of a few protestants was used to discredit their co-religionists who had no desire to be involved in treasonable activities, and to raise the religious motive as a scapegoat. The real reasons which lay behind the rising were secular and political; partly genuine grievances and partly the result of misrepresentation and self-deception. Failure resulted from dependence upon the impact of compelling leadership, which, by its nature, could affect only a small area. Beyond the reach of that leadership the grievances did not appear sufficiently compelling to overcome the fear and repugnance of rebellion. Sympathy was created, but it could not be turned into active support widely or quickly enough to save the movement from collapse.

[1] *Grey Friars,* p. 87.
[2] Harpesfield, p. 154.

4

ARRESTS AND TRIALS

I

The collapse of the rebellion in Kent, and its failure to material-
ize elsewhere, was decisive for those who had taken part, but
it did not alter the basic situation. English opinion was not
reconciled to the marriage, and the government had survived
without victory. The time was opportune for some politic concession, but none was made because each party drew what conclusions it wished from the events we have examined. To Mary
they proved that in the last analysis her people would support
her, and consequently strengthened her conviction that opposition to her policies was the work of heretics and agitators. To
Renard they proved that there could be no safety for Spanish
interests in England as long as Elizabeth and Courtenay
remained as foci for discontent; while to Noailles they merely
demonstrated that greater secrecy and better organization
would be necessary in future. The most significant deduction,
however, was that made by Gardiner. He subscribed to the
religious interpretation more wholeheartedly than anyone,
once the immediate danger was over,[1] and concluded that the
Queen's government could never be safe until heresy was
exterminated.

These various interpretations led to fundamental disagreements over the treatment of the prisoners. Mary had been

---

[1] This, of course, represented a reversal of his previous attitude. While the
rebellion was threatening, and while it was in progress, it had been Gardiner's
enemies who had put forward the religious interpretation, blaming Gardiner for
his policy of reaction. When danger threatened, each side blamed the other for
causing it, but when there was a victory to be exploited their attitudes were
promptly reversed.

badly frightened, and was at first 'inclined to severe justice', but once her indignation had abated she became, as usual, subject to the conflicting counsel of her various advisers and ceased to exercise a determining influence. Renard was anxious to avoid any policy of indiscriminate severity lest it be attributed to his influence. The Emperor had urged that 'due severity should be used towards the principal rebels, and clemency to the rank and file'.[1] He worked assiduously to bring Courtenay and Elizabeth to trial, and did his best to keep out of the public eye. Gardiner's policy was almost the exact reverse of Renard's. Preaching before the Court on Sunday, 11 February, he dwelt at length on the necessity of safeguarding the commonwealth, ' . . . which coulde not be unlesse the rotten and hurtfull members thereof were cutt off and consumed. . . .' 'Wherby', an eye-witness wrote, 'all the audyence dyd gather ther should shortly followe sharpe and cruell execution'.[2] Such, it seems clear, was the Chancellor's intention, but he was handicapped by his continued determination to protect Courtenay. The fact that the Earl was a catholic gave his position a certain superficial consistency, but it was to lead him into dangerous subterfuges. One result of his determination was to emphasize the guilt of the actual rebels, and minimize that of the conspirators.

With Renard and Gardiner thus at odds, the confusion was completed by the attitude of Paget. He and his faction had gained greatly in stature from the defeat of Wyatt,[3] and for a while Pembroke and Clinton were the idols of the Court. This influence Paget used to frustrate the policies of the others. Personal hostility towards the Chancellor, and dislike of his religious programme probably played a large part in determining this attitude, but it was not without other justifications. After so equivocal a victory, and in view of the continued

---

[1] 18 February 1554. *Cal. Span.*, Vol. XII, p. 112. These instructions were addressed to the Count d'Egmont, but intended for both envoys.

[2] *Q.J*, p. 54.

[3] Renard to the Emperor, 14 March. *Cal. Span.*, Vol. XII, p. 151. Gardiner was very worried by this development, as it enabled some of them to gain access to the 'inner Council', which he and Renard had initiated in an attempt to cut down the factional strife. As a result of his hostility no proper recognition was given to Pembroke and Clinton for the services they had rendered.

tension, there was certainly a case for all-round leniency as the best guarantee of future quiet. When it seemed that a wholesale extermination of the leaders was in prospect, on 12 February, Renard reported 'A new revolt is feared, because the people say that so much noble blood ought not to be shed for the sake of strangers'.[1] Consequently Paget was determined to preserve as many as possible of the rebels and conspirators from the block. Above all he was friendly towards Elizabeth.

These divisions were fatal to any coherent action. Renard's struggle to persuade the Council to put Elizabeth and Courtenay on trial went on for several weeks, but in the end he was defeated on both counts. Suspicions against Elizabeth were naturally very strong, and the Spanish interest in her removal was obvious. When she was committed to the Tower, Mendoza wrote to the Bishop of Arras: 'It was indispensable to throw the Lady Elizabeth into prison, and it is considered that she will have to be executed, as while she lives it will be very difficult to make the Prince's entry here safe, or accomplish anything of promise'.[2] The imprisoned conspirators and rebel leaders were examined in an attempt to make them implicate her, and the evidence was sifted for incriminating words and deeds, but very little was obtained. A typical specimen was the report sent up by the Sheriff of Gloucestershire, that, at a recent gathering of the county gentry, Sir Nicholas Arnold had been unwise enough to stand up and denounce the Spanish marriage, 'declaring the vilenes . . . of them' (the Spaniards). He had gone on to talk of the Lady Elizabeth, but ' . . . more I hard not to my remembrans', wrote the Sheriff ingenuously, 'for my hering is not of the best'.[3] Such hints and suspicions were inadequate, for the Princess was popular, and had powerful friends. The confessions extracted from the prisoners were more promising, but

---

[1] Renard to the Emperor, February. *Cal. Span.*, Vol. XII, p. 96. Xenophobia had not ceased with the collapse of the rising. Renard went on: ' . . . many foreigners have departed, because marks have been found on their houses'. A massacre seems to have been feared.

[2] Don Juan Hurtado de Mendoza to the Bishop of Arras, 19 March. *Cal. Span.*, Vol. XII, p. 162.

[3] SP, Vol. III, no 13.

still not conclusive. On 25 February Sir John Bourne reported to the Chancellor that he had 'laboured to make Sir Thomas Wyatt confess concerning the Lady Elizabeth',[1] but so far with no result. However, Wyatt remained the most promising field of enquiry, and it seems that the delay in his trial, and still longer delay in execution, resulted from the hope that he could be persuaded to incriminate her. How far that hope was realized remains uncertain to this day. At his trial on 15 March Sir Thomas alleged that he had written to the Princess, and received a verbal reply of a non-committal nature. It was later claimed that after his conviction he drew up a full statement in writing, accusing both Elizabeth and Courtenay of complicity in his designs, but on the scaffold he declared ' . . . yt is not so good people, for I assure you neyther they nor any other now in yonder holde of durance was privie of my rising. . . .' Despite this denial it is probable that he made some such statement under torture, or in hope of pardon, and then retracted when he saw that it would not avail to save his life.[2] Lord Chandos later testified in Star Chamber that Wyatt had made such a confession on the morning of his execution,[3] but the 'statement in wryting' was not produced against Elizabeth, and has not since been found.

There was other evidence, but it was purely circumstantial. Croftes had visited Ashridge on his way to Herefordshire, and

[1] Ibid. no 34. Despite this temporary setback, Wyatt seems to have talked freely on other points. According to Renard, 'without being tortured at all' he accused Courtenay, Pickering, and Sir Nicholas Pointz (Renard to the Emperor, 12 February). It may also have been Wyatt who caused suspicion to be cast on the aged Anne of Cleves.

[2] Sir Thomas's courage under examination does not seem to have been as great as his courage in the field, but his behaviour on the scaffold certainly makes it look as if he was attempting to undo the damage he had done. Dr Weston, who was appointed to be with him at his execution, interrupted his last speech, saying 'Merke this, my masters, he saythe that that which he hath showed to the counsell in wryting of my lady Elizabeth and Courteny ys true' (*Q.J.* p. 74). There may have been justification for Weston's anxiety, but the bad form of his action was much resented.

[3] ' . . . I, being lieutenant of the Tower when Wyatt suffered, he desired me to bring him to the Lord Courtenay; which when I had done he fell down upon his knees before him in my presence, and desired him to confesse the truth of himselfe, as he had done before, and to submit himself unto the queen's majesty's mercy' (*Q.J.* p. 72 note(e)).

urged her to move away to Donnington. Lord Russell confessed to carrying Wyatt's letters to her,[1] and a servant of hers,
Sir William Saintlow, had been rash enough to appear in
company with Isley and Knevett at Tonbridge.[2] However, she
had not left Ashridge, or replied to the letters received, and
although Saintlow's arrest on 15 February was a serious embarrassment, he made no statement to inculpate his mistress.
Despite her discretion, she was for a time in serious danger.
Her very existence was a threat to the government and a presumption of guilt. As soon as the seriousness of the outbreak was
known, on 26 January, a summons had been sent, addressed by
the Queen to her 'Right dear and entirely beloved sister',
requesting her attendance at Court.[3] This had been ignored,
and there were rumours that Ashridge was being fortified. On
9 February, as soon as there was leisure to think of it, Lord
William Howard was sent down with peremptory orders to
bring her to Westminster. She arrived, in the grip of a real or
feigned illness, on or about the 18th, and ' . . . many men
dyversely thought of hir sending for'.[4] A month later, as a
result of Wyatt's statements made at his trial, she was removed
from the honourable confinement of the Court, and committed
to the Tower. This move was engineered by Gardiner, and was
the climax of the Princess's peril, but, ironically enough, the
Chancellor was unable to follow up his success because he was
forced to suppress a crucial piece of evidence. Early in the rising
one of Noailles' despatches describing the outbreak had been
intercepted. Enclosed with it was a copy of a letter recently sent
by Elizabeth to the Queen. Unfortunately for Gardiner the
despatch made unambiguous reference to his own interview
with Courtenay, and the part which the latter had been
expected to play. This embarrassing circumstance forced the

---

[1] Ambassadors to the Emperor, 8 March. *Cal. Span.*, Vol. XII, p. 140.
[2] Southwell to the Council, 24 February. SP, Vol. III, no. 32.
[3] Petyt MS no. 538, Vol. 47, f. 315 Calendared in *The Second Report of the Historical Manuscripts Commission*, App. p. 154.
[4] *Q.J*, p. 63. Lord William Howard wrote a full report of his interview with Elizabeth upon his arrival at Ashridge. She declared that she was too ill to move, but was contradicted by the physician who was consulted. SP, Vol. III, no. 21.

Chancellor to 'lose' the inconvenient documents when his library was sacked by the rebels.[1] By the beginning of April Elizabeth's enemies were forced to admit defeat. On 3 April Renard reported to the Emperor that by English law the Princess could not be touched, and the proposal to marry her to a foreign Prince was revived in consequence.[2] On 19 May she was allowed to withdraw into house-arrest at Woodstock, for the Queen's anger had passed, and the danger was over.

The attempts to bring about Courtenay's conviction also failed for similar reasons. It was easy to make out a *prima facie* case against him, for he had been very indiscreet, but it was impossible to prove an overt act, because in fact he had done nothing. A quantity of armour was found in his house, and several strange costumes which might, or might not, have been disguises. It was alleged that he had a secret cipher for communicating with Carew, and that he had arranged a relay of post horses to carry him down to Devon.[3] The Duke of Suffolk admitted having said that he would place the crown on Courtenay's head, but denied that he meant it, and at his trial Wyatt had said 'towching Courtney' that ' . . . sir Edwarde Rogers went betwene Courtney and hime, and that he sente him word to procede in the same . . . '.[4] More damning accusations were alleged, but, as with Elizabeth, never produced. By virtue of his office, Gardiner had full charge of the investigations, and appointed a partisan of his, Sir Richard Southwell, to conduct them.[5] Renard was naturally convinced that the Chancellor was suppressing the evidence, but there was not much that he could do about it, and on 8 March he wrote that

[1] Council to Wotton, 22 February. *Cal. For.*, Vol. II, p. 60. Noailles demanded the return of his despatches, but Gardiner stuck to his story. How the copy of Elizabeth's letter came to be there in the first place is still a mystery.

[2] Renard to the Emperor, 3 April. *Cal. Span.*, Vol. XII, p. 201. The Duke of Savoy and Don Carlos were both mentioned as possible candidates.

[3] Ambassadors to the Emperor, 8 March, ibid. p. 139.

[4] *Q J*, p. 69.

[5] Southwell, together with Sir Thomas Pope and others, was appointed on or about 11 February (*Q J*, p. 65). Another Commission, headed by Sir Nicholas Hare, was appointed to examine prisoners on 16 February (*APC*, Vol. IV, p. 393). Whether these two groups worked together or were distinct in their functions, I have not been able to discover.

despite all efforts only misprision of treason could be proved. In the event Gardiner was so successful that his protégé was never brought to trial. On 25 May he was transferred from the Tower, where he had been lodged on 12 February, to Fotheringay,[1] whence he was to be released in the spring of the following year. If the evidence against him had in fact been suppressed it was done so skilfully that no trace of it now remains. In the familiar surroundings of prison the Earl seems to have been far more discreet and in command of himself than in the world outside.

II

The position of the Earl and the Princess, and the conflict over their fate, strongly influenced proceedings against the conspirators. They were more guilty than the majority of the rebels because their treason had been deliberate and constructive, but their guilt was less obtrusive, and more interests were involved in their protection. The Council seems to have felt that the main danger lay in not knowing the extent of their machinations, so that after strenuous efforts to arrest and examine them, the subsequent proceedings were conducted slackly or not at all. Edward Warner had been apprehended while the rising was still in progress, but the turn of the others did not come until the pressure on official time and energy was less extreme. A number of letters were sent out between 7 and 10 February for the safeguarding of the country, and the apprehension of the conspirators, but the first group did not reach the Tower until the evening of the 20th.[2] This consisted of William Winter, Sir Nicholas Throgmorton and William Thomas. The last named had been lying ill at the rectory in the village of Bagendon, in Gloucestershire throughout the period of the rising, and had not left that retreat until the 15th, so that his arrest must have followed speedily.[3] There is no

---

[1] *Q.J*, p. 76. From there he went into exile, in accordance with a plan mooted before the rising.

[2] *Q.J*, p. 63.

[3] The examination of John a Mynde, the parson, and others, was conducted on 22 February (SP, Vol. III, no. 30).

evidence to show how the others had been occupied. Croftes, whose activities had been a great source of anxiety,[1] arrived on the 21st, accompanied by Sir Thomas Grey, whose flight from Astley had ended with his arrest at Oswestry about the 11th or 12th.[2] Sir William Pickering had already escaped to France, as had Carew. Sir Edward Rogers and Sir Nicholas Arnold arrived on the 24th.

Their examinations seem to have been conducted for the purpose of incriminating Elizabeth or Courtenay, or both, and it may be for this reason that they have not survived. Once they were in custody the Council's interest in most of them waned. Except for Wyatt, Harper and Suffolk, against whom the main charge was that of rebellion, no indictment was proffered until 7 April. On that day a True Bill was found in the Guildhall before the Lord Mayor against Throgmorton, Croftes, Arnold, Carew, Pickering, Rogers, Winter and Warner. They were charged with conspiring together with Wyatt, Harper, and others in London on 26 November 1 Mary, with the object of seizing the Tower, and levying war against the Queen to deprive her of her royal title.[3] Carew and Pickering were out of reach, and Winter, Warner, Rogers and Arnold were never brought to trial. Winter was pardoned on 10 November in the same year, Arnold on 4 March 1555, and Rogers and Warner on 2 July following.[4] The recognizances taken upon their release in January 1555 never seem to have been exploited.

[1] There were still rumours of a rising in Wales, which was thought to be Croftes' work, and of mysterious messengers passing through Oxford on their way to the West. On 7 February the Council had sent orders to Ludlow and Hereford for the safe-keeping of those towns, but in fact Croftes appears to have done nothing.

[2] A manuscript chronicle of Shrewsbury records 'The Lord Thomas, brother to the Ducke of Suffolke was taken at Oswestrie in Wales by master Rycharde Myttoon of Shrosbery, being then baylyff . . .' (N. Owen and J. B. Blakeway, *A History of Shrewsbury*, London 1825, Vol. I, p. 351). A Crown case was later opened against Mitton for the property which Sir Thomas was alleged to be carrying (KB27/1177 Rex. r14d). An indenture, dated 15 February, gave the prisoners into Mitton's custody to escort them to London (*APC*, Vol. IV, p. 396) and he claimed the property to offset against his expenses.

[3] KB8/29, r 2.

[4] *Cal. Pat.* Vol. II, pp. 203, 293, 48.

Only Throgmorton and Croftes stood to the indictment. They appeared together at the Guildhall on 17 April, but Croftes pleaded a technicality in bar of trial and Throgmorton alone was tried on that day. After a very able defence, lasting from seven o'clock in the morning until five in the evening, he was acquitted, and there were rejoicings in the City. The trial was a *cause célèbre* and several full accounts of it exist,[1] so there is no necessity to dwell on it here, but one or two points are worthy of comment. When Fitzwilliams was produced as a defence witness, he was not allowed to testify, although Cuthbert Vaughn, who had been twice reprieved from execution, was produced for the Crown. On the other hand it seems clear that Throgmorton had acquired some access to legal books, which was officially denied him. As was usually the case with sixteenth-century treason trials, the issue was political, and the legal framework largely formal, so that the action of the jury was treated as a hostile political demonstration. Throgmorton was probably guilty, although the customary methods of weighting the scales against him make it hard to be sure, and his acquittal was a serious setback to the government. The jury were '. . . commanded to be redy before the counsell at an howres warnyng, on the losse of Vᶜ li a pece . . . .'[2] On 25 April they were brought into Star Chamber, whence two were despatched to the Tower, and the remainder to the Fleet. They were not released until the middle of December, and then only on payment of heavy fines.[3] Throgmorton himself was kept in prison, and not released until the following January, by which time many of the convicted rebels were already free and pardoned.

Despite this severity, the Government only narrowly escaped a second defeat when Croftes was brought to trial on the 28th. He pleaded that his offence did not amount to treason, since he had not been guilty of an overt act. The Court ruled that Wyatt's action had involved all the conspirators in his treason,[4] but

---

[1] Cobbett, Vol. I, pp. 870 et seq., *Q.J*, p. 75.
[2] *Q.J*, p. 75.
[3] Foxe, Vol. VI, p. 579.
[4] 'Nota per Bromeley Chief Justice . . . si pluisors enter de conspiracy a fair comotion ou a levier guerre encount le Roigne ou son Realme pur alter et change

' . . . he colde not be fonde of the Quest which was warned passing viii, so they were fayne to send for Hartopp and serten curryars and others. . . .'[1] This second jury duly brought in the required verdict, but the weakness of the government had been further demonstrated. Croftes was not executed, and after a period of imprisonment he was pardoned on 16 February 1556.[2] There is no trace of his having paid any fine or composition.

In the event the only man to suffer purely for his part in the conspiracy was William Thomas, whose fate was probably sealed by Wyatt's admissions concerning his proposal to kill the Queen. After his arrest, on the night of 25 February, Thomas tried to commit suicide by 'thrusting himself under the pappes with a knife',[3] but he bungled the stroke, and his trial was merely put off to give him time to recover. He was indicted on 8 May, accused of plotting the Queen's death and of holding treasonable conference with Carew at Mohun's Ottery on 27 December, as well as of the conspiracy proper.[4] He was tried the same day, and executed on the 18th. Unlike most of his fellows, he maintained the patriotic motives of his action to the last, but his death seems to have aroused little interest. In view of the serious nature of the plot, it is understandable that Renard should have been dissatisfied with this solitary sacrifice, and have threatened to suspend preparations for the Prince's visit.[5]

Renard, however, was alone among the Queen's advisers in treating the conspiracy seriously once the danger was over. Both Paget and Gardiner had an interest in minimizing its importance and protecting those concerned, so that the execution of Thomas was little but a sop. He was the least influential

---

Religion, si nul act insue sur ceo ceo nest Treason per lestatute de anno 25 E 3 mes si un de eux apres leva le guerre per reason de cest conspiracy, et les auts seont in lour measons sans auter act fair ils sont touts Traitours per le dit Statute. . . .' Dalison's Report in W. Benloe, *Select cases in King's Bench 1530–1624*, pt II, p. 15.

[1] *Q J*, p. 76.
[2] *Cal. Pat.*, Vol. II, p. 124.
[3] *Q J*, p. 65.
[4] KB8/30, r 1.
[5] Renard to the Emperor, 18 May. *Cal. Span.*, Vol. XII, p. 261.

of the prominent conspirators, and the most thoroughly discredited, so that his sacrifice aroused the least controversy. It was otherwise with the rebels proper. In defending them Paget was in a minority against Gardiner and Renard, and was forced to proceed with extreme caution, but his success was considerable. The Council's actions against them after their defeat show a steady decline of energy and animosity, which reflects the influence of Paget and his friends. They were not greatly concerned to prevent the initial round-up, which was conducted with enthusiasm, but the large numbers who escaped trial, and the very large proportion of those convicted who were later pardoned, reveals the ascendency which they gained over the Queen's mind once her first anger had abated. Renard was filled with rage and despair by this situation, and his reports during February and March were full of bitter descriptions of the way in which the ringleaders were escaping the axe.[1] In his letters of 22 and 27 March he wrote that Paget and a group of his supporters had taken advantage of the fact that Gardiner was absent from the Court on Easter Sunday, 18 March, to approach the Queen in her oratory and persuade her to honour the holy day by releasing a number of the prisoners.[2] When the Ambassador later upbraided her for her weakness she pleaded that it was an English custom. It seems that, although Paget was alone among the first rank of the Queen's advisers in working for a policy of leniency, he was well supported at a lower level of the Council, and had the great bulk of influential opinion behind him.

III

The collapse of the midland foray was followed by an energetic, but brief, search for the participants. Suffolk himself seems to have intended to escape westwards, and take ship to Denmark.[3]

---

[1] 'I . . . have done my best to admonish the Queen to have the prisoners promptly punished. . . . However, all has been of no avail.' Renard to the Emperor, 22 March. *Cal. Span.*, Vol. XII, p. 168.

[2] Ibid.

[3] Bowyer's second testimony.

For this, however, he relied upon Bowyer, who was a native of
Somerset, to act as his guide, and Bowyer, disgruntled by
missing his share of the cash distribution, refused. Consequently
the Duke and his brother John went into hiding in Astley park.
They were betrayed almost at once,[1] and on 2 February the
Earl of Huntingdon wrote to the Sheriff and J.P.'s of Rutland:
'. . . by the providence of god the Duke of Suff. and the
Lord John his brother are this day apprehended and in my
custody. . . .'[2] The prisoners were removed to Coventry, and
after a three-day stop at the house of Christopher Warren, one
of the aldermen,[3] reached London escorted by the Earl and
'other gentyllmen to the nomber of CCC horse' on the 10th. Sir
Thomas, as we have already seen, escaped and was not arrested
for nearly two weeks, but the movements of the others involved
are obscure. Medley's goods at Tilty were inventoried, in
accordance with a Council letter dated the 16th,[4] and he
probably surrendered to the authorities soon after as his effects
were placed in the hands of his wife on the 22nd, and he himself
was committed to the Tower on the 26th.[5] Thomas Dannet was
arrested about the middle of the month, and entered the same
prison on the 24th, on which day Leonard Dannet was also
moved there from the gatehouse, in company with Sir Nicholas
Arnold.[6] John Bowyer and Thomas Rampton were both caught
almost at once, the former in Stratford on Avon and the latter
at some place unspecified. They reached London on 10 and
11 February respectively. With the exception of John Wullocke,
who made good his escape, there is no certain information
concerning the others. William Burdet was described as
'remaynyng in ward' when instructions were issued for his
pardon to be drawn on 17 June,[7] but we do not know how or

---

[1] The story is told in full by Holinshed (Vol. IV, p. 14). William Dugdale,
The Antiquities of Warwickshire (edited by William Thomas, London 1760), Vol. I,
p. 80 b, gives circumstantial details.
[2] B.M. Egerton MS 2986 f. 11. Several of Suffolk's servants were arrested at
the same time, but most were soon released.
[3] *Q.J*, p. 53.   [4] *APC*, Vol. IV, p. 393.
[5] *Q.J*, p. 66. *APC*, Vol. IV, p. 401.
[6] *APC*, Vol. IV, p. 399.
[7] *APC*, Vol. V, p. 41. This was a pardon for life only.

when he came there. Presumably Bartholomew Wullocke, Foster, Grene, Symcockes, Glover and Astlyn suffered some kind of confinement, since no special search was organized for them, and there is no mention of their escape. None of them were brought to London, however, and none were actually tried, so it seems probable that they were imprisoned locally, and released after a short period like many other malcontents.

The three Grey brothers, Medley, Foster, the two Wullockes, the two Dannets and Burdet were indicted at Leicester on 10 February,[1] and Burdet was presented a second time at Coventry on 3 March.[2] Grene was also presented separately at Leicester,[3] but, rather surprisingly, neither Rampton, Bowyer, nor any of the Coventry group seem to have been subjected to legal process. Rampton was examined at the Tower on the day of his arrival, and the Commissioners were clearly satisfied of his guilt, for on the 24th a letter was sent to the Constable of the Tower, directing him to ' . . . delyver the body of Rampton to Robert Dickyns, John Sutton, and Robert Gery, to be conveied by them to Coventree to be futher ordered there.'[4] The chronicler put it more bluntly: 'This daie Thomas Rampton . . . caried into the country to Coventry ther to be arained and to suffer death';[5] but in the event Rampton was neither tried nor executed. He seems to have taken advantage of the increasing tendency to leniency during and after the last week in February, but exactly what happened we do not know. His pardon was enrolled during October.[6] Bowyer was also examined, on the same day, by the Earl of Huntingdon. For some inexplicable reason the Earl then released him, and he made his way back to Leicestershire.[7] Thereafter he disappeared for over four years, reappearing in the Fleet in June 1558. On the 14th of that month he was interrogated a second

[1] KB8/28 r 3.
[2] KB27/1172 Rex I (iii)d.
[3] Cal. Pat., Vol. I, p. 503.
[4] APC, Vol. IV, p. 399.
[5] Q.J, p. 65.
[6] Cal. Pat., Vol. II, p. 242, 26 October 1554. In this pardon Rampton is not described specifically as being either indicted or convicted.
[7] Second deposition of John Bowyer, SP, Vol. XIII, no. 26.

time, and the Council noted ' . . . it appereth that he confesseth
to have been privey to the treasoune of the late Duke of
Suffolke, and a doer therein, and never syns laboured for his
pardon.'[1] He had never been formally indicted, and may well
have considered that a sufficient excuse for not requiring a
pardon. The presentation was made at length on 7 November
1558 at Leicester,[2] but ten days later the Queen was dead, and
he was shortly after pardoned. Aylmer was for some obscure
reason not indicted until 12 September. He was never tried,
but his pardon did not appear on the Patent Roll until
8 February 1560, over a year after Bowyer's.[3]

A month after his arrest Thomas Dannet was released,
without any recorded security,[4] and promptly escaped to the
Continent to join his old diplomatic colleague, Pickering. In
April Wotton wrote, recommending that they both be pardoned
for their good services.[5] Just over a month later, on the order of
the Council, his goods were inventoried and delivered to his
wife.[6] He was pardoned during October, and seems to have
returned to England almost at once.[7] Probably his 'escape' was
arranged, and his pardon purchased by an undertaking to work
against the exiles in France, whose activities were causing the
government much embarrassment. Whatever the reason, his
flight left only the Duke and his two brothers to stand their
trials, as no further action was taken against Medley, Foster,

---

[1] APC, Vol. VI, p. 331. It is not clear how Bowyer came to be arrested a second
time, or whether this imprisonment had any connection with his former offence.

[2] Cal. Pat., Elizabeth Vol. I, p. 60.

[3] Ibid, p. 279. It may have been at this time that he fled to Strasbourg.

[4] Q.J, p. 71.

[5] On 29 April Wotton wrote that both Pickering and Dannet were loyal, and
had slipped away from the other exiles towards Italy because they feared their
lives to be in danger. Wotton recommended that if they 'came safe away' they
should be pardoned. He seems to have received several intelligences from them.
Cal. For., Vol. II, p. 79.

[6] APC, Vol. V, p. 37.

[7] This pardon was unusual from several points of view. It was pleaded in person
in the Michaelmas Term 1554 (KB27/1172 Rex VI) when the date of the pardon,
20 October, was recorded on the Plea Roll. The formal enrolment on the Patent
Roll did not take place until 30 January following (Cal. Pat., Vol. II, p. 290).
This suggests that a form of pardon was sent to Dannet in exile, and he returned
upon the strength of it before the official documents were issued.

Burdet, Leonard Dannet or Bartholomew Wullocke. It seems that the government appreciated the true nature of the rising, and decided to deal severely only with those ultimately responsible. As a peer of the realm, the Duke was tried by his brethren before the Earl of Arundel, as Lord High Steward. The legal processes were completed on 16 February,[1] and on the 17th he was 'caried to Westminster . . . by the clerke of the cheke and all the garde almoste. . . .'[2] The indictment accused him of levying war against the Queen at Leicester and alleged that he had ' . . . vicesimo nono die Ianuarii . . . fecit proclamacionem . . . quod predictus Dux dare vellet . . . qui voluit . . . adherere ipsi Duci in executione nephandissime et proditorie guerre et rebellione . . . stipendium sex denarii per diem.'[3] He pleaded not guilty, claiming ' . . . that yt was no treason for a pere of the realme as he was to raise his power and make proclamacion onely to avoyde strangers out of the realme.'[4] If this plea was designed to seek the protection of the Statutes of Repeal, it was an unavailing technicality, for in the next breath the Duke admitted meeting the Earl of Huntingdon 'in arms'. There is no mention of this incident elsewhere, but it was in this connection that Suffolk claimed ignorance of the Earl's Commission, adding 'I met him indeed, but with fiftey men or thereabouts, and would not have shranken from him if I had had fewer'.[5] The panel of 18 peers condemned him unanimously, and on his return to the Tower ' . . . he landed at the water gate with a countenance very heavy and pensyfe, desyring all men to praye for him.' He was executed the following Friday, 23 February, on Tower Hill 'betwyn ix and x of the cloke afore none'.

Thomas was tried at Westminster on the same indictment on 9 March.[6] He also pleaded not guilty, and the substance of his defence was the same as his brother's ' . . . that as God sholde judge his soule he meant none other thing but the abolyshing of strangers, and yf that were hye treason, the

---

[1] KB8/28.   [2] *Q.J*, p. 60.
[3] KB8/28, r. 3d.   [4] *Q.J*, p. 60.
[5] Ibid.   [6] KB8/31.

Lorde be mercyful. . . .'[1] The venire was awarded at once, but as soon as the jury had been sworn, he changed his plea 'and was cast (to lose h)ys hed'. It was strongly suspected at the time that Thomas was the real leader of the family, and the inspirer of his brother's foolish move,[2] so there was small hope of mercy. He was executed on Tower hill on 24 April.

The proceedings against John Grey were rather more complicated. Both the Tower chronicler and Machyn agree that was arraigned on 20 February,[3] but there is no mention of this trial on the plea roll. According to the record his trial opened at Westminster on 27 May, he pleaded not guilty, and the venire was awarded for 11 June.[4] We learn, however, from a contemporary law report that he claimed trial by his peers on the ground that he was Marquis of Dorset by virtue of the attainder and death of his brothers.[5] This plea could hardly have been made, however, on 20 February, when only Henry was attainted and both were still alive. Consequently it must have been made in May, and the incident in February remains unexplained. The claim was disallowed, and the recorded venire resulted. Like Thomas, when the jury was sworn John changed his plea, and was condemned. Alone of the three, however, he escaped the axe, through the 'diligent travail' of his wife, a sister of that good catholic Sir Anthony Browne, Viscount Montague. He was released on 30 October, and pardoned on 17 January following.[6]

---

[1] Q.J, p. 67.

[2] Noailles, at least, was convinced of this. In his report to the King on 28 January he wrote, 'Le duc de Suffolck . . . il s'est retiré . . . avecques ses deulx freres, qui sont gens de plus grand esprit et conduicte que luy; et ne faicts doubte que millord Thomas l'un d'iceulx suyvant ce que je vous en ay, sire, faict entendre par cy-devant, ne soit bientost pour remuer menasge; et comme celuy qui a desclairé à quelqu'un de ses amys et des miens en ces propres mots, que voyant la faulte que a faicte Courtenay, il est deliberé de tenir son lieu, qu'il fault qu'il soit roy ou pendu' (Vertot, Vol. III, p. 48).

[3] Machyn, p. 56. The Tower chronicler adds the detail that he was forced to ride because he had the gout. Q.J, p. 63.

[4] KB27/1171. Rex II. Strangely enough, Machyn also confirms this date. Machyn, p. 64.

[5] W. Benloe, *Select cases*, part II, p. 15.

[6] *Cal. Pat.*, Vol. II, p. 151.

IV

Those who remained in Devon after the flight of Sir Peter Carew were not long at large. On 28 January news reached St Leger that Sir Gawain Carew was at the house of his nephew, John Carew, at Bickleigh. The latter, when apprehended, admitted that it was so, but claimed that his uncle had appeared unbidden and was not an offender to his knowledge.[1] St Leger took him, and went to his house with an escort of thirty men, but he did not need his soldiers, for Sir Gawain gave himself up without a fight. The same day, following another lead, Gibbes was arrested at the house of Sir John More.[2] Both were imprisoned in Exeter castle, but no action seems to have been taken against their hosts. Reporting his success to the Council the following day, St Leger stated that both the prisoners acknowledged their fault, and submitted to the Queen's mercy.[3] He added that he would proceed next to the arrest of Champernowne, but it was rumoured that William Thomas was already in flight. In fact, by the time this letter was written Thomas was already on his sick-bed at Bagendon.

As soon as they were in custody, depositions were taken from Carew and from various servants and others, but they do not add substantially to our knowledge of the previous events.[4] These documents, together with inventories of the goods and chattels of the Carews and Gibbes, were sent up to the Council by St Leger and Dennis on 4 and 5 February.[5] In his letter of the former date St Leger enlarged upon the peace and good order of the shire, news which reached London most opportunely to strengthen resistance against Wyatt's final bid.[6] Once

[1] St Leger to the Council, 29 January. SP, Vol. II, no. 26.
[2] Ibid.   [3] Ibid.
[4] One John Portington, a servant of Robert Dennis, testified that Sir Gawain had made his escape from Exeter after the garrisoning of the city, by scaling the wall. (SP, Vol. III, no. 10 (2)). At the same time a certain John Graynford wrote to St Leger and Dennis, outlining the story of Sir Peter's escape, which he had from an unnamed source (SP, Vol. III, no. 5, Enclosure dated 3 February).
[5] SP, Vol. III, nos. 5 and 10.
[6] This was a shrewd blow against the rebels' propaganda. Q J, p. 42.

the confusion was over and they were in possession of the facts, the authorities showed no inclination to be vindictive towards the Devon rebels. Despite its part in the overall plan, and the initial alarms which it caused, the situation there was local, and the danger soon passed. The government wisely avoided making martyrs, and the episode rapidly faded from memory. There is hardly a trace of it in the records of the county or the City of Exeter. When arrested Sir Arthur Champernowne 'tendered his services like a loyal subject', and no proceedings were taken against him. Presumably he was soon released. Nor was any action taken against those who fled with Sir Peter. The only names which appear in any legal record for their part in the disturbances are those of Sir Peter himself, Sir Gawain, and William Gibbes.

After just over a month in Exeter castle, the latter two arrived in London on 3 March, and were imprisoned in the Tower.[1] By that time the real danger was past, and they seem to have remained unnoticed in prison throughout the summer, except that the Council granted the profits of Sir Gawain's lands to his wife on 15 June.[2] No indictment was proffered until 13 September when a True Bill was found before the Commissioners of Oyer and Terminer sitting at Exeter,[3] which was presumably found 'in absentia' as the prisoners remained in London. The government was clearly not disposed to treat their cases seriously, and neither was brought to trial. On 27 January 1555 Dr Wotton wrote from France to the Council to intercede for Sir Gawain, who was his brother-in-law.[4] In May proceedings against him were halted, and he was pardoned in July.[5] Gibbes was pardoned in October of the same year, and his goods and chattels restored to him.[6]

The position of Sir Peter Carew was more serious in every

[1] Q.J, p. 66.
[2] APC, Vol. IV, p. 403.
[3] KB27/1176. Rex III.
[4] Cal. For. Vol. II, p. 152.
[5] Cal. Pat. Vol. II, p. 291. The pardon was pleaded in the Michaelmas Term 1555. KB27/1176 Rex III.
[6] Cal. Pat. Vol. III, p. 119; KB27/1176 Rex XXIV.

way, except that he was out of reach. Not only was he the leader, and one of the original conspirators, but he continued to harass the government by treasonable activities in France. His name was included with the other conspirators on the Guildhall indictment of 7 April, but the main Bill against him was that found at Exeter in September. There the substance of the London indictment was repeated, and it was further alleged that Carew, 'impie inverse et erronie religionis', had uttered the following words to the Duke of Suffolk: 'If the quene wold forebeare this marriage wyth the Spanyard, and use a moderation in matters of relygion, I wold dye at her foote, but otherwise I will do the best to place the Lady Elizabeth in here stede',[1] adding that 'he durst be one of the hundred gentylmen that should take the Queene and put her in the Tower'. These words show to a remarkable degree the same mixture of bravado and bad conscience that can be traced in the utterances of Wyatt and Suffolk, and are a good illustration of the confused thinking that afflicted the whole movement. The indictment went on to charge Carew with levying war against the Queen at Mohun's Ottery on 17 January, of inducing the Earl of Devon to lead the rising, and of departing the realm without royal licence. Because of his flight, Carew was never tried, but he seems to have been treated as attainted from the moment of his first presentation. In the event he was the only man to suffer materially for his attempted rising, but the circumstances of that suffering belong to another chapter.

V

Most of the rank and file of the Kentish rebels, as well as a number of leaders, were taken in London as soon as Wyatt had surrendered, but some escaped, and some had never come so far. The Kentish gentry, anxious to display that loyalty which had not before been much in evidence, showed considerable energy in the resulting round-up. Southwell, reporting to the Council on 10 February, wrote

[1] KB27/1176, Rex III.

Accordynge to your Lordships commandment and my dewtye, I have apprehended Peter Mapesden, Richarde Parke, William Tilden, Alexander Fysher, William Grene and William Smythe, and foras much as your Lordships hath lefte to my discressyon the apprehension of such others as were in this vile treason, either forward or leaders, I have also apprehended some other, and will more as speedeley as I can; I have comytted such as be of substance as yet to Alyngton Castel where I have a gard for them; and such as be powre, and yet so lewyd as my dewty will not suffer me to (free) them, I have bestowed to the gayle of Maydestone.[1]

He had taken over Allington as his headquarters, and from there directed operations all over the county. Bands of men were raised in Rochester and Canterbury to comb the country-side and guard the prisoners. These were joined, about the 17th, by 300 of the Earl of Pembroke's horsemen, and the prisons of Kent were soon so full that serious disruption was threatened to the life of the county. Southwell wrote on 24 February asking for the speedy appointment of a special commission, for 'sondrie of them be husbandmen and sondrie artificers, and all is at a stay for the period of their imprisonment'.[2] Frequently it seems that the Sheriff examined the prisoners himself, or took statements from witnesses, and forwarded the results to Gardiner. The small number of these that survive are of no particular importance, and it is unlikely that they were of great interest to the Chancellor.[3] The facts of the matter were usually clear enough; the only doubt was the extent of the punishment.

In London progress was rather more rapid. Wyatt himself, William Knevett, Thomas Brooke, the two Mantells and Alex-ander Brett were in the Tower by 5 p.m. of the day on which they surrendered.[4] Within the next two days they were joined by George Brooke, Sir William Brooke, Anthony Knevett, Hugh Booth, Thomas Fane, Robert Rudstone, Sir George

[1] Southwell to the Council, SP, Vol. III, no. 18. Several of those named had been in trouble before, see APC, Vol. IV, pp. 373, 375, 27 November and 2 December 1553.
[2] SP, Vol. III. no. 32.
[3] Southwell sent up one batch by 11 February (ibid. no. 22), but the only one which now survives is a statement by the villagers of Hadlow, that the alarm bell was rung there by order of Sir Henry Isley (ibid. no. 12, dated 9 February).
[4] Q J, p. 51, gives a graphic description of Wyatt's arrival.

Harper, Edward Wyatt,[1] Edward Fogg, George More and Cuthbert Vaughn. A few, like William Staunton, Brian Fitzwilliam, and Edward Randall, made good their escape, but others were intercepted and brought back: Sir Henry Isley, fugitive since his defeat at Wrotham, Thomas Culpepper and William Cromer. At the same time their humbler adherents were lodged wherever room could be found for them. When the prisons were full ' . . . they were fayne to keep the poorest sort by iiii xx on a hepp, in churches'.[2] Indictments were presented, and the trials commenced almost at once. The first was that of 33 Londoners, conducted in King's Bench on the 10th from a Middlesex indictment found the previous day.[3] To expedite the process they had been charged with levying war against the Queen in Middlesex, but probably their most serious offence had been desertion at Rochester bridge. All were condemned. On Monday, the 12th, two further trials were despatched, one before King's Bench and the other before the Lord Mayor and his fellow justices of Oyer and Terminer sitting at the Old Bailey.[4] In the first case 65 Londoners and Kentish men were condemned on a Middlesex indictment, in the second case 82 on a London indictment.

Two other Commissions began to operate on Tuesday the 13th.[5] One for Surrey, headed by Sir Thomas Bromley, the Chief Justice of King's Bench, began sitting in the old Court House at Southwark, and a second Middlesex Commission, headed by the Marquis of Winchester, sat for the first time at Westminster.

[1] Described officially as 'of Allington, Yeoman', and unofficially (by Gardiner) as 'lyttle Wyat, a bastard of no substance' (SP, Vol. III, no. 22). It is uncertain whether he was an illegitimate son or younger brother of Sir Thomas. He was pardoned on 29 April 1554, and seems to have lived until 1590, when the burial of one Edward Wyatt was recorded in the Boxley Parish Register. (Transcript preserved among the Wyatt MSS [no. 37]).

[2] Q.J, p. 59.

[3] KB27/1169, Rex VII. They were presented on a Middlesex indictment to remove the necessity of having to call in a jury from another shire in the event of any of the accused 'putting himself upon the country'. It was notoriously difficult to convene juries outside their counties of residence.

[4] Cal. Pat., Vol. III, p. 125. KB27/1169, Rex VIII.

[5] KB8/26, 32. Each of these pouches contains the complete proceedings of one Commission. It seems probable that Bromley did not sit, as Sir John Mordaunt is referred to as presiding.

The operation of the former was very simple. On the first day True Bill was found against a mixture of Londoners, Kentish men and men of Southwark, 170 in number, for assembling in warlike array at Southwark, marching to Kingston and giving battle to Robert Butcher, Edward Standen and other loyal subjects. The Court was then adjourned until the 21st, when it reassembled in the Shire House. A further 14 men were then presented on a similar indictment, and the whole number tried on the same day. 182 were convicted, and two acquitted. The adjournment seems to have been called to enable the authorities to make sure that no more offenders were lurking in London. The Tower chronicler noted that on the 18th

There was proclamacyon made in Chepesyde by a trompeter, that yf eny man had eny of the saide rebells, or knewe wher they were, (he) shoulde bringe theym unto the Marshalsea; or elles if they were hurt, sicke, or colde not come in person, their names shoulde be brought to the Marshalsea the morrowe followinge.[1]

The last indictment probably represents the response to this command.

The Westminster Commission appears to have been mainly for the trial of the leaders. On the first day True Bill was found against Wyatt, Harper, Culpepper, the Knevetts, the Mantells, Brett, Rudstone, Cromer, Vaughn and Fane for assembling with an armed force at Brentford and attacking London. Two days later, on the 15th, a similar indictment was found against 16 others, including William, George and Thomas Brooke. On the 16th, two further indictments which had originally been found in King's Bench on the 12th were reproved to bring them within the jurisdiction of the Court. These involved 69 men, bringing the total arraigned before the Commission to 97. The first group, with the exception of Wyatt and Harper, was tried on the 15th, when, according to the Chronicler, Brett and Vaughn pleaded '. . . that they ought to have their lives according to the lawe', because 'ther was promised a pardon . . . by an heralde in the felde . . . and if the quenes pardon promised by

---

[1] *Q J*, p. 62. Machyn says that they were commanded to go to Southwark (Machyn, p. 56). There is no mention of any search being conducted.

an herald, which in the felde is as hir owne mouth, be of no value or auctorytye, then the Lord have mercy upon us!'[1] According to the record, however, the whole group pleaded guilty. There was no venire,[2] and all were condemned. The second trial, held on the 19th, involved most of those indicted four days previously. Pelham,[3] Brian Fitzwilliam and William Staunton had fled. John Thorneton had also disappeared, and was later to be outlawed. Of those who did appear, Sir William and George Brooke were remanded as their pardon was already under consideration, and another man, Henry Blisse, was remanded and promptly disappeared from the scene. Although the Brookes had pleaded not guilty, no venire was issued, and they were returned to the Tower by order of the Council.[4] The remainder, with one or two exceptions, were tried that day and the 20th, and were convicted *en masse*. On the 22nd two more were presented on a similar indictment, and convicted on the 26th, bringing the proceedings of the Commission to a close.

By the 22nd the great bulk of the trials was over, and it was decided to clear the prisons. About 430 men had been convicted, only a fraction of whom had actually been executed. There were some in custody who had been indicted but not tried, and some who had not even been indicted. On that day 250 of them 'copled together ii and ii, a rope runninge between them . . . ' were brought to the Court, 'and there of the queenes highnesse received there pardones for lyve. . . .' Amid scenes of great rejoicing, and many shouts of 'God save Queen Mary' they were led to Westminster Hall, and there released. Three

---

[1] *Q.J*, p. 59.

[2] A writ of Venire Facias, directed to the Sheriff, instructing him to convene a jury.

[3] Sir William Pelham, the White Coat Captain approached by Boughton. It was at first thought that he had been killed in the fighting (Renard to the Emperor, 8 and 24 February), but on 1 March Renard reported 'William Pelham, who was said to have been killed in the fray, has been taken on the Scottish border, and has been brought back to suffer with the rest' (*Cal. Span.*, Vol. XII, p. 130). There is no record of his trial or execution, but his name appears on the Act for the confirmation of attainders (*Cal. Pat.*, Vol. III, p. 44) and no pardon is recorded for him.

[4] *APC*, Vol. IV, p. 395. 19 February 1554, KB8/26. r 7.

days later a further 'CCC and upwards' were pardoned in the same way.[1]

For some of them, however, this was not the end of the story. They returned to Kent only to find that the delayed Commission of Oyer and Terminer for the county was just beginning its sittings in Maidstone under the presidency of Lord Abergavenny.[2] According to Proctor a fair number of them were 'troubled by the magistrates' on their return home, and it took a royal command to end this officiousness. Even allowing for this, however, the Kent Commission bore remarkably little fruit. In two main sittings at Maidstone and Canterbury, it received some 230 indictments. Only 42 of them resulted in convictions,[3] a very small total in view of the number who must have been arrested to fill the prisons as described, even allowing for the fact that some of the more guilty were sent to London for trial.

Outside Kent, and the immediate vicinity of the capital, the government conducted nothing in the nature of a punitive campaign, and even there it was of short duration and limited scope. There was nothing comparable to the terroristic methods which had been used after the widespread risings of five years before. The disturbances in the Midlands and southwest were quickly forgotten, because the commons were not identified with them, either by the original intention, or by subsequent persecution. Only in the south-east was there anything in the nature of a popular rising, and only in the southeast did ordinary people suffer in consequence.

[1] Rawlinson. Proctor (p. 93) says that altogether 600 were pardoned in this way, and the two estimates agree closely.

[2] This Commission was appointed on 24 February, the same day that Southwell wrote asking for it. *APC*, Vol. IV, p. 399.

[3] The Maidstone session began on 7 March (*Cal. Pat.* Vol. II, p. 89 etc.), and that at Canterbury on 27 March (KB27/1173, Rex V, etc.).

5

THE INFLICTION OF PUNISHMENTS

I

There is no accurate record of the number of executions, but a fair amount of evidence exists upon which to base an estimate. On 12 February about 20 or 30 gallows were set up in London, and an uncertain number at Southwark, as well as some in Kent. Henry Machyn, the undertaker, who may perhaps have had a professional interest in the matter, carefully listed 45 executions in London on the 14th,[1] and mentions no others. An uncertain number were executed in Southwark the following day, and on the 18th twenty-two more, including Brett, were sent down to suffer in Kent.[2] On the 24th three more were delivered to Southwell, and on the 28th the two Mantells, the two Knevetts, Henry and Thomas Isley, George More and Cuthbert Vaughn trod the same path.[3] At a later date Rudstone, Digges, Goldwell and one of the Fanes were also sent down. Of these, all the last group, together with Brett, Vaughn and four others, were reprieved.[4] Brett was again despatched to execution on the 28th, but Vaughn was saved by 'the importable suit of his wife' and returned to the Tower on 12 March.[5] On 18 March a writ of Supersedeas was issued in favour of Rudstone and his companions, who also returned to custody.[6] Thus it seems that 19 of the first group and 7 of the second

---

[1] Machyn, p. 55. He also mentions some names, 'Boyth the fottman . . . Vekars of the gard. . . . Polard a waterbeyrar', which can be identified from the trial records.
[2] *Q J*, p. 61, Machyn, p. 55.
[3] *APC*, Vol. IV, p. 399, 24 February; *Q J*, p. 66.
[4] *APC*, Vol. IV, pp. 394, 399.
[5] *Q J*, p. 68.
[6] *Cal. Pat.*, Vol. I, p. 266 (Warrant to Gardiner to issue the writ).

actually suffered. Since Machyn's figure for London is also supported by Grafton's Chronicle and the Chronicle of the Grey Friars,[1] we may accept it. For the same reason we may assume that there were no further transfers to Southwell. The evidence for those tried before the Kent commission is quite clear, all but three were pardoned,[2] so the only unknown element remains the Southwark hangings. Renard estimated that between 100 and 120 had suffered, but it is certain that this figure was too high because the Ambassador was deliberately kept in ignorance of reprieves which he would have opposed.[3] We have actually counted 71 executions, and it is highly probable that the total was well under 100. Noailles' exaggerated remarks about the country being cowed by a deluge of blood can be discounted. It would have required far more than 100 deaths to have cowed London, let alone the whole country. A death roll that size was better calculated to irritate than to terrify.

The group which suffered most heavily was the Londoners. If we assume that the normal practice was followed, and that as far as possible the victims were despatched in their home localities, they lost 45 out of the 76 convicted. By contrast the Kentish men lost less than 30 out of 350. Proctor remarks that 'of the common sort very few were executed, save only of the White Coats',[4] and this evidence bears him out in striking fashion. The more so since of the 30 Kentish men, 8 or 9 were leaders, and not 'of the common short'. Omitting those also

---

[1] Richard Grafton, *A chronicle at large*, edited by Henry Ellis, London 1809, Vol. II, p. 543. Stow's *Annals* gives the figure as 50 (p. 1052).

[2] KB29/187–191, *Cal. Pat.*, Vols. I–III.

[3] Renard to the Emperor, 24 February. *Cal. Span.*, Vol. XII, p. 125. Both Renard and Noailles were temporarily impressed by the severity of the first few days. On 20 February Renard wrote 'everywhere one sees nothing but hanged men', and he hoped that the sharp lesson would be salutary. On the 17th Noailles wrote to Montmorency 'There has never been seen such hanging as has been going on here every day, and mostly innocent men' (Aff. Etr. IX, ff. 137–8). At first he thought that this would provoke a new rising (ibid. ff. 135, 137–8), but two weeks later he was lamenting the fact that the English were too cowed to stir (ibid. ff. 153–4). Both were in London, and Noailles seems to have exaggerated both in his statements and expectations.

[4] Proctor, p. 91.

accused of conspiracy, 18 of the leaders were convicted, so they lost almost exactly half. Influence was on their side, but the need for exemplary punishment was against them, and it is clearly not true, as has been asserted, that they suffered much less heavily than the rank and file.

The only executions which seem to have directly resulted from the provincial ventures were those of the Duke of Suffolk and his brother Thomas. It is certain that no deaths resulted from the Devon rising, and very unlikely that there were any unrecorded hangings in the Midlands. One note by Machyn, however, bids us beware on this point. On Tuesday, 6 February, he wrote in his diary: 'The sam day was ii hangyd upon a jebbet in Powles churche yard; the on a spy of Wyatt thodur was undershreyff of Leseter, for carrying letturs of the duke of Suffolke and odur thinges.'[1] There is no record of any other hangings during the course of the rising, but we cannot be quite sure that there were none. Two deaths must also be attributed to the Duke's rash venture which did not directly result from it. On 12 February his daughter Jane and her husband Guildford Dudley were beheaded; a spectacular but pointless sacrifice which earned the government no goodwill. They had been condemned the previous August, and the movement of political events had long since left them behind, but the official interpretation of Suffolk's attempt demanded their removal, which had the great merit of being uncontroversial.

Sir Thomas Wyatt himself was the last of the Kentish rebels to die. Tried, as we have seen, on 15 March, he seems to have entertained hopes of mercy almost to the end, and his son was later to claim that those hopes were only defeated by private malice.[2] He was eventually executed on 11 April in an atmosphere of conventional penitence, but the people

---

[1] Machyn, p. 54. Stow (p. 1049) elaborates this slightly, giving the under-sheriff's name as 'John Egerley, servant to the Duke of Suffolk'.

[2] 'And verilie those neare about her (the Queen) at that tyme had evident tokens of all good hopes, till some one man in aucthoritie, on an olde grudge . . . (raised a petition against him). Also a message from the Prince of Spaine that he would not come in if the knight weare not first made awaie....' (Wyatt MSS no 10, f. 4).

pressed to dip their handkerchiefs in his blood, regarding him as something of a martyr.[1]

II

A total of about 480 were convicted; 76 from London, 37 from Southwark, about 350 from Kent and about 15 from other places. In addition there were several who were indicted, and later pardoned, but not tried, and some whose names appear only on their pardons. Altogether 333 pardons were enrolled in Chancery, but only about 50 of these referred to men duly convicted, so the list clearly contains a number of unanswered questions. If we admit about 90 executions there are still some 340 convicted rebels who disappeared without trace. The only feasible explanation is that these men were some of those pardoned in the street by Mary. Since they were mostly humble men of no particular wealth, the verbal pardon was presumably considered sufficient. This is supported by the evidence of the Bethersden Church Wardens' accounts,[2] the only ones surviving for a village significantly affected by the rising. A total of 24 parishioners appear in the records, of whom 19 are also mentioned in the accounts as paying church dues. Of those 19, 14 received written pardons and 5 did not.[3] All the latter were of the poorer sort. At the other end of the scale there are some 285 pardons recorded for men who were never convicted, and about 65 of whom had not even been indicted. This naturally leads to the assumption that the

---

[1] Like many other condemned offenders, Wyatt seems to have regarded the fact of failure as being in itself a proof of guilt. François de Noailles reported on 12 April that the spectacle at his excecution was ' . . . tres desplaisant à presque tous ceulx qui lay ont assisté, ce qui fut assez tesmoigné par le grand nombre des personnes qui vindrent secretement tremper leurs mouchoirs en son sang, comme jurans et promettans en icelluy la vengence de la mort de ce vaillant et hardy Capitaine, qui n'avoit faict aucun doubte de s'exposer à tout péril pour la conservation de la liberté publique'. (Aff. Etr. IX, f. 161.) Harbison, p. 138. Which shows how quickly a legend can become established. After the execution Wyatt's head 'remayned not . . . x dayes unstolne awaye' (Q.J, p. 74).

[2] *Churchwarden's Accounts of Betrysden, 1515–1573*, printed in Record Branch of the Kent Archaeological Society (Ashford 1928). Introduction by Francis Mercer.

[3] Those quoted appear after the rebellion, as well as before it.

existence or absence of a written pardon was not determined by the guilt of the party, but rather by his need to redeem lands and movables. Among those receiving pardons there seem to have been three distinct groups: those who were pardoned 'for life', without restitution, and later redeemed their property by separate instruments; those who received pardon and restitution in return for a fixed sum; and those who received their quittance without payment.

The last group was by far the most numerous. Of the 333 pardoned the Exchequer records show only about 90 as having paid any fine or composition. This discrepancy is partly accounted for by a mass pardon, containing 245 names, which was issued on 4 June 1558,[1] and partly by the fact that only Sir Peter Carew among the provincial rebels was assessed for such a fine. All those upon the mass pardon were humble men, and only about 40 of them paid small sums ranging from £1 to £5, the pardon itself being without fee. It is not clear why there should have been such a long delay in issuing this document. Those named upon it had not been kept in prison, and most of them had probably already received the Queen's verbal pardon. Perhaps the cause was simply administrative inefficiency.

The men of Leicester and Devon were treated with noticeably less rigour than those of Kent and London. Whereas most of the leaders of the latter appear among the 50 or so remaining names on the Exchequer Rolls, the former, commons and gentry alike, seem to have escaped almost unscathed. Medley and Leonard Dannet were pardoned on 4 and 5 May,[2] and the following February were standing security for the bonds extracted from Leonard Digges, Rudstone and Cromer.[3] Foster was pardoned on 16 June, Burdet on 8 July, Bartholomew Wullocke on 23 July and Grene on the 24th, all without composition.[4] Thomas Dannet, pardoned on 20 October,

---

[1] *Cal. Pat.*, Vol. IV, p. 52.
[2] *Cal. Pat.*, Vol. I, pp. 381, 400. KB27/1171, Rex III.
[3] E159/334 Recognizances of the Hilary term, r 5. E159/338 Recognizances of the Trinity term, r 71 (and in other places).
[4] *Cal. Pat.*, Vol. I, p. 130, (KB27/1172, Rex V.) Ibid. pp. 499, 500, 503.

Rampton and the Coventry group (26 October) were similarly fortunate.[1] Gibbes, although he was not discharged until October 1555, was specifically regranted his lands and chattels,[2] and neither Sir Gawain Carew nor Sir John Grey appear to have paid for their prominence, although the latter had almost lost his head.[3] John Wullocke, John Aylmer and John Bowyer, who were not pardoned until after the accession of Elizabeth,[4] were naturally not mulcted.

The picture in the south-east was substantially different, the majority of those who had any means being granted their pardons and restitutions separately. On 24 March the Council wrote to Lord Cobham (in the Tower), informing him that the Queen was graciously pleased to order his release at the intercession of the Count d'Egmont, and to extend her clemency to his eldest son at the instigation of his wife.[5] The same day they were released, in company with the Marquis of Northampton, Thomas Culpepper and Henry Fane. Renard, clearly out of step with his colleague, was furious, and told the Queen that such clemency was out of keeping with the danger of the time. Culpepper's pardon was enrolled on 5 April, Fane's on 28 April, and those of the three Brooke brothers on 3 and 5 May.[6] Cobham, not having been indicted, does not seem to have been given a pardon, but he paid in a fashion for the indiscretion of the whole family. At some later but unspecified date he acknowledged an obligation to the Queen of £452, the payment of which was not to be completed until after his death.[7] None of his sons paid anything in their own right, so that on the whole they escaped very lightly. The others were

[1] *Cal. Pat.*, Vol. II, pp. 33, 290. Thomas Dannet was in government service again by the end of the reign, but thereafter he falls into obscurity.
[2] Gibbes was apparently required to enter into a recognizance of 1000 marks (*APC*, Vol. V, p. 282) but this was never forfeited.
[3] Grey's pardon was granted to include all forfeitures. Gibbes and Carew were bound in recognizance in January 1555 to pay fines at pleasure, but no such fines appear to have been either paid or assessed. See below, p. 125.
[4] John Wullocke was pardoned on 22 February 1560 (*Cal. Pat.* Elizabeth, Vol. I, p. 278, and Bowyer on 9 December 1558 (*Cal. Pat.* Elizabeth, Vol. I, p. 60).
[5] SP, Vol. IV, no. 4.
[6] *Cal. Pat.*, Vol. I, pp. 179, 381, 390.
[7] E401/1219.

not so fortunate. Fane was forced to enter into an obligation of 400 marks on 15 February following, in order to redeem his property, and it took him three and a half years to clear the debt.[1] Culpepper was even harder pressed. His assessment was £800, accepted on 7 March 1555, of which he had paid only £266 by the end of the reign. When Elizabeth came to the throne he petitioned to be released from the balance, on the grounds that the sum was larger than his lands were worth.[2]

The destinies of Rudstone, Cromer, Digges and William Isley followed a somewhat similar pattern. The last named was probably pardoned in the first instance on the intercession of his mother's brother-in-law, Sir John Mason, who continued to interest himself in his young kinsman, and interceded with the Queen again in November 1554 for the restoration of his property, probably because the family was living at his expense.[3] William was pardoned on 18 April 1554, and on 2 March following entered into a recognizance of £1000 for his father's lands and chattels. The last instalment of this debt was not paid until May 1560.[4] Cromer and Rudstone also enjoyed the protection of an influential kinsman. They were the nephews of Dr Nicholas Wotton, Mary's Ambassador in France, who was tireless on their behalf. On 23 February 1554 he wrote to Sir William Petre, begging him to do what he could for them,[5] and it would seem that Petre did well. Rudstone was reprieved on 18 March, released shortly after, and pardoned on 1 April.[6] Cromer was discharged on 24 April, and pardoned on the 28th.[7] About the middle of May they entered into a joint obligation to pay £500 for the return of their movables, and the Council wrote to Southwell on 19 May to

---

[1] The last payment was made on 25 October 1557. E401/1225.

[2] There is some doubt about the assessment. *Cal. Pat.* says £800, while the Rec. Roll says £400. Culpepper actually paid 4 instalments of £66. 13. 4. His petition to Elizabeth exists among the Malet MSS, Calendered in *The Seventh Report of the Historical Manuscripts Commission*, App. p. 432.

[3] *Cal. For.*, Vol. II, p. 134. 5 November 1554.

[4] E401/1240.

[5] *Cal. For.*, Vol. II, p. 62. 23 February 1554.

[6] *Cal. Pat.*, Vol. I, p. 261.

[7] Ibid. p. 390.

effect this restitution.[1] On 2 July their confiscated lands were returned to them on a 21-year lease at a fixed rent,[2] and on 10 August Wotton wrote again to Petre thanking him for his efforts,[3] as well he might. On 12 February following Cromer and Rudstone entered into a joint obligation of 4000 marks for the return of their lands in full ownership, thus bringing their total indebtedness to £3166. 13. 4. This huge sum they continued to pay in half-yearly instalments of £166. 13 .4. down to June 1558, when they entered into separate obligations for the balance then outstanding (about half). They then continued to pay reduced instalments until the residue was remitted in 2 Elizabeth.[4] Leonard Digges was pardoned, apparently without any special intercession, on 1 April 1554, and on 31 May entered into an obligation of £49. 17. 8, presumably for the redemption of his movables.[5] On 20 February following he entered a second recognizance, of 400 marks, for the redemption of his lands, which he paid off in instalments, finishing in May 1558.[6]

It was not an accident that so many redemptions were bargained in February 1555. On 10 January preceding, a Commission had been appointed, headed by the Marquis of Winchester ' . . . to call before them all offenders in the late rebellion of Thomas Wyatt, . . . except such as remain in ward in the Tower or elsewhere, and to compound with them for the redemption of their lands and goods. . . '.[7] If any should object to their assessments, they could ' . . . answer to the indictments', provided, of course, that they had not already been pardoned. This Commission seems to have sat on and off for the remainder of the reign, taking recognizances and making out forms of pardon. Except for those already pardoned, the normal procedure was for the applicant to enter a recognizance for about

[1] *APC*, Vol. V, p. 24. *Cal. Pat.*, Vol. I, p. 331.
[2] Ibid. p. 317.
[3] *Cal. For.*, Vol. II, p. 114.
[4] E401/1208–E401/1248, E159/339.
[5] E401/1210, the first instalment of this had already been paid.
[6] E401/1208–E401/1228.
[7] *Cal. Pat.*, Vol. II, p. 104.

¼ more than his assessed redemption, agreeing to pay the assessed sum in specified instalments, and naming suitable securities. The Commissioners would then make out a form of pardon for him which might or might not include a statement of the assessment. The applicant would then sue that pardon, which would be recorded on the Patent Roll years before the payment was complete, although the form of the pardon might make it appear that payment had already been made.

One group of 17 such pardons for sums ranging from £10 to £200 was sued out in February,[1] at the same time as the assessments already considered. This group included all those mentioned by Southwell in his letter of 10 February 1554. Their names had been included in the 'Act for the confirmation of Attainders' passed during the autumn, and they were presumably thought of as ringleaders, but, being mostly yeomen and prosperous tradesmen, they were of more value alive than dead. All completed their payments at the time appointed, in October and November 1556.[2] A further group of 18 received a similar discharge on 15 December 1555.[3] Some of these appear on the Receipt Roll as 'William Smith et al.',[4] and paid a collective redemption of £21.6.8. Clearly they were men of lesser consideration, and the Council was in no hurry to issue their pardon, as the date of their obligation was 13 February.[5] 18 more were pardoned on 15 May 1557, for individual obligations ranging from £1 to £5, the greater part of which had been discharged in single payments during February 1557.[6]

In addition to these there were the 40 or so small obligations taken before the mass pardon of June 1558, and about half a dozen individual discharges. Most of the former were taken in October 1557,[7] and since there are no relevant recognizances

[1] Ibid. pp. 92 et seq.
[2] E401/1219.
[3] Cal. Pat., Vol. III, p. 46.
[4] The Memoranda Roll lists six names: William Smith; John Bele, butcher; Thomas Crosse, cutler; Henry Robinson, tailor; Nic. Bennett, labourer; and John Newman, pewterer; all of Maidstone. E159/337, Michaelmas Recorda, r 194.
[5] Ibid.
[6] E401/1219.
[7] E401/1225.

of later date than that, it may reasonably be assumed that the
Commission was then wound up. Of the individual cases the
most interesting are Sir George Harper, Jane Wyatt, Sir
Thomas's widow, and Sir Peter Carew.

For some unaccountable reason Sir George, who stood
indicted of both conspiracy and rebellion, and was seemingly
second in guilt only to Wyatt himself, was never tried. He
remained in prison until 18 January 1555, and was then
released in company with the other conspirators. Their pardons
followed during the next few months, Harper's being the last,
on 6 November.[1] Before that, on 21 August, he had entered
into a recognizance to pay £1000,[2] and some indication of his
wealth is given by the rapidity with which he discharged the
debt. The last £100 was paid on 14 April 1556.[3]

Jane Wyatt had five young children to bring up, and her
plight aroused the Queen's compassion. On 14 June 1554 she
was granted an annuity of 200 marks to preserve her from the
charity of her kinsfolk. In the autumn of 1555 she was allowed
to redeem her late husband's moveables for £254.19.10, to be
paid in instalments,[4] and at about the same time the residue
of the estate, valued at £64. 14. 7., was returned to her.[5] The
last portion of her obligation was discharged on 15 May 1557.

Sir Peter Carew seems to have been regarded as attainted
from the moment of his first indictment. On 15 April 1554,
before the Exeter Bill had been presented, the Council 'took
order' for some of his lands, and on 26 October a substantial grant
was made to George Jernegan, wherein Carew was expressly
described as 'attainted of High Treason'.[6] Despite this, however, and despite his continued activities in France, on 15 June

---

[1] *Cal. Pat.*, Vol. III, p. 12.
[2] E405/241 f. 12.
[3] E401/1216.
[4] E401/1213.
[5] *Cal. Pat.*, Vol. III, p. 159. The bulk of Wyatt's estates had been granted to
those who had helped in the suppression of his rising, such as Southwell, Cheney,
and George Clarke (*Cal. Pat.*, Vol. I, p. 135, Vol. II, pp. 67, 311). Some parts of it
later reverted to the family. In June 1568 a 21-year lease of lands at Boxley to the
value of £38. 1s. 4d. was granted to Edward Wyatt (*Cal. Pat.* Eliz. Vol. IV, p. 184).
[6] *Cal. Pat.*, Vol. II, p. 30.

Sir Peter's goods and moveables were placed in the hands of his wife, and on 22 September she was licensed to send him 'material relief'.[1] Perhaps the Council were already entertaining hopes of finding him 'serviceable'. In April 1555 he secretly visited his father-in-law, Sir William Skipwith, in Lincolnshire, in search of further financial support, and may have canvassed other worthies in that county.[2] Soon after he must have made up his mind to return to his allegiance, and partly through the intercession of his wife with Philip, received a promise of pardon some time during the autumn. Miss Garrett has reasonably surmised that there were conditions attached to this promise which found expression in the kidnapping of Sir John Cheke near Brussels on 15 May following. Certainly he was in possession of a pardon, enrolled upon 9 December,[3] when he was ostensibly captured with Cheke, and committed to the Tower.

What followed remains something of a mystery. Carew was kept in the Tower, and on 2 June Michieli reported 'One of the chief members of the Privy Council who busied himself with this arrest, and was perhaps the author of it, has said that ... it would be desirable ... to find him guilty of something ... his presence here being of no benefit.'[4] This remarkably cynical utterance suggests that the Councillor concerned (possibly Paget), knew of the pardon and considered it valid, but thought the opportunity too good to miss. If he had not known of the pardon he would not have thought it necessary 'to find him guilty of something'. The December pardon had specifically covered both indictments, and also contained a clause regrant-

[1] APC, Vol. V, p. 75.
[2] In the Hilary Term 1556, William Lord Willoughby brought an action against one Arthur Thimbleby of Lincolnshire under the Statute of 2 Richard II against slandering a peer of the realm. The words alleged were: 'Sir Peter Carewe dyd lande at Hull, and from thenscame to Wyllyam Skypwythes house at Ormesbye, and there did lye one nyght and so went to a place called Frampton nere Boston, and there the lorde Willoughbye and sir Wyllyam Skypwythe dyd appoynte to mete hym, and Raffe Persall, gentylman, receyved letters from the said Sir Peter Carewe to ayde the said Sir Peter Carewe with money' (KB27/1177 r. 170).
[3] Cal. Pat., Vol. III, p. 45.
[4] Cal. Ven., Vol. VI, p. 475.

ing all lands and goods forfeited, to be held of the gift of the
Crown by the same rents and services as before; but it seems to
have been treated as a pardon for life only. On 9 July 1556,
while Carew was still in the Tower, a Commission of Devon
gentlemen was appointed 'to inquire concerning the lands
which Peter Carew, knight, who for divers high treasons committed ... 26 Nov. 1 Mary was outlawed and attainted, held in
the county of Devon'.[1] Eventually he was forced to acknowledge
a debt to the Crown of £2000, and on 20 September 1556 he
received a detailed regrant of his lands, 'forfeited by his
attainder now pardoned'.[2] He pleaded his pardon in King's
Bench the same term, and on 1 December requested that 'some
order' be taken for the payment of his debt, whereupon the
instalments were determined, and sureties taken.[3] Whether
this 'debt' was a genuine fine, or merely a strenuous enforce-
ment of old debts arising out of Carew's extensive deals in lead,
is not at all clear.[4] His dealings with the Exchequer of Receipt
were complex, and not always very clearly recorded, so it is
not certain how much of this £2000 he actually paid, or when.
Judging by other similar transactions, most of it was probably
paid eventually. At least no sort of action seems to have been
taken against him in the Upper Exchequer for its recovery.

On the whole the fines assessed seem to have been paid
satisfactorily. Out of 92 separate obligations, 57 were certainly
met in full, and several others, including Carew's, probably
were. We cannot be certain in some cases because the total
assessment was not recorded. In 18 cases Exchequer process
was necessary to expedite or enforce payment, but in only two
was there a clear and successful default. Out of an estimated

[1] *Cal. Pat.* Vol. III, p. 248.
[2] Ibid. p. 551. These lands remaining in the hands of the Crown were regranted
direct, and those already granted away in reversion.
[3] *APC*, Vol. VI, p. 27.
[4] The sum mentioned in the Council Register is £820, which corresponds to the
amount still outstanding on a recognizance of December 1553 of £920 for 230
fodders of lead. A fresh recognizance was taken from Carew late in 1556 for this
sum, probably as a result of the Council's action. It is not clear whether this £820
was held to be a part of the £2000 or not, as Carew seems to have been dis-
charging several recognizances simultaneously (E159/337 Michaelmas Recognizances r 34d).

total assessment of £8650[1] on cases arising out of the rebellion, £5600 was paid between January 1556 and May 1560. By the latter date payments had virtually ceased, but it is quite possible that a certain amount had already been paid when the Receipt Rolls first began to record such payments at the former time, as a result of the Exchequer reforms of the previous year.

For the most part the pattern is clear enough, and there does not seem to be any vital defect in the evidence, but one or two curious anomalies call for comment. When the conspirators were released in January 1555 they were bound in substantial recognizances 'to their good abearing, ordre and fyne at pleasure'.[2] The list included Rogers (£1000), Warner (£300), Gawain Carew (£500), Harper (£4000), Arnold (£2000), Throgmorton (£2000) and Gibbes (£100). In addition Sir James Croftes (£500) and Cuthbert Vaughn (£300) were bound for their 'good abearing' only. No distinction appears to have been made between Throgmorton, who had been acquitted, and those who had not been tried, while Croftes and Vaughn, who had been convicted, were not bound to a fine at pleasure. As far as I can ascertain no payments were made on any of these recognizances, except that of Harper whose fine was assessed at £1000 as we have seen, and there is no evidence that they were ever called upon to pay. Vaughn was pardoned for life only, but it appears that Croftes, Carew and Gibbes redeemed their lands and chattels without payment. It is not certain that the property of the others was ever impounded, and even Thomas received some posthumous consideration. A small grant of the land forfeited by his attainder was made for the support of his widow in December 1554.[3] This leniency was in accordance with the tendency already noticed, but rather surprising in view of the wealth of the men concerned, and a damaging comment on the government's methods. True as it may have been, there is a hollow ring about the

---

[1] This does not include the £2000 assessed on Carew. See Appendix II.
[2] APC, Vol. V, p. 90.
[3] Cal. Pat., Vol. II, p. 176.

praise which the Elizabethan poet accorded to the Queen's actions in this respect.

> 'And sure Queen Mary was most mercyfull
> Though nursed upp in superstition,
> Was ever English Prince so bountifull
> To subjects? Mark her Restitution
> Nott of their Bloode alone, butt of their landes
> Which then remayned in her princelie handes.'[1]

It also appears that a few minor men who appeared before the Commissioners and were assessed for fines gained their redemptions without actually paying. The pardons of Thomas Fane, John Harper, Christopher Bachelor and Thomas Rayner are recorded on the Patent Roll as being in consideration of sums ranging from £10 to £100,[2] but none of these names appear on the Receipt Roll. This omission raises the question of whether other obligations upon which no payments were actually made escaped the record. The list of recognizances appearing in the Memoranda Roll is clearly very incomplete,[3] and if there were a large number of payments started and not completed, such carelessness would be plausible. However, the general impression is one of thoroughness and efficiency, so that these anomalies are more likely to have been individual cases, whose explanation lies elsewhere.

The most striking fact which emerges from the proceedings following the rebellion is the lack of any consistent policy. Leniency in the Midlands and south-west, although rather exceptional, was justifiable under the circumstances, especially as two of the four principals paid the full penalty. In Kent and London, however, the punishments administered were not justifiable by any rational standard, since they resulted from a conflict of ideas. They were not individually absurd, but lacked any constructive value for the stability of the regime. For a few days the government acted as though it intended to pursue a

---

[1] 'Legende of Sir Nicholas Throgmorton'.
[2] *Cal. Pat.*, Vol. II, pp. 50, 94. Vol. III, pp. 45, 405. KB27/1174, Rex VII.
[3] Many of those who are recorded in the Receipt Rolls as paying on dated obligations, do not appear among the recognizances on the Memoranda Rolls, even when process is later entered against them.

course of terror, but then abandoned this approach in favour of indiscriminate mercy. The executions which were carried out were very unevenly distributed. In the Medway towns and villages, whence the chief strength of the rebels came, there were less than 30, hardly more than would have resulted from a severe assize, and no attempt was made to follow the common practice of carrying out an exemplary execution in every affected village. It seems clear that many of those initially arrested were released without punishment or process, and the total number who suffered in body or estate was less than five per cent of the number involved. Among the gentry the incidence of punishment was not so much inadequate as arbitrary. Wyatt, Thomas and Isley suffered; Croftes, Harper and William Brooke escaped. Rudstone and Cromer paid over £3000; the Brookes less than £500, and Rogers and Winter nothing at all. These facts demonstrate that neither the guilt of the individuals concerned, nor their wealth, nor the need for future security was allowed to determine the course of justice. The same divisions and conflicting purposes which had paralysed the government while the rising was actually in progress minimized the impact of its victory.

Consequently Wyatt's failure was neither a beginning nor an end, but rather the acutest phase in a crisis which continued with fluctuating intensity from the autumn of 1553 to the autumn of 1558. English opinion was not reconciled to the marriage. Its domestic and international implications were unchanged. The changes which took place were personal changes in Mary and Gardiner. Never again did Mary display the mercy that allowed so many of her secular enemies to escape on this occasion; and both she and the Chancellor turned their minds definitively to the task of restoring England to the catholic church. Both convinced themselves that the grievances which had caused the rebellion were either feigned or grossly exaggerated, and therefore no attempt was made to moderate the pro-Spanish policy. This attitude, combined with the fact that so many of the opposition leaders had survived the wreck, made the continuance of sedition inevitable and serious danger very likely.

6

THE PERMANENT CRISIS

I

The bitter wranglings between Gardiner and Paget, which allowed so many conspirators and rebels to escape, appeared for a while to threaten even more serious consequences. For upwards of a month Noailles remained optimistically certain that the brief severity and subsequent vacillations of the English government would provoke a fresh uprising. 'Of the twenty-five or thirty who compose the Queen's Council', he wrote, 'there are not three who approve the said marriage . . . and in general gentlemen as well as others in the land are utterly opposed to it.'[1] He therefore attempted to persuade Henri to make up for having missed the substance of an opportunity by grasping at its shadow. He urged the king to send back Carew and his companions at once to make another attempt, this time to be adequately supported, and to proclaim an open house for all English malcontents.[2] In making these suggestions he was moved by the conviction that war between England and France was in any case inevitable, and this would be the most profitable way of commencing hostilities. Henri, however, although he seems to have shared his ambassador's conviction, was not prepared to take the initiative. He allowed provocative incidents to occur; mustered ships as if for a descent on the south of England, and permitted Noailles to threaten and goad the English Council; but he committed himself to nothing, and sent no instructions to London for positive action.

[1] Noailles to Montmorency, 17 Feb. 1554, Aff. Etr. IX, ff. 137–8 (Harbison, p. 159).
[2] Ibid.

The English government, indignant as it was at this behaviour, was naturally anxious to avoid a breach. Consequently, when no further rising materialized the prospect of hostilities temporarily receded. On 21 March Henri wrote to Noailles:

I see no way to break off or stop the marriage unless those of the country who ought to know the harm which will come to them from it and the slavery to which it will subject them put their hand to the matter; nothing has been or will be left undone on my part to encourage them in this, as I assure myself and as I pray you to believe. . . . You have done me a very welcome service in taking pains to remove the opinion which the Queen and her ministers wish to impress upon the people, that it is I who am encouraging the seditious and favouring the mutinous in her realm, for I know very well that although I wish to benefit the nation, it has such an inveterate hatred for this crown of mine that the common people will find difficulty in accepting any grace or favour from me.[1]

He remained constant to the policy outlined in this letter for the next three years. In spite of Noailles' periodic urgings he refused to risk either men or money in England, but willingly entertained those English exiles who went to France. The subsistence which he granted them and the encouragement which he gave to their schemes varied with the circumstances of the moment, but he consistently turned a deaf ear to the complaints of the English government. Wotton, the English Ambassador, soon realized that he could expect no co-operation in his efforts to sabotage the exiles' activities. In London Noailles remained continually alert for promising intrigues, and surreptitiously fostered propaganda against both the Spaniards and the government.

As the prospect of Philip's arrival in England grew more immediate the danger of war returned. It was widely feared that the peace would not survive his landing, and Noailles decided to exploit the reluctance of the English Council in a last-minute bid to frustrate the whole enterprise. At an audience on 10 May he asked pointedly whether the fleet bringing

[1] Aff. Etr. IX, f. 22 (Harbison, p. 160); Royall Tyler, Transcripts in the P.R.O. pp. 233, 239, 260–1.

Philip to England would observe the neutrality of French shipping. He was told, equally pointedly, that it would fight only if attacked. Neither side had yet ratified the treaties of friendship in force at Mary's accession, and Noailles concluded: 'The king his master . . . thinketh he is none otherwise bound to the observation of them than of his own good will and inclination, and as her Highness shall by her doings and shewing of friendship, give him cause to do. . . .'[1] The implication was only too obvious, as was the Queen's anger, and the Ambassador quickly realized that he had gone further than his master would countenance. His action was disavowed in Paris, and he was forced to take refuge in rapid explanations. The incident seems to have done him no harm, however, and he was soon advocating other threatening gestures, with the result that by the end of May each side was convinced that the other was about to declare war.

War did not occur because Henri was preoccupied with his forthcoming campaign against the Netherlands, which made him increasingly anxious not to have an enemy on his northern flank; and because the English Council was in no fit state to take the initiative. The quarrel between Paget and Gardiner had come to a head in the Parliament which opened on 5 April. The former, inspired partly by personal hatred, and partly by a genuine dislike of the Chancellor's religious policy, engineered the defeat of his Bill against 'heretics and erroneous preachers'. By playing on the fears of the temporal lords that their ecclesiastical spoils were in danger, Paget succeeded in persuading them to reject this important measure on 1 May.[2] The consequence was his own eclipse. So great was the Queen's indignation that he went in daily fear of arrest, and eventually escaped

---

[1] Council to Wotton, 10 May 1554; SP, 69, Vol. IV, no. 185.

[2] *Journals of the House of Lords.* London, 1846, Vol. 1, pp. 459–60. The Lords later pleaded as an excuse that they had acted out of fear for their property, although Renard had reported in March that the Chancellor was proposing to offer them safeguards (Renard to the Emperor, 22 March 1554. *Cal. Span.* Vol. XII, p. 170), and a measure entitled ' . . . that the Bishop of Rome nor any other spiritual person shall convent for Abbey lands' had been passed by the Commons only four days previously (*Journals of the House of Commons,* edited by T. Vardon and T. E. May, London 1852, Vol, 1, p. 34).

disgrace only by self-abasement.[1] He was allowed to retire to his estates about the middle of May, having forfeited both the confidence of the Queen and the friendship of Renard. Immediately rumours began to gather round him. He spent long hours closeted with Sir Philip Hoby, whom Renard described as 'the craftiest heretic in England', and it was feared that the desire for revenge had driven him to conspire with the Queen's enemies. Gardiner seems to have feared him more in retirement than as a rival for power, and the shadowy plots which Renard was always discovering linked the disgraced Councillor with others whom he mistrusted, such as Arundel and Clinton, in a monstrous web of intrigue.[2] There is no proof that Paget ever indulged in treasonable activities, and he was later in high favour with Philip, but he never outlived Mary's distrust or again enjoyed great influence at Court.

Gardiner's unchallenged supremacy did not, however, bring unity or coherence to the Council. Quarrels between the Chancellor and the secular peers continued with undiminished vigour, and whatever Noailles might think, the warring factions had no intention of voluntarily sinking their differences in an attack on France. Renard's pessimism ebbed and flowed as the time of Philip's arrival drew nearer. The nobility, he wrote at the end of June, were ready to rise, ' . . . but the people are more cautious than they have been in the past, for they see that the nobility care more about their own private ambition than about the public welfare'.[3] Both Ambassadors lived in a state of tense anticipation throughout June and July, but in the event Philip's landing on 20 July, and the wedding which followed it, passed off without incident. Although there were undoubtedly many people in England who hated the Spanish marriage per se, most of the opposition to it resulted from doubt and confusion over its possible consequences. Wyatt had based his popular appeal upon the claim that the Prince's landing would be preceded or accompanied by a military occupation,

[1] Renard to the Emperor, 13 May 1554. *Cal. Span.* Vol. XII, p. 250.
[2] Same to same, 13 and 22/25 May. *Cal. Span.* Vol. XII, pp. 250, 258.
[3] Same to same, 28 June. *Cal. Span.* Vol. XII, p. 290.

and there was, as we have seen, a general and justifiable tendency to distrust the marriage treaty as a safeguard.[1] However, some doubts were allayed by the wise provision of a joint Commission for Sir Thomas Holcroft and Briviesca de Munatones to judge disputes which should arise between the nationalities;[2] and influential gentlemen were further reassured by the appointment of a complete English household for Philip. Everything possible was done to avoid creating the impression that the Prince was coming to take control of the country, and these efforts were crowned with success. Six months before, it would not have seemed possible that Philip should sail without interception, land without opposition, and progress across the south of England without incident. Impressed by the strenuous advice of his father and Renard[3], he behaved with a tact and graciousness far in excess of anything that he later achieved, and briefly fortune seemed to favour his enterprise.

Even Renard allowed himself a brief indulgence in satisfaction: ' . . . his Highness personally has produced the most agreeable impression on the English', he wrote; 'Also, the royal couple are bound together by such deep love that the marriage may be expected to be a perfect union;'[4] The fact, however, could not long be concealed that the initial success of the marriage merely raised in a more potent and immediate form the unresolved problem of its political consequences. For the time being the Emperor was anxious not to involve England in his perpetual conflict with France, but no Habsburg ally could evade its responsibilities indefinitely. The marriage would be worse than useless if Philip could not entrench his dynasty in England, and merge its resources with those of his

[1] See above, p. 18, concerning the doubts expressed in the first parliament of the reign, which seem to have been representative.

[2] The Articles of the Commission are set out in SP, Vol. IV, no. 10, 'that in all punisshementes wher the same is to be made extraordinarilly and by discretion of the judges, consideracion be had to the usage of the nation of thoffendar'.

[3] Renard sent many letters of good advice to Philip, but the Emperor sought rather to exercise his control indirectly. On 1 April he wrote to the Duke of Alva (who was to accompany the Prince to England): 'For the love of God . . . see to it that my son behaves in the right manner; for otherwise I tell you I would rather never have taken the matter in hand' (Cal. Span. Vol. XII, p. 185).

[4] Renard to the Emperor, 29 July 1554. Cal. Span. Vol. XIII, p. 4.

other territories. Noailles and his English allies were quick to grasp this situation; with its grosser terrors purged away the Spanish match could be seen as a political gamble, the dividends of which were still to be won. It did not matter greatly to the French whether the English government was changed by revolution or merely paralysed by division and disorder. What was vital was that the Habsburgs should not secure an effective grip. Consequently after a very short time plots and conspiracies again became rife, and the leaders of opposition, constitutional and otherwise, consulted with the French Ambassador upon their tactics and progress.

II

The first hope, both of the Emperor and of the English supporters of the alliance, lay in the prospect of issue. The English hoped that the Burgundian inheritance, which by the terms of the marriage treaty was to be the portion of such issue, would secure English commercial interests from arbitrary interference without turning England into a mere dependant of a continental power. The treaty bristled with stipulations protecting the country from outside interference:

The said most noble Prince shall not promote admitt or recyve to any Office Administration or Benefit in the sayd Realme of Englande . . . anye Straunger . . . That the sayd most noble Prynce shall doo nothing whereby anything bee inovated in the State and Right, eyther publike or private, or in the Lawes and Customes of the sayd Realme. . . .[1]

The intention of the English negotiators had been to secure the political and economic advantages of close continental ties without any sacrifice of English autonomy, and the treaty reflected their purposes accurately. The Emperor's hope, of course, was different. Any child born to Philip and Mary would be only a quarter English, and could be reasonably expected, if Philip asserted himself over its education, to keep England firmly within the Habsburg orbit. In any case, once his son

[1] Statute 1 Mary st. 3 cap. 2. *Statutes of the Realm*, Vol. IV, p. 222.

was firmly established as the father of an heir to the English throne, the details of the treaty would scarcely matter against the reality of his power. It was no doubt this consideration which moved him to accept a treaty so unfavourable to his interests.

In the autumn of 1554 few in England were looking so far ahead. The immediate fear was that Philip would himself attempt to seize the reins of government, a course from which the slower and more lawful prospect of legitimate inheritance might deter him. Provided that an early *coup d'état* could be avoided the course of time might bring its own solution. In any case, apart from more material considerations, a child of the union would act as a focus of loyalty for both nationalities and help to diminish the friction that was producing daily out-breaks of violence. Consequently, when rumours of the Queen's pregnancy began to circulate in September, Renard seized on them with glee. 'If it is true,' he wrote on the 18th, 'everything will calm down.' He did his best to further such reports,[1] and enlarged enthusiastically upon the benefits portended. Simpler people rejoiced at their Queen's success in the fundamental duty of womanhood;

> Nowe singe, nowe springe, oure care is exil'd
> Oure virtuous Quene is quickned with child.[2]

and although there were from the first some who scoffed at the news, and called it a device of the Spaniards, by October London was quieter than at any time during the previous twelve months.

By Christmas, in spite of factious murmurings, it seemed probable that Mary's policies would be crowned with success. The third parliament of the reign, which opened on 11 November, although it struck a hard bargain with the Crown for the security of secularized lands, had legislated to end the twenty-year-long schism, and had restored the heresy laws to the Statute Book. Cardinal Pole had returned in triumph bear-

---

[1] Renard to the Emperor, 18 September 1554. *Cal. Span.* Vol. XIII .p. 51.
[2] *S.T.C.* 17561. Printed by W. Ryddael 1554.

ing the Papal absolution which the Lords and Commons had received on behalf of the realm with every sign of joy.[1] Apparently the government had won a major triumph. The Imperialists greeted it as a miracle, and believed that this essential preliminary had guaranteed their ultimate supremacy.

Equally important were the negotiations still in progress concerning the guardianship of the Queen's expected issue should she die while it was still under age. Up to this point Philip had secured nothing but the title of King; the benefits of fatherhood and the fruits of hard-earned goodwill were still to be gathered. Consequently high hopes were entertained of a Bill which had been introduced in the Commons just before the recess. This proposed to give Philip the guardianship of Mary's children in the event of her death, and to extend to him immediately the full protection of the treason laws.[2] More important still there was a move afoot to grant him the right of succession in the event of Mary's death without issue. This would have involved the virtual abrogation of the marriage treaty, in which it had been expressly provided that

. . . in cace no Children being lefte, the saide moste noble Quene doo dye before him, the said Lorde Prynce shall not chalendge any Right at all in the sayd Kingdome but without any impediment shall permytte the Succession therof to come unto them to whom yt shall belong. . . .

The origin of this proposal, so extraordinarily out of keeping with the Commons' normal attitude, is obscure. Some in the lower house seem to have feared a plot by the Lords to regain their Edwardian supremacy as soon as Philip's back was turned.[3] Renard's laconic report does not name the sponsors.

Whatever the reason, this extreme measure disappeared

---

[1] There are many eye-witness accounts of this emotional outburst. See for example the report sent by Don Pedro de Cordova, December 1554, *Cal. Span.* Vol. XIII, p. 118.

[2] SP, Vol. V, nos. 1, 2. The Commons rejected a Lords Bill passed down during the third week of December on the grounds that it gave the King inadequate protection.

[3] Renard to the Emperor, 21 December 1554. *Cal. Span.* Vol. XIII, p. 124. The crisis seems to have been connected with Gardiner's proposal to get Elizabeth declared a bastard, which was soon abandoned as too controversial.

from sight during the recess, and the guardianship bill ran into difficulties in Committee. Guardianship itself, as Renard pointed out, was Philip's legal right, and not a concession; while the Regency Council upon which the Chancellor's supporters were trying to insist would have paralysed the government.[1] More serious still, the Lords clearly intimated that they would reject the Bill, since the burden of a Regency Council would fall mainly on them. When the Parliament reassembled the Commons' apparent enthusiasm for Philip had evaporated and a crisis was clearly brewing. Suspicions that any increase in Philip's power, actual or potential, would lead directly to war with France reasserted themselves. During the second week in January a number of peers and commoners absented themselves from the Parliament in protest against the proposed Bill,[2] and Philip's prestige, far from being strengthened, was weaker than at any time since his arrival.

Eventually a Committee of both Houses amended the Regency Bill removing the Regency Council and giving Philip the government of the realm during the minority of his children. However, a clause was also inserted re-affirming the marriage treaty. In this form the measure was passed during the closing days of the session; but all that the King had really gained was the protection of the treason laws. For the rest, all depended more obviously than before upon the Queen's ability to produce an heir.

As the year 1555 advanced, the royal pregnancy, which had been greeted with such enthusiasm in September, became a subject of scandal and concern. If Mary should die in childbed Philip's position in England would be destroyed immediately. If the child should be stillborn it was very unlikely that the thirty-seven year old Queen would ever have a healthy infant.

---

[1] It was proposed that a Council of six earls, six barons and six bishops should be instituted to approve the convocation of Parliament, declarations of war, or the marriage of the heir.

[2] Edward Coke, *Fourth Part of the Institutes*, London 1669, pp. 17–21. An abortive indictment in King's Bench followed (KB27/1177, Rex XXV etc.) and several bills were vainly introduced in subsequent parliaments for their punishment, (*Journal of the House of Commons*, Vol. I, pp. 42, 51).

It is hardly surprising therefore that during the spring some of the Emperor's advisers were urging him to prepare an army to secure his son and his interests if the Queen should miscarry.[1] At the end of April Elizabeth was brought to court 'for the period of the Queen's confinement', presumably as a precaution, and thereafter expectancy grew daily more acute. As May turned into June, and still the prayers for safe delivery went unanswered, the 'scandalous tales' began to multiply. The Queen was sick, or bewitched; there was a plot against her life; she was already dead. On 11 June, Giovanni Michieli, the Venetian Ambassador, wrote that the delivery could not long be delayed, 'and then . . . King Philip will not live in this realm so much like an alien as he does. He has hitherto . . . abstained from interfering and commanding . . . nor has he as yet availed himself of one penny of the national revenue, but supplied it considerably from his own resources.'[2] By that time, however, some better informed than Michieli already knew that there would be no delivery. Mary's condition was the result either of a pathological delusion, or of symptoms of that disease which was to carry her off.[3] The pretence was kept up for some weeks more, and several false reports caused the bonfires to be lighted in the streets, but the trappings of confinement were gradually removed, and at the beginning of August the Court removed to Oatlands. As if to emphasize his frustration and disappointment, Philip immediately departed to join his father in the Netherlands.

The marriage had failed of its dynastic purpose, and the chances of redeeming that failure were so remote as to be scarcely worth considering. It was therefore left to the Imperialists to salvage what they could of their hopes in England. Short of a military invasion the most fruitful prospect lay in

---

[1] Badoer to the Doge and Senate, 15 May 1555. *Cal. Ven.*, Vol. VI, p. 71.

[2] Michieli to the same, 11 June 1555. *Cal. Ven.*, Vol. VI, p. 107.

[3] Throughout her married life Mary suffered this recurrent delusion of pregnancy. Contemporary accounts of her death mention 'dropsy' as a possible cause, and Miss Prescott (*Mary Tudor*, London 1952, p. 379) suggests that a tumour may be indicated. Cancer of the womb appears to be the most probable explanation.

securing Philip's coronation as King. The legal significance of such a coronation would have been small. Philip had been recognized as King by the marriage treaty, and his position as defined therein would not have been altered; nor would he have retained any legal right to the kingdom after the Queen's death. However, the symbolic significance would have been immense. The coronation played a very important part in Tudor royal mystique, not least in fortifying the sacred character of the kingship against the impiety of rebellion. Whatever the theoretical or legal position, Philip as duly crowned King of England would have been in an immeasurably stronger position than Philip, the Queen's husband who was styled 'King'. The position of King-Consort was unprecedented in England[1] and incomprehensible to Englishmen, who had no idea what claims its occupant should have upon their obedience. Faced with this situation, they spontaneously evolved and accepted the idea that the King's coronation would mean the transfer to him of the crown and all its regalian rights, which would thus remain vested in him (and presumably in his heirs) irrespective of the Queen's life or death. This notion, while ostensibly offering Philip all the benefits for which he undertook the marriage, in fact operated strongly against his achieving them. It was almost certainly originated and spread by the Queen's enemies. Favourers of the coronation liked to keep its implications vague; this extreme interpretation had the effect of placing it in the same position that the marriage itself had once occupied—that of *summum malum*. In fact the enemies of the Spanish connection had dramatically succeeded in raising a new bogy.

Beginning almost as soon as Philip's peaceful arrival had discredited the earlier Jeremiahs, this alarm continued with mounting intensity for about two years; until it had done its work and made the coronation impossible. The fact that after the summer of 1555 the Imperialists concentrated all their

---

[1] The precedent of Ferdinand's rule in Castille after the death of Isabella would not have been known to most Englishmen, although it told in favour of their fears.

attention on bringing the coronation about, and Philip made several attempts to blackmail the Queen into forcing it through, confirmed the worst fears. Much of the propaganda occasioned by this threat was of the same obvious kind as that spread by Wyatt and his associates, but the nature of the crisis also called forth some interesting constitutional speculations, notably from the Cheshire agitator John Bradford. In his *Copye of a letter . . . sent to the Earls of Arundel, Darbie, Shrewsbury and Penbroke*,[1] probably written in the spring of 1556, he claimed

Ye saye the Quene hath the Power in her Hands, we must obey her. That is true in all such Laws as be already made and passed by Parlement. But whether ye may lawfully consent, (contrary) to the Discretion of the whole Realm and nation of Englishmen (to the giving away) of the Crowne, and dysannul the Authority that was given by parlement, I leave yt to your Consciences. Yf the Crowne wer the Queen's, in such sorte as she myght do with it what she would, both nowe and after her Death, ther might appear some rightful Pretence in giving it over to a Stranger Prince: But seeing it belongeth to the heirs of England after her death, ye commytt deadly Synne and Dampnation in unjustly giving and taking away the Right of others. . . .

With shrewd insight he compared the prospect to Northumberland's bitterly unpopular conspiracy. The same stubborn legitimacy that had defeated the Duke was invoked against the Spanish King.

I think you can never forgette the unjust Enterpryse of the late Duke of Northumberland and what myserable success yt had. Be ye therefor wyse and beware by other Men's Harmes; for ye may perceave evidently that God wyll take Vengeance upon wrongfull Dooers. Otherwise the Queenes Majestie that nowe is had not been Quene of England at this present.

Bradford wrote in haste, and his arguments display some extremely confused thinking,[2] but since he was writing for a

---

[1] *S.T.C.* 3480. These extracts are from the version printed by Strype, Vol. III(2), no. xlv, which was almost certainly amended from the original. Concerning the production of this work, see my note in *Transactions of the Cambridge Bibliographical Society*, Vol. III, 2, 1960.

[2] For instance he declares that the Queen cannot ' . . . break her father's entail, made by the whole consent of the realme, which neither she nor the realme can justly alter'. A *non sequitur* which no serious theorist of the time would have perpetrated.

popular market that hardly mattered. His main theme was a tirade against the Spaniards, comparing the plight of England to that of Naples and other Spanish-controlled territories. Other writers had preceded him in the same vein,[1] so that by the time that Philip and his advisers turned seriously to the question of a coronation, in the summer of 1555, English opinion was already thoroughly aroused against it.

As early as October 1554 Wotton reported that in addition to the usual stories of commotions in England, rumours were circulating in France to the effect that the English would refuse to crown their new king.[2] The significance of this seems to have been lost on the government, for no formal proposal to that effect was put forward until the new year. By then it was too late to treat the coronation as an unimportant adjunct of the marriage. The Bill introduced in the Commons about 9 January, apparently on Renard's insistence, had missed the tide and was promptly and unanimously rejected.[3] By the time the fourth parliament of the reign was summoned, in September 1555, the matter was foremost in everyone's mind. Michieli, reporting to his government on 16 September, wrote that the reason for the summons was 'either a subsidy or the King's coronation'. However, in the event the subject was considered too dangerous to be raised. Badoer, the Venetian envoy at the Imperial Court, reported on 27 October that the Queen had written to Philip saying that the opposition was so strong that she dared not make the proposal.[4] Rather than risk failure, he advised her to let it rest. The Emperor was less easily put off. For some time he had been urging his son to return to England to strengthen his own and the Queen's position. In November he made a further effort, pointing out that Philip would have neither money, nor a crown, nor an

---

[1] Bradford refers to two of these pamphlets, 'The lamentation of Napelles' and 'The Mourning of Mylayne', which he had seen but which have not survived. Strype, loc. cit.; Garrett, pp. 96–7.

[2] Wotton to the Council, 2 October 1554. *Cal. For.* Vol. II, p. 122.

[3] Harbison, p. 219.

[4] Badoer to the Doge and Senate, 27 October 1555, *Cal. Ven.* Vol. VI, p. 227.

heir unless he went, but the King was not to be persuaded.[1] All he would do was to make vague promises in the hope that those few English lords who adhered to him would secure his position in their own interest. No sooner was Parliament safely out of the way, however, than dark hints began to be dropped that it was the Queen's duty to crown her consort by her prerogative power if the estates were uncooperative, and that if she did not do so, he would not see his way to returning. This continued to be Philip's attitude for upwards of a year, but it was as unperceptive as it was unscrupulous. As Badoer justly pointed out in reporting the matter, Mary's Councillors and the country at large were as opposed to the crowning as was the Parliament, and the Queen could not act in defiance of all three.[2]

Mary was trapped between her husband's importunity and her subjects' obstinacy. At the end of December she wrote to him desperately that she was encompassed with enemies and could not move without endangering her crown; bitterly as she regretted it, she could neither bring about his coronation nor persuade her Council to declare against France.[3] By March Philip was openly saying that England was nothing but a nuisance and an expense, and when Paget went to Brussels the following month he simply reiterated his conditions for returning. According to Badoer the French Ambassador in Brussels, Bassefontaine, seized the opportunity of Paget's presence to rub salt in the open wound. Referring to the coronation he said ' . . . that should they purpose doing this without the consent of the people of England, his most Christian Majesty . . . would be compelled to favour it (England) in order that it should not be forced to do anything against its will.'[4] What he meant by 'favour' was not stated. In accordance with Henri's frequently demonstrated policy the threat was a vague one, but it would have been sufficiently meaningful to Paget at that

[1] Same to same, 19 November 1555. Cal. Ven. Vol. VI, p. 253.
[2] Same to same, 6 and 15 December 1555. Cal. Ven. Vol. VI, pp. 272, 281.
[3] Same to same, 29 December 1555. Cal. Ven. Vol. VI, p. 299.
[4] Same to same, 26 April 1556. Cal. Ven. Vol. VI, p. 420.

moment. For over a month his colleagues in the Council had been painfully unravelling the implications of such 'favour'. An enormous web of conspiracy had come to light which aimed at preventing the Spanish succession by armed intervention, and every thread which the investigators picked up pointed directly or indirectly to the French Court.

III

Rumours of sedition and incipient rebellion were so common in England during these years that it is often impossible to decide which had some basis and which, in Michieli's words, were '... mere suspicion, which ... may be said to have dominion here.'[1] Fresh alarms followed thick and fast upon Wyatt's defeat, but French and English seem to have been at cross-purposes. While Noailles expected another rising, Englishmen expected a French invasion, and in the event neither materialized. The summer of 1554 was filled with rumours of preparations to resist Philip's landing by force of arms, but if there was substance in any of them it did not become apparent. Not until September, when the Spaniards had already had an opportunity to make themselves personally unpopular, was any dangerous enterprise uncovered. On 5 September Noailles reported that a plot had been discovered to surround Hampton Court by night and slaughter all the Spaniards who could be found, an act which should have been the signal for a general massacre of Spaniards in London. The Ambassador added that the Queen and her Hispanophile Councillors would almost certainly have shared their fate.[2] There is no evidence as to who was involved, or how far their plans had progressed, but the constant skirmishes and affrays between English and Spanish give plausibility to the story. The Spaniards at any rate believed it, and when a month later another similar attempt was rumoured, a panic ensued. Incidents of lesser significance, but similar import, occurred from time to time

---

[1] Michieli to the Doge and Senate, 1 April 1555. *Cal. Ven.* Vol. VI, p. 37.
[2] Aff. Etr., IX, ff. 261–2 (Harbison, p. 197).

as long as Philip and his retinue were in England. On Corpus Christi day 1555 a threatening mob gathered outside the church where some of them were worshipping, and a repetition of the Sicilian Vespers was threatened.[1] Mary was deeply distressed by these disturbances:

It is a cause of great sorrow to the Queen if they maltreat a Spaniard (wrote Juan de Barraona), greater than if she herself had to suffer, and she has done enough on her part issuing edicts that prohibit wrong to any Spaniard, but it is of no avail. . . . .[2]

The only result of the Queen's concern was that her subjects called her 'a Spaniard at heart', and the Spaniards decided that she had no authority in her own kingdom. Philip was furious, but equally helpless. 'Not choosing that . . . they should come to blows at the risk of . . . insurrection', as Michieli wrote during the tense month of July 1555, ' . . . but rather to put up . . . with any affront or persecution.'[3]

Out of this perpetual crisis a few incidents emerge as particularly dangerous or significant. Political assassination was not, on the whole, a remedy which appealed to the English, as William Thomas discovered, but because it needed no great resources it was a sore temptation to the extremist. At least two plots seem to have been laid against Mary's life during the two years after her marriage. About one of these, which should have taken effect at the opening of Parliament in November 1555, nothing is known beyond a single reference by Michieli.[4] The other, however, is relatively well documented and might have had incalculable results. On 25 November 1554 the King and his followers demonstrated the 'jeu de cannes' for the benefit of the Queen, and a group of malcontents planned to kill them both while attention was concentrated upon the play. According to one version upwards of 300 people were in the secret, including Francis Verney, and the assassins were only

[1] Michieli to the Doge and Senate, 1 July 1555. *Cal. Ven.* Vol. VI, p. 126.

[2] One of two letters written by Juan de Barraona to his uncle, this one dated 25 October 1554, printed by C. V. Malfatti in *Four Manuscripts of the Escorial*, Barcelona 1956, pp. 92–3.

[3] Michieli to the Doge and Senate, 1 July 1555. *Cal. Ven.* Vol. VI, p. 126.

[4] Same to same, 27 October 1555. *Cal. Ven.* Vol. VI, p. 231.

frustrated by the premature end of the game.[1] Another version, however, puts it in a very unheroic light. One of the conspirators named Hinnes later related how

... he, Aldaye, Cornwaile and other to the nomber of xii wer appointed to have slayne the queenes maiestie and after that the kings maiestie ... (but) ... ther was suche a cowardice and feare in ther bones when thei sholde have done yt that thei made scrupules who sholde begin the onset, for said he that whosoever sholde kill her maiestie sholde have bene put to deth for examples sake whosoever had byn king or queene after . . . . [2]

Their failure of nerve was so complete that no one even suspected what they were about, and the story did not come out for another eighteen months.

The year 1555 was full of alarms. In March a number of men were in trouble for proclaiming that King Edward was still alive. In July a certain Edward Horsey spread a panic right across the south of England by falsely reporting disturbances in Dorset,[3] and in the following month Michieli was creditably informed that a religious rising had broken out in Warwickshire. The rising turned out to be a petty riot, and the government took stringent and successful precautions against trouble in London, but one conspiracy did emerge which demanded serious consideration. This was an obscure episode which occurred at Cambridge. How much danger it really carried is hard to assess, but it provides an excellent example of the tense and restless state of the country, in which agitators of all kinds were finding willing audiences.

On 13 March Renard reported that a plot had been uncovered, and in a further letter of the 27th he gave the details which investigation had brought to light. The conspirators programme was an extraordinary carpet-bag of grievances and popular slogans. If Renard's information was accurate they were

---

[1] Advis, 18 June 1556, Aff. Etr., XIII, f. 20 (Harbison, p. 198). These details came out during the examination of prisoners implicated in the Dudley conspiracy.

[2] Confession of Thomas White, 'concerning Hinnes', 30 March 1556. SP, Vol. VII, no. 47.

[3] APC, Vol. V, pp. 168, 169, 29 and 31 July 1555. Letters were sent to the sheriffs and J.P.s of nine southern counties not to credit these false reports.

proposing the end of enclosures; Courtenay and Elizabeth for King and Queen; the forcible expulsion of all Spaniards, and a return to the reformed religion. The last was apparently an optional extra, included only where the authors thought that it would be well received. To back up this assortment it was also to be proclaimed that the Queen was not really pregnant, but lending herself to a treacherous design whereby a spurious prince was to be foisted on the country.[1] The plot was revealed when one of the ringleaders overreached himself in trying to inveigle a loyal subject. The French, inevitably, had a hand in it.[2]

At about the same time Michieli also reported the plot to his government,[3] and although the two reports agree in substance the Venetian lays much more stress on religious discontent.

The Lords of the Council (it runs), . . . have lately had suspicion that certain inhabitants of Cambridge, more daring and licentious than the rest, not choosing to inconvenience themselves by living according to the present religion, had leagued together and privily collected a large supply of arms for a rising when the moment should seem fit to them, not merely to conspire against the faithful and Catholics termed by them Papists, but, with numerous adherents whom they expect to have to march upon this city, hoping with the assistance of the Londoners who share their opinions, not merely by slaughter and maltreatment to expel all strangers hence, but even to attack their Majesties. . . .

A purposeful and dangerous seeming conspiracy reminiscent of Wyatt, which, Michieli implies, was only prevented by the Council's vigilance and promptness. Several Cambridge men, including a gentleman named Anthony Bowes, had been imprisoned in the Tower, and arrests were taking place daily in London, ' . . . the prisoners being strictly examined to ascertain the basis and origin of the plot and detect the conspirators; so

---

[1] Renard to the Emperor, 27 March 1555. *Cal. Span.* Vol. XIII, p. 147.

[2] Rumours of this nature were common. At about this time a certain Alice Perwicke, the wife of a London Merchant Taylor, was indicted for saying 'The Queen's Grace is not with childe, and another lady shuld be with childe and that ladies childe when she is brought in bedde shold be named the Queen's childe'. *Cal. Pat.*, Vol. III, p. 184.

[3] Michieli to the Doge and Senate, 26 March 1555. *Cal. Ven.* Vol. VI, p. 31.

some severe demonstration and act of justice is expected. . . . '
The Queen and her advisers were certainly disillusioned with
the effects of clemency, but no 'severe justice' was forthcoming
on this occasion. Probably the examinations revealed that the
plot was insignificant or embryonic. A few days after writing
the dramatic despatch quoted, Michieli was inclined to attri-
bute the alarm to exaggerations produced by the highly
charged atmosphere, and this explanation is much more
plausible than Renard's disgusted claim that interested parties
were suppressing the evidence.

A hint in Michieli's first letter that the intrigue was connected with the burning of Rowland Taylor at Hadleigh on
5 February is probably not far from the truth.[1] The burning of
heretics, of whom Taylor was among the first, undoubtedly
increased the government's unpopularity. Beginning when it
did, just as the early optimism of the alliance was collapsing in
ruins, it provided the opposition with yet another stick to beat
the Spaniards and those who favoured them. It was an easy
task for skilled agitators to suggest that the Protestant Divines
were the victims, not of heresy laws resurrected by the English
Parliament, but of Spanish malice. Many of those who suffered
showed exemplary courage and were justifiably respected, but
it would be wrong to suppose that the crowds who demonstrated at their executions, hurling abuse at the bishops and
threatening to attack the officiating officers,[2] were composed
entirely of their co-religionists. From the very beginning propaganda associated this unprecedentedly severe persecution with
the novelty of Spanish influence, and encouraged many who
had no interest in religious disputes to see the protestants as
victims of foreign tyranny. Renard saw the danger clearly and
made frequent but unavailing appeals for caution, saying by
the end of March that he had ' . . . never seen the people in

[1] Ibid. Taylor was particularly popular and influential, and there were widespread demonstrations after his death.
[2] Renard to the Emperor, 5 February 1555. *Cal. Span.* Vol. XIII, p. 138;
Michieli to the Doge and Senate, 8 April 1555. *Cal. Ven.* Vol. VI, p. 45; and
others.

such an ugly mood.'[1] Philip also seems to have been aware of what was happening, but his father's politic advice had to struggle against his own intense devotion to the Church, and although he allowed his chaplain to preach against the evils of persecution in February, he never made any strenuous attempt to stop it. A number of efforts were made to link up individual disturbances provoked in this way into general risings, and the enterprise at Cambridge was probably one such, unusually wide in its scope.

Individually most of the rumours, conspiracies and disorders which fill the diplomatic correspondence of the period were insignificant, but collectively their significance was very great. The Council was kept constantly on the defensive, detecting, examining and assessing subversive activities. Not only did this take up a prodigious amount of official time and energy, but it threw an intolerable strain on the administrative machinery. Renard justly compared the opposition to a Hydra, constantly sprouting fresh heads to replace those which had been removed. The only way to defeat such a monster was by constant vigilance at the lowest level, not only of the magistrates but of the constables and other humble officers. No sixteenth-century government had the resources to ensure such vigilance, and the constant ineffective persistence of Mary's Council served only to impair its normal authority. It was normal for both sides to 'school the people' by deliberately spreading reports in their own interest. As the Emperor wrote to his ambassador in December 1553 ' . . . it will . . . be wise to gain the support of a few of the baser sort who are fond of talking, so that some gifts secretly distributed may make their discourses serve our purpose.'[2] Confronted by such reports, however, it was almost impossible to tell which had been deliberately spread and which were the spontaneous products of fear, confusion and superstition. It was natural for ordinary people to seek to escape from uncertainty by resorting to necromancers and quack prophets, and these practitioners, who were experts at tuning their

---

[1] Renard to the Emperor, 27 March 1555. *Cal. Span.* Vol. XIII, p. 148.
[2] Emperor to Renard, 24 December 1553. *Cal. Span.* Vol. XI, p. 455.

voices to popular demand, consequently gave the government
a good deal of trouble. Prophecies of the Queen's death and
of the elevation of Elizabeth were commonplace, as were those
obscure doggerels whose meaning was left to the audience to
decipher, such as

> When bowes and branchis beginne to budde
> ii meres shall go owt of the Towre
> And make sacryfice wt theyre owne bloud.[1]

It was almost impossible to pin down the responsibility for this
kind of thing, and the authorities were never quite sure how
seriously to take it. Occasionally they felt that there was method
in the apparent madness, and in one case at least they were
justified.

Throughout the reign, and well on into the 1560's, there were
recurrent rumours that Edward VI was still alive, and
prophecies that he would return. Most of these probably
originated in the unbalanced minds of some extreme protestants as they mourned the passing of Zion.[2] In January 1556,
however, pamphlets began to appear in London announcing
not only that the King was alive, but that he was in France,
awaiting a demonstration in his favour. A Greenwich man
named Laurence Trymmyng was arrested for distributing
these pamphlets, and upon examination confessed that they
had been given to him by one William Constable.[3] This
Constable was the same man who had been whipped at the
pillory the previous year for impersonating the dead King,[4]
and he was promptly rearrested with a number of associates.
At the beginning of February he and several others were
hanged. In view of what later occurred it is hard to avoid the
suspicion that determined intriguers were making use of
Constable's little weakness, either to ferment a disturbance or,

---

[1] B.M. MS Harleian 559, f. 11, 'In the year of owre Lord 1554'.
[2] Edward was referred to as 'the Godly Imp', and was frequently and extrava-
gantly praised in the writings of protestant divines.
[3] APC, Vol. V, p. 221, 11 January 1556.
[4] He had previously been arrested in May 1555, but his imprisonment then had
been of short duration and the punishment which he received indicates that he
was considered harmless. APC, Vol. V, p. 122, 11 May 1555.

more likely, to help paralyse resistance to an invasion from France. Whoever they were they remained in obscurity, but the mention of France is significant.

The English were not the only people to look to self-appointed prophets for guidance. King Philip himself was in the habit of consulting astrologers, and in March 1556 he was told that there would be a major conspiracy against him in England that year.[1] It did not need an astrologer to make such a deduction from the perpetual intrigues of the islanders, but the date of the letter in which Badoer reported the prediction—15 March—suggests that this prophet was in possession of precise and particular information. Several days previously a conspiracy had come to light which the English government was carefully concealing in the hope of increasing its haul. This was a plot hatched between a number of those who had sought refuge in France and their supporters and sympathizers who had remained behind. Its leader among the exiles was Henry Dudley, and in England, although its ramifications were still obscure, suspicion was already beginning to reach both wide and high. By 18 March the government could hold its hand no longer, and almost 20 arrests were made. On the 24th Michieli reported that the matter was serious and the Council were very worried.[2] Both Michieli and the Council had cried 'wolf' before, but it soon became clear that this was no ordinary petty intrigue of the kind which had become so depressingly familiar. Influential men and trusted officials were involved, and the complicity of the French Ambassador was beyond all reasonable doubt. Much still remained obscure, but the general intention of the conspirators was to overthrow the Queen by a mixture of armed insurrection and invasion, and it seemed certain that they were counting on French money, arms and reinforcements.

Such an attempt was the natural consequence of developments which had taken place since Wyatt's failure. Several survivors of the earlier rising appeared among its leaders, and

---

[1] Badoer to the Doge and Senate, 15 March 1556. *Cal. Ven.* Vol. VI, p. 376.
[2] Michieli to the same, 24 March 1556. *Cal. Ven.* Vol. VI, p. 384.

others were implicated. The failure to demand Noailles' recall had enabled the existing channels of subversion to be re-opened with a minimum of delay.[1] The failure of the Queen to produce an heir, and her refusal to admit defeat by settling the succession on her sister had left the country under the threat of indefinite Spanish rule. Failure to prevent the spread of seditious propaganda had weakened the governments' authority, and encouraged its opponents to believe that it was weaker than it was. Constant quarrels among the Councillors, and between the Queen and her advisers, aroused in foreign observers and English critics a contempt which was not altogether justified; Wyatt and Dudley, Noailles and Renard, all underestimated Mary's powers of survival. Above all, failure either to reach an understanding with the French King, or to bring effective pressure to bear upon him, meant that English malcontents were always sure of a refuge and base, and could usually count upon encouragement and support. The new conspiracy, like its predecessor, arose naturally from its context and was not an isolated event, but an acute phase in the perpetual crisis of the reign.

[1] On the subject of Noailles' network, see E. H. Harbison, 'French intrigue at the court of Queen Mary', in *American History Review*, xlv (1940), pp. 533–51.

7

THE ENGLISH EXILES IN FRANCE

I

There were two quite separate streams of exiles from England during this period, one flowing mainly into Germany, the other to France. In the introduction to her census of exiles Miss Garrett wrote

... the first must be considered a genuinely religious movement, even though ... an undercurrent of politics ran so strongly as ultimately to dominate its activities; the other was frankly political, openly anti-Spanish, and only 'protestant' in so far as that term covered hostility to the Spanish match.[1]

Both groups wished to see the overthrow of Mary, but only a small proportion of the refugees in Germany were prepared to assist actively in the process. Their weapon was the printing press, and from Strasbourg, Geneva and Emden they smuggled great quantities of vitriolic pamphlets into England. The exiles in France were men of a different stamp. Survivors of Wyatt's rebellion, joined later by fugitives from a dozen lesser conspiracies, they were men of the sword rather than the pen. Today their attitude would be described as 'direct action'; and like most men of action they easily became bored, quarrelsome and despondent when their plans did not meet with quick success.

Henri's attitude towards these adventurers was straightforward in principle, but often tortuous in its application. He had no intention of distributing gratuitous charity. If the Englishmen wanted his money and support they would have

---

[1] Garrett, p. 33.

to be of service to him, to wait on his convenience, and above all to avoid implicating him in international incidents from which he could not escape. In March 1554, at a time when both Henri and Noailles were inclined to back the exiles strongly, the latter wrote

Since they (the English Council) feel themselves so irritated and outraged by Carew, it might be possible as well as beneficial if he would restrain himself a bit more, both in his presence and in his language, keeping himself concealed and changing his residence until necessity should force him to show himself. Meanwhile (it would be well) to offer the Queen's Ambassador every means of arresting him in order to amuse his mistress and to discourage her still further from declaring her ill will.[1]

Although he remained hopeful the French king never took very seriously the possibility that these exiles would overthrow the English government. If that was to be achieved at all, it would have to be from inside the country. Carew, Dudley, and those who adhered to them represented a strong card in Henri's diplomatic hand, but one which it would be dangerous to over-play. Consequently he was most prepared to aid them in adventures which committed him least. He lent them ships for their piratical expeditions, allowed his own subjects to take part, and gave them facilities to dispose of their prizes. These were acts of which he could easily and safely deny all know-ledge. Similarly he was quite prepared to allow them to intrigue against Calais and the Pale. If they succeeded it would precipi-tate a war, but the prize would already be won; if they failed, the risk was negligible. However, when it came to planning expeditions against England the King was much less enthusi-astic. This meant the risk of war for a highly problematical gain, because the exiles had neither the numbers nor the resources to launch a major attack without large-scale backing, of the kind which could not be denied. Twice he toyed with the idea, and both times drew back. It is not surprising that the

[1] Noailles to Montmorency, 17 March 1554, Aff. Etr., IX, f. 16. Noailles had had a stormy interview with the Council two days before, in which he was up-braided by Gardiner for his own and his master's complicity in the recent rising (Harbison, p. 162).

more hot-headed of the exiles complained vigorously ' . . . that the franche men ware . . . untrue men that wold promys myche and dow notheyng and yf they deyd show aney plesure they wold loke to reseve x tymes as myche agayne.'[1] Between promises and disappointments their morale fluctuated wildly, but it was more often low than high.

Not all the Englishmen in France at this time were political fugitives, or anxious to associate with these extremists. Cross-channel traffic was heavy, and only in moments of acute danger was any serious attempt made to keep a check on travellers. The crayers which plied between Southampton or Winchelsea and Newhaven were always prepared to take passengers—if they could pay the fare.[2] Many of those who crossed were outlaws for debt, or theft, or forgery. Others had 'fled for fear', without any specific offence.[3] Some of these were the victims of private feuds, and some had kept a step ahead of detection. If we count those Englishmen, mostly students and merchants, who were resident in France for legitimate reasons there must have been several hundreds of these expatriates. All shades of political opinion seem to have been represented amongst them, and although most tended to be hostile to Mary's government, only a relatively small number were prepared to carry their hostility into action. The fact that the fifty or so whose names are preserved in the records were mainly of this persuasion is natural, because it was with them that the authorities were most concerned. Edward Randall's estimate of July 1554, that this hard core never numbered more than 150, must be treated with reserve.[4] At that time Randall was anxious to belittle them, and

---

[1] Examination of Martin Dore, August 1556; SP, Vol. VII, no. 59. Appendix III.

[2] See, for example, the statement by Robert Gyre of Southampton how the crayer operated by himself and Robert Marten was hired by Richard Uvedale to take 'two strangers' to Cherbourg: 'theye agreed for iiii li for settinge them a lande there'. But it is not clear whether this meant £4 each. SP, Vol. VII, no. 34, 25 March 1556.

[3] Wotton to Queen Mary, 17 April 1554. *Cal. For.* Vol. II, p. 73. Also p. 191, 23 October 1555, concerning Richard Bunny. Bunny had been sent to the Fleet in March 1554 for misdemeanour in his office as Treasurer of Berwick. He had forged a note for £95 in the hand of Northumberland. By the autumn of 1554 he had escaped, first to Basle and then to France (Garrett, p. 99).

[4] Wotton to the Queen, 29 July 1554. *Cal. For.* Vol. II, p. 108.

the constant comings and goings meant that such an early assessment had no meaning for the reign as a whole.

The situation was further confused by the fact that most of the prominent exiles were professional soldiers, and a number of professional English captains were serving in the French army. The position of Thomas Crayer seems to have been typical of many. In March 1554 he was clearly in the service of Lord Grey, to whom he wrote acknowledging a payment and requesting recall to England.[1] By December of the same year he was at the French court, and eighteen months later Nicholas Wotton wrote to the Council 'Crayer will give all information of their (the exiles) proceedings, and though he has here a pension of 300 crowns and a little less in land for life, yet if he could obtain a meaner living than this in England he would not remain'.[2] Crayer was personally friendly with such fellow-soldiers as Carew, Dudley and Tremayne, and it is impossible to analyse his loyalties in simple political terms. At the end of 1556 he and one Tutty had commissions to raise English mercenaries for the French king, and Wotton wrote that they '. . . would fetch (their) men out of England unless her Majesty takes some order to let it.'[3] Leaving the realm without licence turned all such men into fugitives and offenders, although most of them could have had little interest in the political implications of their actions. Once in France their technical proscription naturally inclined them to associate with the exiles, even if they had no intention of joining them. This made it doubly hard for observers to assess the strength and composition of the rebel groups. The reverse tendency also operated. When their plots failed the exiles drifted into the French service. In December 1556 it was rumoured '. . . that Dudley shall be the captain of all the English who serve' in the forthcoming war. Henri encouraged this, generally preferring the Englishmen as

[1] Captain Thomas Crayer to Lord Grey, 24 March 1554. *Cal. For.* Vol. II, p. 66. With this letter Crayer enclosed a note from Carew and Pickering recommending one John Adams for a place in his company!
[2] Wotton to Sir William Petre, 13 July 1556. *Cal. For.* Vol. II, p. 238.
[3] Same to the Queen, 30 November 1556. *Cal. For.* Vol. II, p. 277.

hired soldiers rather than as expensive and unpredictable allies.[1]

Unlike the exiles in Germany, who had frequently migrated with their entire households, those in France were either single men or had left their wives and families behind. There was a strong streak of irresponsibility in their behaviour which troubled all who had dealings with them, but their military potential could not be ignored. Philip was most unwilling to see so many good soldiers, who were technically his subjects, serving in the ranks of his enemies. Consequently he was often willing, as in the case of Carew, to intercede with Mary for the pardon of individuals.[2] For a while in the summer of 1554 it was even rumoured that the whole caucus of the rebels in Normandy was about to defect to the Imperial camp, although in the event they dispersed.

The main burden of dealing with this tangled and dangerous problem fell upon the English Ambassador in France. Wotton was a shrewd and able diplomat, neither so optimistic nor so gullible as Noailles, but the weakness of his government left him at the mercy of events. Henri did not want a war with England, but he knew that the English wanted it still less, and so, like his ambassador, he was prepared 'to give them a ripe one between two green ones'.[3] Wotton was the recipient of a number of these 'ripe ones' as he fruitlessly protested against the countenance given to Carew and Dudley, or the piratical activities of the Killigrews. Henri's normal tactic was to deny all knowledge of the activities complained of. When Carew first landed in France he blandly assured the Ambassador 'I have not seen him, nor know him not', and continued innocently 'Marry, I

[1] How far the 'entertainment' frequently mentioned by Dudley's associates (see below, pp. 186-192) implied commitment to the King's service is not clear. Henri seems to have given sums of money and pensions to individuals without obligation, but regular rewards such as that given to Crayer were reserved for those who accepted his commissions.

[2] The Venetian envoy at the Imperial Court wrote: 'the King (Philip) ... does whatever he can to win the support of Englishmen.' Badoer to the Doge and Senate, 24 November 1555. *Cal. Ven.* Vol. VI, p. 258.

[3] This picturesque phrase appears to have been Noailles' own description of the blustering tactics which he adopted with the English Council. Renard to the Emperor, 12 Feb. 1554. *Cal. Span.* Vol. XII, p. 97.

have heard speak of one of that name in times past that was Master of the Horse in England.'[1] As late as June 1556, the King could still reply to a bitter complaint of piracy with a disingenuous promise to make enquiries.[2] Montmorency was more honest, but scarcely more helpful, and Wotton early realised that there was no real hope of obtaining the extradition of the offenders. The only concrete result of his formal diplomacy was an agreement reached in August 1556 for the suppression of an illegal mint operating at Dieppe.[3] In the absence of any effective sanctions to bring Henri to a more co-operative frame of mind, the Ambassador was forced to resort to less open methods to safeguard his mistress's interests.

His main objective was to obtain information. Like every other Ambassador he employed spies and agents, but Wotton was not only concerned to detect the practices of the French government. With the domestic situation in England so unsatisfactory, even a small-scale landing by the exiles could have unpredictable results. Consequently it was essential that the Council should be kept informed of their movements and intentions. In the spring of 1556 Bretville, now working as French agent, wrote that ' . . . if Dudley were to land with a thousand men, he would quickly have twenty thousand, and the best'[4]; and Wotton was the first line of defence against such an enterprise. His main asset was the powerful intercession which he could offer for the pardon of any offender who appealed to him, an asset which he sometimes used with more enthusiasm than discretion. From the first he was convinced that more of the fugitives had gone to France in a panic or for trivial reasons than with deliberately subversive intentions, and the frequent approaches made to him seemed to justify this opinion. However Wotton, like Montmorency, made the

[1] Wotton to the Queen, 12 February 1554. P. F. Tytler, *England under the reigns of Edward VI and Mary* (London, 1839) Vol. II, p. 289.

[2] Giacomo Soranzo, Venetian Ambassador in France, to the Doge and Senate, 23 June 1556. *Cal. Ven.* Vol. VI, p. 493.

[3] Wotton to the Queen, 4 August 1556. *Cal. For.* Vol. II, p. 244. This was probably the mint originally established to serve the conspirators in the spring of the same year. See below, p. 191.

[4] Bretville to Montmorency, n.d., Aff. Etr., IX, f. 660 (Harbison, p. 281).

mistake of assuming that these individuals knew which side they were on. 'The English', wrote Soranzo, 'are of little faith, both towards their sovereigns and towards each other',[1] and his opinion was amply corroborated by the behaviour of these exiles. One of Wotton's first protégés was that Edward Randall who had been an associate of Wyatt. By the end of May 1554 he had procured his pardon, and Randall remained in France for the remainder of the summer, working as a government agent. It was largely through his persuasions, wrote Wotton at the end of July, that Carew had forsaken his purposes and gone into Italy, an action instrumental in breaking up the first rebel caucus in Normandy.[2] In August 1554 Randall returned to England, bearing the Ambassador's letter of recommendation. He received from Philip a commission as colonel of infantry and an annuity of 200 crowns, and sustained the character of a loyal subject. At the same time, however, he was in communication with Noailles, urging him to persuade Henri to invade, and so enthusiastically did he present his case that it required an authoritative rebuff from the Constable to silence him.[3]

This kind of double dealing was common, and Wotton later came to realize that he must deal circumspectly with such men. William Staunton, another of those who worked for him in the summer of 1554 and was pardoned as a result, later took a leading part in the Dudley conspiracy. Subsequent petitioners, such as Brian Fitzwilliam and Henry Killigrew, found their welcome cooler.[4] As he became more accustomed to the situation, Wotton treated all the information which he derived from such sources as suspect. When he was approached in December 1554 by one Roger Edwards, a Welshman who professed to be a defaulter from the Constable's service, the Ambassador

[1] Soranzo's Narration of England, 1554. *Cal. Ven.* Vol. V, p. 532.
[2] Wotton to the Queen, 29 July and 10 August 1554. *Cal. For.* Vol. II, pp. 108, 113.
[3] Randall's scheme was for Henri to arm and equip 1500 English exiles and Gascon musketeers, place Carew at their head and send them across (Harbison, p. 230).
[4] Brian Fitzwilliam to Wotton, 12 July 1555. *Cal. For.* Vol. II, p. 178. Wotton to the Queen, 30 November 1556. Ibid. p. 277.

treated him with distinct reserve and forwarded his intelligences direct to the Council.[1] In the case of William Lant, a north-countryman introduced to him by the London merchant Hugh Offley, he was even more suspicious. Lant changed his own story twice, and finally came out with a vague warning about a huge conspiracy in which the greatest in England were involved. Unable to get any convincing details out of him, Wotton came to the conclusion that he was a 'naughty fellow' and a 'very false liar', probably employed by the French to spread alarm and despondency in England.[2] Many of the rumours and 'tales' which the Ambassador picked up were of a similar nature, and he 'gave them little credence'. When in doubt as to the value of his information he tended to communicate it privately to Sir William Petre, not wishing to trouble the Council officially with matters which might turn out to be groundless.[3]

Wotton's position was a difficult one in every sense. Both the exiles and the French government recognized him as an astute and persistent antagonist, and he was more than once on the verge of being declared *persona non grata*. At the same time he was the centre of a net of espionage and counter-espionage which he never fully controlled or even understood. His own nephews had been involved in Wyatt's rising,[4] and he was embarrassed by the presence among the exiles of such colleagues and friends as Sir William Pickering and Sir Nicholas Throgmorton. Pickering, indeed, caused more than embarrassment for he was familiar with the diplomatic ciphers, which had to be changed in the spring of 1554. There were, however, advantages in these contacts for it was through Wotton's friendly persuasions that Pickering abandoned the rebels in April 1554 and Throgmorton was induced to return to his

---

[1] Wotton to the Council, 24 December 1554. *Cal. For.* Vol. II, p. 147. Edwards gave himself out to be a Monmouth man, son of one Arnold Edwards. Ibid. p. 144, 12 December 1554. Miss Garrett does not mention him.
[2] Wotton to Petre, 21 January 1557. *Cal. For.* Vol. II, p. 286.
[3] As he explained in a letter to Secretaries Bourn and Boxall after Petre's retirement, (6 May 1557.) *Cal. For.* Vol. II, p. 302
[4] See above, p. 81.

allegiance three years later.[1] Sir Nicholas had fled on 20 June 1556, and Wotton greeted him on arrival with a warning '. . . by no means to have any communication with the rebels'. This warning seems to have been heeded for he kept in touch with the Ambassador, who reported in October 1556 that he had ' . . . a faithful mind to her majesty and his country.' He was pardoned on 1 May 1557,[2] and managed to return to England before the outbreak of war. Many others were not so fortunate. On 6 May Wotton wrote sadly that most of his penitents would be stranded unless their welcome was speedily assured.[3] In the event they remained abroad until the next reign.

Apart from his difficult trafficking with informers, the Ambassador maintained a regular secret service in which his secretary John Somers played a key part. The names of his agents are never mentioned, because as he explained his letters were always liable to be intercepted,[4] but they seem for the most part to have been Frenchmen. Somers acted as go-between to save these men from the hazardous task of visiting the Ambassador's lodging. The regular agents were paid by the month, and were not scrupulous about screwing up their prices if they got the chance. On one occasion Wotton wrote to Petre: 'The person who has offered to supply her Majesty with secret information of the French court demands 50 crowns *per mensem.*'[5] This was more than he could pay without special authorisation, which suggests that he was working on a more limited budget than his French and Imperial counterparts. It was not the least of Wotton's worries that he was always short of money.

The Ambassador was not the only man who kept spies in France. Lord Grey, the Captain of Guisnes, had his own agents,

[1] According to Wotton, Throgmorton 'often visited' him during the autumn of 1556. Wotton to the Queen, 29 October 1556. *Cal. For.* Vol. II, p. 273.

[2] *Cal. Pat.* Vol. III, p. 476.

[3] Wotton to the Secretaries, 6 May 1557. *Cal. For.* Vol. II, p. 302.

[4] Wotton to Petre, 9 May 1554, 30 November 1556. *Cal. For.* Vol. II, pp. 89, 276.

[5] Wotton to Petre, December 1555. *Cal. For.* Vol. II, p. 200.

mainly to give him warning of any possible attack on the Pale. There also seem to have been free-lance spies who communicated direct with the Council. Such a one was Edgar Horngold of Guisnes, who wrote to Secretary Bourne in March 1554 giving a circumstantial account of Carew's activities in Normandy.[1] Any Englishman whose business took him to France was liable to find himself involved in these transactions, sometimes with serious consequences for himself. Among those examined during the investigations of March and April 1556 was a certain Martin Dore, a Southampton merchant.[2] According to his own story he went to France in November 1555 on a business trip. Ending a fruitless journey just before Easter, he had reached Dieppe on the way back when he '. . . hard report that the passing (into) ynglond was layd that noman myght com over into france, nor from france into ynglond but that he was stayed and (sent) unto the consell. . . .' This news persuaded him ' . . . to stay untell a more quyet teyme'. On reflection, however, he decided that his remaining in France under such circumstances might be misinterpreted, and so he 'imageneyd whyche way I myght devyse to serfe the queynse heyghenyse whareby I myghte the better be abull to answer for my beyng yn fraunce,' and decided to undertake a little sabotage among the Queen's enemies. He therefore made it his business to seek out Christopher Ashton, Francis Horsey and others and persuade them that Dudley was 'a prowde man (and) not wyse'. He also told them, as one who had inside information, that the French would default on their promises, and that it would be '. . . best for them to go into italy whyle there money deyd laste and to seycke to serfe there. . . .' Unfortunately for him, while dining one night on board ship the vessel was captured by royal ships and Dore was brought to his account. There is no record of whether his elaborate *apologia* was accepted. Most of the information which it contained was circumstantial and of little direct value to the

---

[1] *Cal. For.* Vol. II, p. 67.
[2] Examination of Martin Dore, 1556. SP, Vol. VII, no. 59. See Appendix III concerning the date of this examination.

investigators, but it provides an interesting glimpse of the hand-to-mouth existence of the exiles. Frustration, inactivity and intermittent poverty had warped their sense of political reality and left them a prey to exaggerated hopes and suspicions.

II

Of the various outlets through which these dangerous energies might run, the most natural was piracy. The channel had always been infested with pirates, against whom the royal fleets of England and France acted spasmodically and inefficiently.[1] Star Chamber and Admiralty litigation show that the mariners and gentry of the west country were frequently prepared to take the chance of seizing a passing merchantman, and in wartime could not be relied upon to discriminate between friend and foe.[2] Politically, piracy was an innocuous activity because it was not an act of direct hostility, and in any case responsibility was extremely hard to bring home.

Many of the Englishmen who sailed from the North French ports during Mary's reign were pirates first and enemies of the government only incidentally. The two best known, Peter and Thomas Killigrew, had begun their career in the previous reign and their activities had very little to do with patriotism.[3] The decision to aid and harbour them was a political one, taken against the professional judgement of the vice-admiral at Brest, but their voyages would have taken place in any case. When Peter Killigrew was in the Tower, in September 1556, Sir John Baker wrote to Sir Henry Bedingfield

. . . to receive of Peter Killigrew all such licences and other instruments as he has made to him by the Admiral of France and his predecessors or any other of the French King's officers whereby he or his brother was licensed to use any exploite . . . upon the see. . . .[4]

---

[1] Lord Seymour of Sudeley was not the only official accused of complicity with the pirates, although he was the highest.

[2] See *Select Pleas in the Court of Admiralty*, R. G. Marsden; *Selden Society*, vi (1892), pp. xi–lxxxvii.

[3] See above, p. 40.

[4] *Third Report of the Historical Manuscripts Commission*, Appendix, p. 239; Sir John Baker to Sir Henry Bedingfield, 5 September 1556.

The result must have been disappointing, for a month later Wotton wrote from France that it would be exceedingly hard to establish the King's position, since the written authorities were in the hands of the Admiral.[1] What these 'authorities' were is not quite clear. Baker's letter implies some kind of privateering commission, but Wotton was concerned only with the ownership of Killigrew's principal vessel, the *Sacrette*. The *Sacrette* was a cause of intense irritation for over two years, but Henri knew well enough that Mary would not be able to persuade her Council to break the peace over a nest of pirates, however indignant she might be.

The relations between professional pirates such as the Killigrews and the rebels seem to have varied from cordial co-operation to complete indifference. The collapse of Wyatt's rising brought a draft of fresh recruits to the pirate vessels, and Carew seems to have taken to the sea within a few weeks of his arrival, but whether his ships were working in collaboration with those of Killigrew in February and March 1554 is not at all clear. Wotton was advised on 22 February that Carew had ' . . . hired sundry English mariners with their vessels and boats' at Rouen,[2] and on 14 March Renard reported that he had armed the *Sacrette*. At the same time it was rumoured that Henri had given the Killigrews a ship, and by the end of March they were definitely at sea ' . . . with three ships of Englishmen.'[3] The pirates made a number of voyages during the summer, but there is no evidence that they had any hand in Carew's rumoured invasion preparations. The majority of Sir Peter's associates were not seafaring men, and although he personally was known to the men who had rescued him it seems probable that they went their separate ways.

With Dudley the position was rather different. Although Peter Killigrew claimed 'I never saw hym but ons . . . at which tyme he desyred us to lende hem iiiC crownes, sayeing that

---

[1] Wotton to the Council, 8 October 1556. *Cal. For.* Vol. II, p. 261.
[2] Mary to Wotton, 22 February 1554. *Cal. For.* Vol. II, p. 61.
[3] Captain Crayer to Lord Grey, 24 March 1554. *Cal. For.* Vol. II, p. 66. There seems to have been considerable uncertainty as to whether the *Sacrette* was being used by Carew or Killigrew.

there was never a porer man in the worlde than he was ... ',[1] several of his associates were experienced sailors. Nicholas Tremayne had been imprisoned in February 1555 on a charge of piracy,[2] and Francis Horsey commanded one of Killigrew's ships in the summer of 1556, Christopher Ashton the younger was also at sea with them on the same voyage.[3] In October 1556 Wotton reported that Ashton and his company were again at sea ' ... which is thought to be the greatest succour by which these honest men seek to live here.'[4] It is clear from Killigrew's examination that he was strongly suspected of complicity in Dudley's invasion plan. His name was also associated with an obscure plot for the seizure of Jersey which seems to have followed upon the collapse of the original conspiracy.[5] If his personal relations with Dudley were negligible, there was certainly much coming and going among their associates, and each must have been informed of the other's actions.

It would, however, be wrong to suppose that the profits of piracy were used to finance the conspirators' schemes. Men like Ashton and Horsey served in the Killigrews' ships to supplement their meagre and irregular pensions from the French king, not to contribute towards a common 'war chest'. The English government was never quite sure whether it was dealing with one problem or two, but it seems clear that in spite of a certain amount of co-operation there was no real identity of interest. This conclusion is supported by the fact that the destruction of the Killigrews' fleet had no visible repercussions upon the exiles' plots. It did not prevent Thomas Stafford's voyage to Scarborough the next year, and Dudley's main attentions had

[1] This characteristic request shows the true Dudley touch! Examination of Peter Killigrew, 21 August 1556. SP, Vol. IX, no. 25.
[2] APC, Vol. V, p. 99, 24 February 1555. No details are given.
[3] Further confession of Peter Killigrew, 21 August 1556. SP, Vol. IX, no. 26. On the familiarity between the Killigrews and several of Dudley's associates, see Appendix III.
[4] Wotton to Petre, 8 October 1556. Cal. For. Vol. II, p. 265.
[5] This enterprise against Jersey is mentioned by Dore as being the objective of the Killigrews' last voyage, and appears twice among the interrogatories put to Killigrew. It may have been abandoned, or frustrated by their defeat.

been transferred from England to Calais before it occurred. In spite of his imprisonment and rigorous examination Peter Killigrew was never indicted for treason, and less than a year after his capture was in command of a royal ship. When compared with the experiences of known rebels such as Sir Peter Carew this rapid rehabilitation suggests that Killigrew was never seriously identified with the main purposes of the exiles.

The summer of 1556 began promisingly enough. On 19 June Wotton reported that the pirates were at sea with four or five ships, and had taken good prizes.[1] One of these was a Spanish merchantman which was carried about the middle of June, and its cargo sold in France.[2] A number of English ships were also taken, and Wotton began a fresh round of protests towards the end of the month. About the middle of July, however, the pirate fleet was caught by the Queen's ships off Plymouth, and in a decisive engagement six of their vessels were captured.[3] Only a handful of men in one small boat managed to escape. The French government was probably as much relieved by this turn of events as anyone, since the rovers had sometimes been injudicious enough to attack French vessels, but its official reaction was an extraordinary one. The Constable demanded the return of the pirates' best ship, the notorious *Sacrette*, on the grounds that it had been lent to Killigrew by the king for the duration of the Franco-Imperial war![4] Killigrew himself denied this. In his examination of 21 August he described how his original ships had been confiscated at Brest, probably during the spring of 1553.

. . . in consyderation whereof after the return of my brother . . . we were sewtors to thAdmirall to be meanes unto the Kinge that we myght have the Sacrett for ii yeres with such furnyture to serve hem, whiche was grauntyd us. And after upon service (discharged) demanded the gyfte of the saide shippe with such ordonance which

[1] Wotton to Petre, 19 June 1556. *Cal. For.* Vol. II, p. 229.
[2] At his examination on 21 August Killigrew confessed to taking the Spaniard 'aboute xi weeks past'. They had killed six of her crew, and kept the rest as prisoners until the Queen's ships rescued them. SP, Vol. IX, no. 26.
[3] Michieli to the Doge and Senate, 21 July 1556. *Cal. Ven.* Vol. VI, p. 536. Michieli's report that Killigrew had escaped was mistaken.
[4] Harbison, p. 305.

was grantyd us, and which was (conveyed) to us by the Lord Admyrall in Newehaven in Lent was twelvemonth. . . .[1]

Wotton was left to sort out this tangle as best he could. If any deed of gift existed, it was in the hands of the French Admiral who would not, of course, produce it. Investigations at Newhaven made no progress because of the peoples' bitter hostility to the English, and the question remained unanswered until it was caught up in the wider issue of war.

The disappearance of the Killigrews from the scene did not put an end to English piracy from France, but greatly reduced it. Ashton was the only substantial operator left, and he does not seem to have had the professional skill of the Cornishmen. Political considerations played a large part in his actions, and he busied himself with schemes like that for the seizure of Portland castle which Wotton unearthed in the spring of 1557. The fact that the Ambassador's protests on this score were greatly diminished during the autumn of 1556 and the spring of 1557 indicates that the incubus had been temporarily removed.

For those exiles whose main preoccupation was the overthrow of the English government, piracy was a profitable sideline, and the distinction between the professional and amateur pirate was one of degree rather than kind. At the same time the political importance of those pirates who were not conspirators was created by the action of the French government. Henri protected Killigrew no less assiduously than Dudley, which tended to obscure the fact that they represented very different threats to England, in spite of frequent overlaps in their fields of operation.

III

The French king could not, and did not, expect to make large gains from these activities. Their main value to him was as a weapon in minor diplomatic skirmishes. Very much more significant from the French point of view was the possibility

[1] SP, Vol. IX, no. 25.

that the exiles might succeed in engineering the surrender of
Calais. Henri had brought with him to the throne an intense
ambition to dislodge the English from their continental foot-
holds.[1] The weakness of Northumberland's position had enabled
him to regain Boulogne in 1550, and the succession crisis of
1553 seems to have brought him within an ace of securing
Calais as well. On 13 July the Duke despatched Henry Dudley
as his personal envoy to negotiate for French assistance.
Dudley's mission was futile because the government which he
represented collapsed within a few days of his departure. On
his return he was arrested and examined, apparently confessing
that, in exchange for French aid '. . . the Duke had promised
to hand over to the French Calais, Guisnes and Hames, the
English possessions on the mainland, and Ireland.'[2] The source
of this information is suspect, but there was certainly some truth
in it.

Northumberland's fall did not diminish Henri's appetite for
intrigue in that direction, and Wyatt's rebellion once more
brought Calais into the 'front line'. Diversions in Scotland and
the Pale were among the French suggestions offered to the
conspirators as methods of assistance. Unwilling to believe for
some weeks that they had really missed their opportunity,
Noailles and Henri D'Oysel, the French Ambassador in Scotland—particularly the latter—continued with the schemes for
these diversions long after the rising had collapsed.[3] From
February to May 1554 rumours of impending French attacks
upon the Pale were constant. At the beginning of March Lord
Grey wrote to the Council from Guisnes, begging for reinforcements to meet the expected onslaught, a request with which the
government hastened to comply.[4] Carew and his followers were
associated with these threats from the outset. Calais was a
frequent resort for undesirable characters wishing to lie low,

[1] 'L'idée de la conquête de Calais l'obseda pendant tout son règne', Lucien
Romier, *Origines Politiques des guerres de religion*, Paris 1913–14, Vol. I, p. 29.
[2] Renard to Prince Philip, 5 September 1553. *Cal. Span.* Vol. XI, p. 208. Wotton's
original despatch has not survived.
[3] D'Oysel to Noailles, 2 March 1554. Aff. Etr., IX, ff. 143–4 (Harbison, p. 154 n).
[4] Lord Grey to the Council, 10 March 1554. *Cal. For.* Vol. II, p. 65.

and it is certain that some of these were in communication with the exiles and the French in the hope of being able to profit by their position. The Pale also seems to have contained a large proportion of protestants, and at the beginning of April Renard wrote that the Captains of both Guisnes and Calais were suspect as heretics.[1] On 10 April the Council notified Wotton that a 'practice against Calais' had been discovered and was being investigated, but no details were given.[2] A month later Renard also reported that the French had an understanding with traitors in the town, and on 13 May he wrote that one Jaques Granado had been arrested for such treasonable activities.[3] No clear picture emerges from these various hints, and it seems that at this time the exiles confined themselves to rather half-hearted attempts at undermining the morale of a garrison which was nearly two years in arrears with its pay.

The dispersal of the exiles in August 1554 temporarily reduced the danger from that direction, but the state of Calais itself continued to give cause for anxiety. By March 1555 it had been decided to move against the lawless and heretical elements in the town, and the Earl of Pembroke was despatched thither armed with a special Commission. This immediately caused rumours that a fresh attack was expected, but the threat was general rather than particular. Pembroke's activities in Calais were part of a wider scheme of precautions taken against the possibility of the Queen's miscarriage.[4] Pembroke made some arrests, and reported that religious disaffection was widespread. There was urgent need of a good preacher and firm ecclesiastical administration. However, in spite of constant threats and recommendations, very little was done to strengthen the Pale. A year and a half later the garrisons were still grossly understrength, and religious disturbances were again encouraging French attentions.

---

[1] Renard to the Emperor, 7 April 1554. *Cal. Span.* Vol. XII, p. 214.
[2] Council to Wotton, 10 April 1554. *Cal. For.* Vol. II, p. 71.
[3] Renard to the Emperor, 13 May 1554. *Cal. Span.* Vol. XII, p. 253. Renard had already written that Granado was intriguing in the Low Countries, and should be watched.
[4] Michieli to the Doge and Senate, 12 March 1555. *Cal. Ven.* Vol. VI, p. 18.

In October 1556 Wotton discovered another, and this time serious, practice against Calais. Frustrated in their attempt to invade England, Dudley and his followers turned their attentions in that direction. About the middle of the month Wotton noticed that one Nicholas Devisat, sometime tutor to the children of the Duke of Somerset, had taken up a post in the Comptroller's household.[1] A few days later he discovered that a notorious intriguer named Chesnes had also gone thither, and investigations revealed that a plot had been under way for almost a month.[2] Through an unnamed informer among the exiles he was told that Dudley had established contacts within the garrison and among the townspeople, and that a number of his associates were with the French troops which were quietly mustering at Boulogne.[3] Henri seems to have hoped that the protestants, incensed by spasmodic attempts to suppress them, would rise against the city authorities if given sufficient encouragement. Dudley encouraged him in this belief, promising, as a beginning, to engineer the surrender of the fortresses of Guisnes and Hammes. Since his brother, Edmund Sutton, Lord Dudley, was Captain of the latter, his promises carried conviction. However, either because of his own dilatoriness, or Wotton's prompt warnings, Dudley's schemes came to nothing; in spite of their close relationship there was no political sympathy between Lord Dudley and his brother, and the former remained in his allegiance. The boundary dispute which was being used as a pretext for troop concentrations reached deadlock about the beginning of December, but the almost simultaneous arrival of the Earl of Pembroke with substantial reinforcements cooled the French enthusiasm for a sudden stroke.[4] By the middle of December Michieli reported

[1] Wotton to Petre and Bourn, 19 October 1556. *Cal. For.* Vol. II, p. 267.
[2] Wotton to the Queen, 20 and 29 October 1556. *Cal. For.* Vol. II, pp. 267–73. Chesnes is described as ' . . . the man who intrigued the fall of Marano, fourteen years ago.'
[3] Wotton to the Queen, 20 October and 30 November 1556. Ibid. pp. 267, 278. The Ambassador was told that the conspirators had intelligence with some merchants in the town, ' . . . who like nothing the fashion of religion now used in England.'
[4] Wotton to Petre, 12 December 1556. *Cal. For.* Vol. II, p. 280.

that the rumours had died down, and that the Calais Council was on the alert for any fresh intrigues.[1] The crisis had passed quickly, but had been dangerous while it lasted. Wotton wrote that 'it lacked but a little that Calais was not delivered to the French king . . .', implying that if Dudley had used his opportunities energetically the English reinforcements would have arrived too late.[2]

By the beginning of the new year complacency was reasserting itself within the Pale. In spite of the increasing probability that England would become involved in the Franco-Imperial conflict, and despite the fact that a plot by Devisat to fire the Calais magazine had been unearthed, the Council remained confident. On 13 January Wotton warned the government that the situation was still precarious. The French had not given up their purpose, nor the exiles their intrigues.[3] However, preoccupation with other matters led to further neglect. Even after the outbreak of war the garrisons were left under strength and underpaid, a disproportionate reliance being placed upon the strength of the fortifications. When the Pale was eventually overrun in January 1558, suspicions of treachery were naturally revived, but no such explanation is necessary to account for the ease of the conquest. In March 1558 Michel Surian, the Venetian Ambassador at the Imperial Court, wrote ' . . . that since more than six years the French have been practising against Calais.[4] In many of these practices the English exiles had been principals, but in spite of this fact, and in spite of constant warnings, no more than a spasmodic vigilance could be maintained. The very frequency of the plots against the town, and the fact that they had been frustrated, induced a false sense of security. Dudley, Ashton, and several others of the second exile group were still in France at the time of the fall of Calais, but there is no evidence to suggest that they played an active part in its capture.

[1] Michieli to the Doge and Senate, 14 December 1556. *Cal. Ven.* Vol. VI, p. 867.
[2] Wotton to the Queen, 13 and 21 January 1557. *Cal. For.* Vol. II, pp. 281–235.
[3] Ibid.
[4] Surian to the Doge and Senate, 24 March 1558. *Cal. Ven.* Vol. VI, p. 1476.

IV

From the point of view of the English government these rebel plots were intensely annoying, and at times alarming, but they did not represent the principal danger. The most disturbing possibility was that of a descent on England itself. If it acted on its own, a small force of returning exiles could probably be contained without much difficulty; although in some places even that was not certain. If, on the other hand, it was supported by the French fleet, or reinforced by French troops, the consequences could not easily be foreseen. Henri's extreme reluctance to embark upon such an adventure was not realized in England. Noailles made certain of that. Rumours of invasion were constant, and could not safely be ignored.

Apart from the crisis occasioned by the Dudley conspiracy, the period when this danger was most acute was, as we have seen, the spring of 1554. The gathering of the French fleet in early March caused serious and justifiable alarm in England, although a number of observers believed that its object was to intercept Spanish shipping.[1] At that stage the exiles' enthusiasm was high, and they had powerful allies at the French court in the persons of the Guises. On 14 March Renard reported with complete certainty that the French were planning to seize the Isle of Wight, and bring the Scots across the border ' . . . in order to give the factions a chance to rise.'[2] The south coast defences were reinforced, but the Ambassador was very dubious of the country's ability to resist a determined attack without Imperial assistance. Before the end of the month news had reached the Council that the French fleet would number 200 sail, and that the Vidame of Chartres had gone in haste to Scotland; ' . . . and (they) stick not to say openly that if the king of Spain comes to England, the French king will send his

---

[1] Especially, of course, any attempt by Philip to land in England. Renard to the Emperor, 8 March 1554. *Cal. Span.* Vol. XII, p. 138.

[2] Renard to the Emperor, 14 March 1554. *Cal. Span.* Vol. XII, p. 153.

foot to the aid of the commons. . . . '[1] Carew's stock was very high in Normandy, where he talked in large and blustering terms of the ancient union with England, invoking it against the present unnatural alliance between England and Spain.[2] He gathered 'a great retinue', including such new arrivals as the Staffords, but did not dare to act without Henri's approval. In the middle of April his followers were boasting of their intention to oppose Philip's landing, and of their powerful connections in England, but by the end of the month defections had sapped their morale. On the 29th Wotton wrote that they were planning two small-scale landings in the immediate future, one in the Isle of Wight, and the other at Lee in Essex.[3] In the event the King appears to have prohibited both these adventures, for nothing was done and by the end of May the exiles were complaining loudly that Henri would not employ them, and was keeping them short of money. Desertion from their ranks became common, and Wotton was bombarded with appeals for pardon. For obvious reasons the French king preferred to bolster his influence in Scotland, which could provide him with a stronger and more manageable lever against the English government.

It is very doubtful whether Carew had the powerful contacts within England at which his followers so frequently hinted. The disgrace of Paget, and Renard's continuous suspicions are not really evidence. He certainly had a number of friends, especially among his wife's relations in Lincolnshire, who corresponded with him and supplied him with money.[4] There is nothing to suggest that these friends had either the means or the intention of fostering rebellion. By 1556 the situation was rather different. Dudley's plots were hatched on both sides of the Channel, and it was the implication of key officials such as Richard Uvedale, the Captain of Yarmouth castle, which made

---

[1] 'The French King has provided 80 ancients of footmen to send to the seas. . . .' Crayer to Grey, 24 March 1554. *Cal. For.* Vol. II, p. 67.

[2] Edgar Horngold to Secretary Bourne, 28 March 1554. *Cal. For.* Vol. II, p. 67.

[3] Wotton to the Queen, 29 April 1554. *Cal. For.* Vol. II, p. 79. This information apparently came from Pickering.

[4] Concerning Carew's visit to Lincolnshire in April 1555, see above, p. 123.

them especially dangerous. In his plans for invasion, however, Dudley was handicapped no less than Carew by Henri's equivocations. At first the King received him well, then rebuffed him. On 11 March Montmorency wrote that 'discreet and secret help' would be given to the conspirators,[1] but a week later the circle in England was broken up, and with the English government on the alert most of the plausibility had gone out of the scheme. For a while the exiles continued with their plans apparently undeterred. They had already been in touch with Courtenay in Venice,[2] and some time in May they seem to have sent a further messenger—Henry Killigrew, the youngest of the three Cornish brothers. However, by that time there was no chance that Henri would either support or finance a major enterprise. The proposed attack dwindled to the proportions of a raid 'either on Harwich or Yarmouth', and there were rumours that the whole band would be sent to Scotland.[3] Wotton heard as late as August that Courtenay was still expected in France, but the information seems to have been one of the many 'tales' with which he was afflicted.

By October 1556 Dudley was again at court, and 'well entertained', but his eyes were on Calais and the Imperial war rather than on England. It was left to the irresponsible extremist Thomas Stafford to make the only actual raid which emerged from these restless plots. Thomas and his brother in law, Sir Robert Stafford,[4] had fled to France in March 1554, when the former had had the audacity to present himself to his

[1] The reason given for this decision was that the truce with the Emperor had not been ratified, but the ratification arrived the next day (Harbison, p. 286).

[2] '. . . the vedam had sent unto my lord cortney that yf yt shuld plese hym to come into france, he wold provyd for him xxx M crowneys and aney other theyng that he had bised shuld be at hys commandement. Treymayne sayd that my lord cortney sent the vidame word agayn . . . that yt was not for hym to enter aney Keyngs realm upon any subgets promys. . . .' Examination of Martin Dore, SP, Vol. VII, no. 59. Tremayne himself seems to have been the messenger. Courtenay was officially exonerated, but several mysterious letters of his remain unexplained, and one of the conspirators accused him of planning to sell £200 worth of land to help finance the plot. Hinnes' confession, 30 March 1556, SP, Vol. VII, no. 49.

[3] Wotton to the Queen, 13 July 1556. Cal. For. Vol. II, p. 238.

[4] Third son of Sir Humphrey Stafford of Blatherwick, and a notorious adventurer (Garrett, p. 293).

uncle, Cardinal Pole. The Cardinal expelled him from the house and he seems for a time to have returned to England.[1] By October 1556 he was back in France, where his violent and pointless quarrels with his brother-in-law attracted the sarcastic attentions of Wotton.[2] By November the Ambassador was reporting ' . . . Stafford gives himself out to be a lord, and next heir to the Crown. . . .' These pretensions were not completely groundless, for he was of royal descent, but they were politically ridiculous. If he hoped that the French would adopt him as a rival to Elizabeth for the succession, he miscalculated wildly. If the French wanted an alternative claimant to the English throne they had a much more plausible one ready to hand in the person of the young Scottish Queen.[3] However, Henri was not averse to using him as a catspaw, and in January 1557 he was entertained at court, where he assumed ' . . . the full arms of England on his seal, without any difference.'

Stafford seems to have remained at the court until the middle of April, when one of Wotton's spies who was closely associated with him reported to the Ambassador that he had collected armaments and hired a ship.[4] He was studying maps of a place in Sussex which the informant could not identify, and there was talk of a young man named Thomas Brooke ' . . . who is kin to the Captain of Scarborough.' By the end of April Wotton wrote that Stafford had taken up four or five hundred men of all nations and there was talk of a descent on 'Scarborough, Hull, Dover or the Camber.'[5] As a postscript to his letter of 27 April he added that he had just been informed that Stafford had set sail on Easter Day, 18 April, with two vessels, one of

---

[1] Garrett, p. 294.

[2] 'If ever there was a tragico-comoedia played, surely these men played it.' Wotton to Petre, 8 October 1556. Cal. For. Vol. II, p. 264.

[3] There were a number of rumours that Henri would advance the claims of Mary Stuart, and it was one of Sir Robert's accusations against his brother-in-law that he was ' . . . a traitor to the French king, claiming the English throne himself, whereas the true claimant is the Scots Queen.' Wotton to the Queen, 13 January 1557. Cal. For. Vol. II, p. 283.

[4] Wotton to Petre, 14 April 1557. Cal. For. Vol. II, p. 294.

[5] Wotton to the Queen, 27 April 1557. Cal. For. Vol II, p. 298. When he wrote on 6 May, Wotton still did not have any news of the raid, which reached him some time between then and the 14th.

them commanded by the formidable John Rybawde.[1] By the time that his letter reached London the raid was already over. The attackers had actually taken Scarborough Castle, and Stafford had proclaimed himself 'protector of the realm', but he gained no adherents and on 28 April the castle was retaken by the local levies under the Earl of Westmorland. Stafford and 30 of his adherents were imprisoned, and he was executed on 28 May.

At his trial he strongly denied that he had been dependent upon French aid, and Henri hastened to disclaim all responsibility, but the King had played his half-hearted and underhand game once too often. The news of Stafford's raid came in the midst of a desperate tussle within the English Council over the desirability of aiding Philip in the war. It turned the scale, and although war was not declared at once, the decision to do so was taken.[2] The other exiles laughed at Stafford's mischance, calling him 'King of Scarborough', but the manner of his failure effectually prevented any further attempt of a similar nature. The final alarm before the outbreak of war came on 14 May, when Wotton wrote that Ashton had designs on Portland castle.[3] Ashton, the Ambassador considered, was a much more dangerous man than Stafford, and French assistance was nearer, but nothing came of his scheme if it ever really existed. At the end of May the Council ordered special precautions in the Channel, but they were not needed. On 7 June, after the formal preliminaries, war was declared between England and France, and the exiles ceased to play any significant part in relations between the two countries.

Although their plots came to virtually nothing, the presence of these exiles in France was an important political fact from the spring of 1554 to the summer of 1557. Not only did they form a constant irritant in Anglo-French relations but they gravely complicated the domestic crisis both by their threat-

[1] Ibid. Alias Jean Ribaut. He is elsewhere mentioned as a companion of Dudley's. Deposition of Henry Wasse, 9 May 1556. SP, Vol. VIII, no. 55.
[2] Harbison, p. 326.
[3] Wotton to the Secretaries, 14 May 1557. Cal. For. Vol. II, p. 306.

ened actions and by their mere existence. Their real strength, and the real danger which they represented, were less significant than the image which they succeeded in sustaining in England. It would not, however, be true to suggest that that image was a mere *tour de force* of propaganda. Dudley, like Wyatt, has been discounted because he failed, but his attempt was far from absurd. In that he differed radically from Stafford. His conspiracy was the second of the two major attempts to overthrow Mary by force, and not altogether unworthy of comparison with the first.

8

DUDLEY'S CONSPIRACY

I

As the Commissioners proceeded with their lengthy and exhaustive enquiries, which followed hard upon the first arrests in March 1556, the Council began to show signs of acute alarm. The ramifications of the plot seemed to be endless, involving an ever-increasing number of gentry and officials. The complicity of those in high places was darkly hinted at, and Mary would trust only her most devoted catholic councillors to carry out the investigations. The Commission consisted of Rochester, Englefield, Waldegrave, Jerningham and Hastings; 'As for all other noblemen, they meddle nothing, and if any suitors speak unto them, they wish them good speed . . . and will them to resort unto the Commissioners. . . .'[1] This was no ordinary plot, devised by a small group of unemployed servants, but a major alliance between those two forces which the government most feared, the disaffected gentry and the exiles in France. Like Wyatt's conspiracy, which it resembled in many ways, it grew out of the heightened tension produced by a turbulent parliament. Unlike the previous threat, however, it was not a deliberately constructed plan so much as a crystallising of ideas and discontents which already existed. It was for this reason that its boundaries seemed so shadowy, and its protagonists so numerous. In a sense all the opponents of the government were implicated, because Dudley and his associates made it their business to spread their net as widely as possible, hoping that when the moment came all those who were distrusted by the

---

[1] Robert Swift to the Earl of Shrewsbury, 22 June 1556. Edmund Lodge, *Illustrations of British History*, London 1791, Vol. I, p. 217.

Council would throw in their lot with the rebels out of fear, if not out of enthusiasm.

Dislike of the Spanish connection and the fear of Philip's coronation were the chief driving forces of the conspiracy, but many other factors contributed. The perpetual fear of the gentry for their ecclesiastical plunder; dislike of the religious persecution, and straightforward personal ambition, were all important. Elizabeth, it was vaguely felt, would be a 'gentleman's Queen'. She was ' . . . a liberal dame, and nothing so unthankful as her sister'. When she was upon the throne, ' . . . then should men of service be regarded', and their property secure. 'If my neighbour of Hatfield might once reigne', as one put it, 'then shulde (I) have (my) landes . . . ageyne.'[1] The actual conspiracy may fairly be compared to the head of a spear, of which such sentiments and motives as these formed the shaft. There was a widespread desire to see Elizabeth upon the throne, and the line which separated that desire from the plot to implement it was exceedingly indistinct.

The summer of 1555, as we have seen, found the government's popularity at a low ebb, and produced a spate of hostile propaganda and a number of conspiracies. None of these came to an issue, but there were several signs that the opposition was regrouping. In the middle of July the Council dispersed a number of gentry who had lingered suspiciously in London after the heat of summer had driven most of their fellows to seek their country houses. Renard described them as 'partisans of Elizabeth', and Michieli mentioned that 'the Dudleys' were amongst them.[2] At about the same time Randall again approached Noailles with a proposal for French intervention. Fifty gentlemen, he declared, had sworn to recover their liberties by the end of August; would Henri recall Carew, and send him to their aid?[3] Probably these gentlemen were the same that the Council had dispersed, but the French govern-

---

[1] Indictment of Lord John Bray. *Cal. Pat.* Vol. III, p. 396.
[2] Michieli to the Doge and Senate. July 1555. *Cal. Ven.* Vol. VI, p. 137. Renard to the Emperor, 10 July 1555. *Cal. Span.* Vol. XIII, p. 227.
[3] Noailles to Montmorency, 15 July 1555. Aff. Etr., IX, f. 489. Montmorency to Noailles, 27 July 1555; ibid. ff. 498-9 (Harbison, p. 272).

ment was in no mood for adventures. With the negotiations at La Marque engrossing his attentions, Montmorency instructed the Ambassador not to be drawn. In August Philip departed to the Netherlands, and this, as the shrewder leaders of the opposition realized, was also a blow to their hopes. When the Spaniard was not actually poisoning the air, the 'people of the realm here wolde not so redely take their partes' in measures of active resistance.[1]

However a new situation was created by the decision at the end of August to summon a parliament. Mary was desperately short of money, and a subsidy was urgently needed. At the same time her officious conscience was goading her to restore to the church those lands and revenues which were still in the hands of the Crown. Both these desires opened opportunities which her enemies were not slow to exploit. By the middle of September rumours were circulating that the subsidy would be sent to Philip ' . . . to further some device for his crowning by force or fraud',[2] and the threat implied by the Crown's renunciation of church property was assiduously emphasized. Long before the parliament met it was becoming a focus for all manner of grievances and discontent, with the shadow of the coronation lying heavily upon it. As a result a very large number of members unsympathetic to the government were returned. In a famous despatch during the session Michieli wrote

The present House of Commons, whether by accident or design, a thing not seen for many years in any parliament, is quite full of gentry and nobility (for the most part suspected in matters of religion) and therefore more daring and licentious than former houses which consisted of burgesses and plebeians, by nature timid and respectful, who easily inclined towards the will of the sovereign.[3]

A bad harvest had exaggerated a situation already full of danger, and when the members arrived at Westminster the political storm signals were set. A few days after the beginning

---

[1] Indictment of Sir Ralph Bagnall. *Cal. Pat.* Vol. III, p. 318.
[2] Michieli to the Doge and Senate, 16 September 1555. *Cal. Ven.* Vol. VI, p. 188.
[3] Same to same, 18 November 1555. Ibid. p. 251.

of the session, the Council closed all the houses of public dancing and gambling in London on the ground that they provided opportunities for seditious assemblies.[1]

Such a move was justifiable, for the meeting of parliament signified more than the prospect of constitutional opposition. The arrival in London of a number of gentry known to be hostile to government policies provided an excellent opportunity for other opposition groups to get in touch with them. As in the similar situation of 1553, intrigue flourished. Some of Wyatt's captains, notably Randall and Staunton, were in the capital, as were the protagonists of the 'jeu de cannes' fiasco of the previous year, Cornwall, Alday and Hinnes. Probably Courtenay's servant and agent John Walker was also there.[2] Noailles' door was constantly open, and Dudley himself, the Horseys and the Tremaynes came and went discreetly as their movements were already under surveillance. The favourite meeting place of the opposition Members and their friends was a tavern known as 'Arundel's', where they gathered to discuss their plans, and grumble with more vigour than discretion. 'With gret wilfullness', an informer later declared, 'they intended to resiste such matters as shold be spoken off in the parleyment other than liked them. ... '[3] Arundel's was not their only meeting place, but it was the one most frequently resorted to. The hospitable house of Sir John Butler provided an alternative,[4] and for casual or contrived meetings there were always the thronged promenades of St Paul's.

It was in these surroundings, some time during November, that the conspiracy was hatched. The separate and distinct threads of ambition and discontent began to be woven into a

[1] Same to same, 11 November 1555. Ibid. p. 243.

[2] Walker's indictment did not mention any participation before 14 February, but he is referred to by other conspirators in terms suggesting a longer acquaintance. *Cal. Pat.* Vol. III, p. 402.

[3] Examination of John Danyell, March 1556. SP, Vol. VIII, no. 35.

[4] Sir John was later the recipient of letters from the exiles in France (examination of William Bury, 16 and 17 April 1556, SP, Vol. VIII, no. 12) but no action was taken against him. Two ladies of the same name were also implicated: Catherine, wife of Antony Throgmorton, John's brother (SP, Vol. VII, no. 30), who was probably his daughter, and Sylvestra, described as 'widow', whose connections are obscure. *Cal. Pat.* Vol. III, p. 400.

single scheme for the removal of Mary and her replacement by Elizabeth. It is difficult to be more precise, because the evidence does not exist. Probably as the session progressed and the atmosphere became more heated, treason began to seem more attractive and expedient. By the time that Parliament was dissolved on 9 December, a plot was in existence of which Dudley was the recognized leader, and rebellion the premeditated aim.

II

The session began on 21 October, and the same day was read the Papal Bull of Paul IV confirming the dispensation previously granted to the holders of monastic property. This was a transparent gesture, for the Bull had been publicly proclaimed over a month before, and the members were unimpressed.[1] Gardiner in his opening speech had declared that the parliament was summoned ' . . . for necessary aid to be made unto her majestie', and the Subsidy Bill was introduced almost at once. Stiff opposition was expected, for, as Michieli wrote, 'The members of the Lower House (give it) freely to be understood that . . . owing to the present year's grievous scarcity . . . Her Majesty . . . should compel all the debtors of the Crown to pay up their arrears, there being not one, or a few of the great personages . . . that do owe . . . some eight thousand pounds and upwards (each). In addition to this, the opponents say that so long as her Majesty is in debt, she should retain . . . the sort of ecclesiastical revenue lately alienated by her from the Crown.'[2] In addition a number of members had privately assured Noailles that they would fight it to the last, and he did his best to persuade others to a similar resolution.[3] However, when it came to the point the Chancellor's eloquence carried the day without even the necessity for a division. The Bill was passed on 28 October. It was Gardiner's last service, for he was already a sick man, and

[1] Memorials of Council proceedings, SP, Vol. VI, nos. 16, 18.
[2] Michieli to the Doge and Senate, 27 October 1555. Cal. Ven. Vol. VI, p. 229.
[3] Harbison, pp. 275–6.

on 12 November he died, leaving the Crown at this vital
juncture without a powerful advocate in either House. His loss
was very seriously felt for the remainder of the session, and
indeed for the rest of the reign.[1] Men of sufficient ability to
replace him, such as Petre or Cecil, could not be trusted;[2]
and trustworthy men like Hastings and Rochester had not the
capacity. Thus, with most of the important issues still to be
joined, the opposition was presented with a gratuitous advantage by the feebleness of the Crown management.

By the end of October the Queen had abandoned all hope
of persuading parliament to consider the coronation, but her
determination to achieve two lesser goals was thereby intensified. One of these was the controversial renunciation of church
lands and revenues, in particular first fruits and tenths. A Bill
for this purpose was introduced into the Lords on 11 November,
and at once provoked sharp disagreements. By the 18th Michieli
reported that the measure was in difficulties, because a number
of the peers, although they were prepared to admit that ' . . .
the Queen may do what she likes with her revenues during her
lifetime', refused to agree to a statutory restitution on the
grounds that it would diminish the revenues of her successor.[3]
Their meaning was obvious, but legally it was a feeble argument, and a peremptory reminder of this from the Queen
herself was sufficient to ensure the passage of the Bill. It was
handed down to the Commons on 20 November, the
Speaker at the same time 'declaring the Queen's pleasure'
concerning it. The lower house, however, was less amenable to
this form of pressure than the Lords. The Bill was discussed on
26 November, and on the 27th the Commons Journal laconically
records 'long arguments upon the bill of first fruits and tenths'.[4]
Behind the scenes Noailles was again doing his best to stiffen

---

[1] For instance Pole's comments in his letter to Philip on 23(?) November. *Cal.
Ven.* Vol. VI, p. 256.
[2] Cecil featured, although not very prominently, in the ranks of the opposition
during this parliament. Sir John Neale, *Elizabeth I and her parliaments 1559–1581*
(London 1953), p. 24.
[3] Michieli to the Doge and Senate, 18 November 1555. *Cal. Ven.* Vol. VI, p. 251.
[4] *Journal of the House of Commons*, Vol. I, p. 45.

the opposition, reinforcing persuasion with ponderous sarcasm. To a group of M.P.s who dined with him just before the final debate he remarked

. . . that they should not be so obstinate about doing (the Queen's) will to the diminution of her revenues, since they had so readily accorded her such a great sum of money (the subsidy) which they well knew was to be used for the aid and succor of him (Philip) whose only aim in the world is to oppress them. . . . [1]

His arguments carried weight, and when the Bill was brought to a division on 3 December the struggle was long and bitter. Eventually, by choosing their time carefully, and locking the doors upon the members for most of the day, its sponsors managed to get it through by 193 votes to 126, a victory which Pole imaginatively described as a 'great majority' when reporting the outcome to Philip. The opposition were deeply chagrined, and convinced that they had been cheated, but, as Noailles wrote, 'en telle assemblée la pluralité des voix l'emporte, et n'y a peu servir l'oppinion contraire de cent gentilzhommes qu'il y avoit parmy le nombre de trois cens personnes'.[2]

Such a setback made the Queen's opponents doubly determined to frustrate the second measure upon which she had set her mind. This was a Bill to recall the exiles in France and Germany upon pain of the forfeiture of all property. By the statute of 5 Richard II, st. 1, cap. 2, upon which the current law was based, the penalty for departing the realm without royal licence was forfeiture of goods. However, many of the fugitives had taken their moveables with them, usually in the form of money, and the difficulty and expense of distraining upon those who had not made this penalty scarcely worth enforcing.[3] The real wealth of all the fugitives who mattered was in land, and the lands of an offender could not be touched until his conviction had been secured. Since he could not be convicted in his absence, his property thus remained safe. The

---

[1] Advis, 26 November 1555; Aff. Etr., IX, f. 565 (Harbison, p. 277).
[2] Noailles to Montmorency, 31 October 1555. Vertot, Vol. V, p. 190.
[3] For a further consideration of this point see 'The Essex Inquisitions of 1556', in the *Bulletin of the Institute of Historical Research*, Vol. XXXV, May 1962, pp. 87–97.

government's measure was couched in the form of a summons, but it was a safe assumption that very few would obey, and the real intention was clearly to cripple the exiles by cutting off their subsistence. The Bill was introduced into the Lords on 31 October, and seems to have passed without undue difficulty, being handed down to the Commons on 26 November. Michieli forecast a stormy passage for it in the lower house, and he was right.[1] There were several reasons why this should have been so. A number of the members had personal connections among the exiles, or were strongly in sympathy with them. Many more were apprehensive of the consequences which might result from the establishment of such a precedent. Following hard upon the Annates Act, this Bill seemed to be a further move in a subtle attack upon the property rights of the gentry. Finally, there was a vague but powerful feeling that the House should assert itself, and that the passage of the Annates Act had in some way been a fraud perpetrated upon the whole Commons.

When the division was reached on 6 December the opposition was very strongly placed, and needed only a leader to carry it to victory. The role was filled by Sir Anthony Kingston of Gloucestershire. Fearing lest the government might repeat the manœuvre which had succeeded before, he secured the keys of the House from the Sergeant at Arms and locked the doors upon the inside. Posting himself beside the door with a number of supporters, he then proclaimed in a loud voice that this measure should not be passed in defiance of many consciences as the other had been.[2] The Bill was defeated, and three days later, on 9 December, Parliament was dissolved. An attempt had been made by the Commons to create a diversion after the defeat of the exiles Bill by raising an issue of privilege, but the Queen was not to be diverted or placated.[3] On

---

[1] Michieli to the Doge and Senate, 11 November 1555. *Cal. Ven.* Vol. VI, p. 244.
[2] Same to same, 16 December 1555. *Cal. Ven.* Vol. VI, p. 283.
[3] *Journal of the House of Commons*, Vol. I, p. 46: 'It is Ordered that Mr Comptroller, with other of the House, shall declare to the Lords that their Opinion is that their privilege is broken for that Gabriel Pledall, a Member of this House, was bound in a recognisance in Star Chamber to appear before the Council within 12 days after the End of this parliament.' The Lords ruled it 'no breach of privilege'.

10 December Kingston was committed to the Tower for his 'contemptuous behaviour and great disorder'. The following day a number of his supporters joined him, including the Sergeant at Arms.[1]

Michieli may have been right about the composition of this House. The returns do not support him unambiguously, but both Noailles and the Council seem to have been of the same opinion. One of the first things that the government attempted to do when the Parliament assembled was to reintroduce the ancient residence qualifications for borough members.[2] The response of the opposition leaders showed both their skill and the fact that they appreciated the significance of the move. They proposed to reintroduce the exclusion of place-holders, a ripost which forced the Council to retreat. There are some interesting resemblances between this House of Commons and those of the 1620's. The dominance of the self-confident gentry, at odds with the Crown; the regular meetings of opposition leaders; the constant circulation of propaganda pamphlets among the members, and even within the chamber; all this foreshadows the days of Coke and Elliot. 'Both the Lords and the Commons,' wrote Badoer from Brussels, 'have displayed the worst possible will in printed books. . . . '[3] The similarity may be partly attributable to comparable weakness in the government leadership, but there was also a similar turbulence among the members, breaking out at times into open violence. During the final debate on the Exiles Bill Sir Edward Hastings, the chief government spokesman, and Sir George Howard almost came to blows on the floor of the House. The dispute continued afterwards at the house of the Earl of Pembroke. The Earl sided with Hastings, greatly to the disgust of many of his retinue, and 'many gentlemen . . . took their leave of him'.[4] Michieli's summary of the situation in the middle of December was shrewd and to the point: 'Audacity and discontent gain

[1] APC, Vol. V, pp. 202–3.
[2] Michieli to the Doge and Senate, 18 November 1555. Cal. Ven. Vol. VI, p. 252.
[3] Badoer to the Doge and Senate, 6 December 1555. Cal. Ven. Vol. VI, p. 272.
[4] Michieli to the same, 16 December 1555. Cal. Ven. Vol. VI, p. 283.

ground daily, but the individuals in question (are) private gentlemen. The chief nobility and principal personages shew themselves well disposed. . . .'[1]

While these events were taking place, and discontent was beginning to shape itself into conspiracy, there was extraordinarily little mention of religion. It was later remembered that the group at Arundel's ' . . . did very sore myslyke such catholicke proceedyngs as . . . the Quene . . . went aboute', and 'did . . . declare themselves to be right protestauntes',[2] but at the time the only open association between opposition and religion was made by the government. That the disaffected gentry were not enthusiastic Catholics is evident, and that they made use of protestant propaganda is also true. But their connections with militant protestantism were even more tenuous than those of Wyatt's followers. Presumably in the event of an insurrection they would have counted upon protestant support but such an alliance would have been a 'marriage of convenience'. There is no evidence to suggest that Dudley relied in any way upon the support of the exiles in Germany, although some of them may have been aware of his designs. By the manner of their opposition to the Annates Act both the Lords and Commons made it clear that they expected the Queen's policies to be short-lived, but their hope was a political one. There was a conspicuous absence of such remarks as 'the restoration of God's Word', or 'the increase of true religion', which were characteristic of the comments of genuine protestants.

Although the Queen was intensely annoyed by the recalcitrance of the Parliament, there was no sign that the government connected this with any deeper or more active resistance. Sir Anthony Kingston was summoned before the Council on 23 December, and released 'upon humble submission' the next day.[3] At the end of the month Michieli wrote that the Queen still considered him to be a good subject, and no move was

---

[1] Ibid.
[2] Danyell's examination, SP, Vol. VIII, no. 35.
[3] APC, Vol. V, p. 208.

made to deprive him of his office as Vice Admiral of the Severn.[1] Whatever the reason for this confidence, and it may simply have been that the Queen's anger had abated, it was ill-founded, for Kingston was already deeply compromised in the French interest.

III

Dudley had not wasted his opportunities. Some time before the middle of November he had established contact with the experienced intriguer Jean de Bretville, a Frenchman long resident in England who had been in the French Ambassador's pay for about two years.[2] Before the exiles Bill was brought to a division he succeeded in bringing Bretville and Kingston together, and in persuading the former to present his case to Noailles in the most favourable terms. Bretville went further. He wrote direct to Montmorency, informing him that Dudley 'had a mind to do the King some service'. The Constable's reaction was cautious; he committed the management of the affair to Noailles, instructing him to discuss the matter thoroughly with Bretville, and to offer Dudley a pension to keep him in the right frame of mind.[3] The Ambassador's report, sent on 16 December, was favourable. Dudley was a man of much promise and some attainment, who was a valiant soldier, and likely to perform whatever he undertook.[4] Bretville also sent a letter by the same messenger, explaining how far the intrigue had already progressed. He had been in touch with Randall and four other Captains ' . . . who are so well attached that they have offered and sworn and promised to Dudley that if he goes to serve his Majesty, they will turn French whenever he pleases. . . .'[5] More important, Sir

---

[1] Michieli to the Doge and Senate, 30 December 1555. *Cal. Ven.* Vol. VI, p. 300.
[2] Harbison, 'French Intrigue at Queen Mary's Court', *American Historical Review*, xlv, April 1940, p. 540 et seq.
[3] Montmorency to Noailles, 26 November 1555. Aff. Etr., XVII, ff. 212–14 (Harbison, p. 280).
[4] Bretville to Montmorency, n.d., Aff. Etr., IX, f. 660 (Harbison, p. 280).
[5] Harbison, loc. cit.

Anthony Kingston was fully behind them.

. . . he can assuredly raise (Bretville wrote) more than six thousand men in his district, and more than sixty of the most important knights of the district. In talking with Dudley, as one who relies much on him, and who hates the spaniards mightily, he said to him 'If you go into the service of the King (of France) and land in my county, I will go to meet you with all my forces to chase these tyrants from our country. This I say to you in the presence of this gentleman (Bretville)'.

Also they had an understanding with 'the Captain of the fort of the Isle of Wight', who had agreed to surrender his charge to the French on demand.

Dudley had probably not decided upon a positive course of action at this stage, but was assembling his pieces to see what kind of a game he could play. The west-country gentry were expected to provide the main military backing. Richard Uvedale, controlling the key fortress of Yarmouth, offered a means of ingress to an invading force. The exiles in France could provide the nucleus of such a force, and Randall's friends suggested a suitable means of augmenting it. The outlines of a plan were present, but it presented several problems. Dudley was realistic enough to understand that if he wished to stimulate a rising in southern England which would persuade all his sympathisers to show their hands, it would be useless to land with a token force. A band of 3000 men at least would be necessary, and he was prepared if need be to build up that band over a period of time.[1] However, the sooner it could be assembled the better, and it was far beyond the resources of the existing exiles. He therefore seems to have decided to follow the example of such men as Crayer, and enlist mercenary bands as though for the service of the French king, relying upon the good offices of their Captains to lead them back to England as an invading force. Suitable and reliable officers were essential, and it was no doubt with this in mind that

[1] Throgmorton told Uvedale that ' . . . he wolde have a greate band of men, and the moste parte of theym shulde be Englisshmen; and there he woulde serve the Frenche Kinge for a tyme until he . . . (had made) . . . up his band . . . to iii thousand. . . .' Uvedale's confession, 25 March 1556; SP, Vol. VII, no. 32.

Dudley spoke ' . . . with all ye gentylemen that be sodyars yt be abowte (London)', and was assured of their friendship.[1] This need must also be the explanation of the extraordinary pains taken to recruit John Danyell, a servant of Lord Grey, to whom Dudley is alleged to have said '. . . I know you, and what a good soldier you are.'[2] In addition to Captains, however, the enterprise needed men, arms and money. To obtain the former Dudley seems to have enlisted the help of all his friends and associates, but to have relied especially upon John Throgmorton and John Bedell. The former was a relation of Sir Nicholas Throgmorton, and the latter a confidential servant of Christopher Ashton. Of Bedell Dudley said ' . . . this is the man that shall ryde about to provide me men',[3] and after himself these two were the most active protagonists of the conspiracy. Shortly after Christmas Bedell told a fellow conspirator that ' . . . all the holydays & after (he) did nothing ells but ryde from on to another . . . his mynd coulde not be in queyt till he hadde brought this matter to some purpose.'[4] At first it was supposed that the role of the French would be to arm and finance the expedition, but Dudley had sufficient experience of the vacillations of the King not to rely implicitly upon such support. Arms could always be purchased in France, but if Henri was not in the mood no money would be forthcoming, either to make such purchases or to pay the professional soliders. If the conspirators wished to have any freedom of action they must have some alternative source of supply to fall back upon.

Throughout January 1556 the leaders of the plot worked upon these problems, but it is not always clear how much progress they made with them. Two lines of communication were opened with France: one through a French denizen of Winchelsea,[5] the other through Southampton with the assist-

---

[1] Declaration by Henry Peckham, 9 May 1556. SP, Vol. VIII, no. 52.
[2] Confession of John Danyell, 11 April 1556. SP, Vol. VIII, no. 6.
[3] Uvedale's confession. SP, Vol. VII, no. 32.
[4] Confession of Thomas White, 26 March 1556. SP, Vol. VII, no. 37.
[5] A certain 'Mr Mynyell' of Winchelsea was in touch with the exiles, and was later arrested and examined by the Council. Examination of William Bury,

ance of Uvedale. The intention seems to have been to use these as undercover routes to transport soldiers to the Continent, but it is difficult to say how far this was realized because Uvedale, who is the main source of information, was naturally anxious to minimize the number of men who passed through his hands. Also we have no evidence to suggest how successful Throgmorton and Bedell were with their recruiting. Nor can we be quite sure how far, if at all, plans were advanced for a rising in the west country. After his release from the Tower Kingston went to Fifield in Berkshire to confer with his friend Christopher Ashton, who gave him the half of a broken coin which it was later alleged was to be matched as the signal for rebellion.[1] Thereafter nothing is heard of Kingston directly until he was examined by the Council on 8 and 9 April.[2] If he canvassed opinion in Gloucestershire, or made any active preparations, it was done so discreetly that no suspicions were aroused. Yet there can be no doubt that he and his friends featured largely in the minds of others. Thomas White, a minor conspirator, later testified that Ashton had told him of

... a noble gentilman that was able to bring a gret part of Wallis at his taile, and then I asked him yf it were my Lord of Pembroke and he said tushe for hym for he is more feared than loved ... and this man I speek of hath may frendes there and is well beloved and able to dryve my Lord of Pembroke owt of Wallis.[3]

Similarly Henry Peckham was informed that Kingston would be ready at three days' notice with 10,000 men, who would cut off the Earl of Pembroke if he offered any resistance, and be in London within twenty days. Even the tactics to be employed for Pembroke's discomfiture were discussed.

... all his (Pembroke's) trust was in his grete horses but ... with v or vi thowsande felowes ... with stakes sharpened at both ends, pikes and galthropes ... rounde about (blocking all except) one

16–17 April 1556. SP, Vol. VIII, no. 12. Renard to Philip, 13 June 1556. *Cal. Span.* Vol. XIII, p. 270.
[1] Declaration by Henry Peckham. SP, Vol. VIII, no. 52.
[2] SP, Vol. VIII, nos. 2, 3. Kingston denied virtually all acquaintance with conspirators, but admitted receiving the coin from Ashton.
[3] Confession of Thomas White, 26 March 1556. SP, Vol. VII, no. 37.

waye at which waye sholde his (Kingston's) ordnannce (point)
beinge such slynges of the largest the Frenche kyng had and suche
peces that wolde fetch further than eny in this Realme, that sholde
be drawen with xx men and so shadowed with more, that ther enemies
sholde nott know wher theyr ordnnance wer and when thei
thought to geve the onset thei sholde divide themselves and dis-
chardge their pieces not seen or thowghte of . . . and having as he
saide vii or viii C of the best hagbuttes in all France that wolde
spitt in ther faces with their shotte sholde make ther horsemen geve
rome and go backe.[1]

This plan showed much good sense, and it avoided the error
of relying implicitly upon heavy numerical superiority. However, it made the rebels more dependent than ever upon
French arms, and consequently upon adequate financial backing. As one of them later remarked ' . . . armour, money and
weapons ys not to be had uppon a sodeyn . . . ';[2] and 'vii or viii C
of the best hagbuttes . . .', an unspecified number of field pieces,
and the 4000 corselets (sets of body armour) which Dudley aimed
to have would be exceedingly expensive. It is hardly surprising,
therefore, that during January the conspirators were toying with
two alternative projects, in case the French should fail them. One
of these was a plan to intercept the £200,000 which rumour
claimed was about to be sent out of England to Philip in the
Netherlands. The ingenious Alday seems to have been behind this
attractive idea, and it was reported that Sir Thomas Cawarden
'. . . and a grete many other gentelmen . . .' were involved;[3] but
since the money was never sent they had no opportunity to make
the attempt. The second plan, which was eventually adopted, was
to remove £50,000 worth of silver bullion in the custody of one
Brigham, the Teller of the Exchequer. The leading spirits in
this subsidiary conspiracy were Throgmorton, Bedell and John
Dethicke, a servant of Sir Thomas Cawarden. At first their
success was absurdly easy. By bribery or cajoling they won over

[1] Ibid.
[2] Deposition of William Rossey, 24 April 1556. SP, Vol. VIII, no. 33. Another
observed 'There are men enough in England, but they lack money'. SP, Vol. VIII,
no. 59.
[3] Second deposition by White, March 1556. SP, Vol. VII, no. 48.

William Rossey, the Keeper of the Star Chamber and a friend of Brigham's. The Teller himself was a man of the strictest honesty, but Rossey, and Dethicke who was also known to him, succeeded through the offices of his wife in getting an impression of his keys.[1] They then went one night to the treasury and weighed the chests. Finding them too heavy to be conveniently carried they resolved to break them open and extract the silver piecemeal. After toying with the idea of storing it at the lodging of Henry Peckham, another of the conspirators, they decided that such a course would be too dangerous,[2] and resolved to hire a crayer and ship it straight to France. Rossey's garden stretched down to the river not far from the treasury, and under cover of night loading would be a simple process. Also, one of them remembered that 'Sir Anthony Kingston . . . was vice admirall of those parts about severn and that all his power and frends by see we sholde not fail to have at our will. . . .'[3] In the event Kingston's services were not called upon but a boat was hired closer at hand in London. The searcher at Gravesend was bribed to let it pass, and if the enterprise had not been betrayed at that juncture it would probably have succeeded.

In France, plans had already been completed to handle a supply of bullion before it was known whence it should come. As long before as the previous September feelers had been put out for the establishment of an exile mint. An obscure individual named Bowes had then gone over, and through the good offices of Boisdauphin, who had been Ambassador in England during the previous reign, had secured an audience with the King. He requested a licence to set up a mint ' . . . for the ayde of his countrymen against the spanyardes', and although Henri 'denied hym his broade seal' the necessary permission was granted.[4] Bowes later claimed that he was acting purely in a private capacity, and that the project 'went not forward' for

[1] Third confession of White, 30 March 1556. SP, Vol. VII, no. 47.
[2] ' . . . they stood in doubtt lest Sir Edmund Peckham wold come to the towne at abowt thatt tyme'. Statement by Rossey, 9 May 1556. SP, Vol. VIII, no. 61.
[3] SP, Vol. VII, no. 37.
[4] Examination of William Hinnes, 28 March 1556. SP, Vol. VII, no. 39.

lack of capital. The latter statement may have been true, but the former seems intrinsically unlikely. However the foundations had been laid, and a mint was actually established near Dieppe, in a castle belonging to one 'Captain Tybalt' some time during January. At the beginning of February Ashton, Bedell and Dethicke were searching in London for skilled workmen to operate it. After one or two false casts they managed to secure the services of an engraver named Andrew Pomeroy to make the dies,[1] and presumably others must also have gone, for the mint went into production and continued to operate throughout the summer. On account of the deplorable state of the English currency, coining was a major profession in England at this time, and a number of the exiles had fled, as we have seen, for that very reason. This particular mint was closed by the French as a sop to English indignation in August 1556.[2] At the time when it was established the conspirators still believed 'that the French king shall aid and assist (us) and will disburse into our hands a hundred thousand pounds'.[3] It was not until the middle of February that this optimism was proved to have been ill-founded.

Bretville's work in England was completed by the end of January, and on the 25th he crossed the Channel to smooth Dudley's path to the French court. In this he was not particularly successful, because the negotiations for the ratification of the Truce of Vaucelles had reached a delicate stage, and Henri was again in two minds about the English enterprise. When Dudley arrived in person during the second week in February the King was displeased, and dismissed him with empty promises.[4] Although this rebuff was not altogether unexpected,

---

[1] Confession of Bawcriffe, March 1556. SP, Vol. VII, no. 58. The first man they approached, one Castell, demanded £50 earnest money, which was more than they were prepared to pay.

[2] See above, p. 156.

[3] Statement by William Hinnes, 30 March 1556. SP, Vol. VII, no. 46. Dethicke attempted unsuccessfully to persuade Hinnes to help operate the mint, and painted a generous picture of French enthusiasm for the venture.

[4] Although he 'willed them to go through with their enterprise', the King made his promises of aid in 'men, money, and other things necessary' conditional upon Philip sending the bulk of his troops eastwards against the Turks! Wotton to Mary, 12 April 1556. Cal. For. Vol. II, p. 222.

it was nevertheless a serious disappointment. Before Christmas, when the enterprise was first mooted, Bedell later recalled, 'Mr Ashton and Mr Dudley didd discorse . . . how they might know what ayde they myt have at the Frenche kyngs hande and so they did write what help they wolde have of hym, or ells note to meddell. . . .'[1] They had received a favourable reply 'within xx dayes', and the Ambassador had also 'given them good comfort' when they discussed the matter with him. The conspirators therefore had some right to feel betrayed, for the King had certainly countenanced the encouragement which had been given to them. The plot was not crippled by this setback, but its chances were reduced by the heavy reliance which thereafter had to be placed upon the success of the exchequer burglary. There remained a chance that Henri might again change his mind, but the hope was a straw and not a factor to be calculated upon.

Meanwhile the practical preparations continued, in spite of the darkening prospects. During the second half of February and the first week of March most of the military leaders crossed over to France. We have a full description of Ashton's departure from Southampton with sixteen followers,[2] but most of the others passed the Channel unnoticed. Among them were Francis and Edward Horsey, Andrew and Nicholas Tremayne, Robert Cornwall, Roger Reynolds and John Dalton. No doubt, as a recent scholar has pointed out, most of these men were only too glad to place the sea between themselves and the English government,[3] but it would be a mistake to represent their action as arising mainly from fear. They were to be the leaders of the invading force—the fragment of the ice-

---

[1] Deposition by Bedell, 30 March 1556. SP, Vol. VII, no. 52. There is plenty of supporting evidence to show that the conspirators were deliberately led to believe that the French would support them. E.g. Uvedale's deposition of 23 April. SP, Vol. VIII, no. 24.

[2] Deposition of John Peers, shipmaster of Southampton, 16 March and 14 April 1556. SP, Vol. VII, nos. 9, 26. Peers declared that he had been reassured as to the propriety of his action by the fact that Uvedale was 'the Queen's servant'. This may possibly be the John Peers, 'rover of the sea', who had appeared before the Privy Council on a charge of piracy in March 1552. APC, Vol. IV, p. 8.

[3] Harbison, p. 286.

berg which appeared above the surface. By far the greater number of those implicated in the plot remained in England; partly because their participation was less obvious, but partly also because that was where they were needed. Dudley's two principal agents, Throgmorton and Bedell, remained at their posts in London arranging the plunder of the Exchequer. The parliamentary gentry went about their business as usual, because their services would not be required until some overt act had taken place—and they had had an opportunity to assess its chances. Richard Uvedale remained 'on his charge' at Yarmouth. In the event of an invasion his role might well turn out to be the most important of all. At his last interview with Dudley, while the latter was awaiting the boat which was to take him to France, they discussed their plans in some detail. 'When I see my tyme to come ageyn and land here in England', Dudley had said, 'I will lande hereaboute even at Portesmouth, ... and thou wilt doe like a good fellowe and healp me.'[1] Ideally, Uvedale was to use his official position to suborn the garrison of Portsmouth, and sabotage the harbour defences so that the invading fleet could use the haven. If this should prove beyond his power, the invaders would come ashore further down the coast 'where the king's camp lay'.

Then (continued Dudley) when I am landed and have my men togyther with me, then will I sende unto you and gyve you knowledge what company I have, and what power I loke to have, ... and if I think myself stronge enough ... I will streight march on forewarde, and if not I will then come to Yarmouth to you with the company that I have, and there we will tary. ...

Naturally, Uvedale later tried to minimize his importance, but it is clear from his own confessions that he occupied a key position, and his constant professions that he 'abhored' these schemes 'in his heart'[2] do not carry much conviction.

Thus by the time that Dudley went to France a clear strategic

---

[1] Deposition of Uvedale, 24, 25 March 1556. SP, Vol. VII, no. 32. 'By God's bloude', Dudley had added, 'I will dryve oute these Spanyardes or I will dye for it,' and ' ... I have a goodly band'.

[2] Ibid. Uvedale alleged that he had made no attempt to carry out his share of the enterprise, but his accomplices in London clearly believed that he had.

plan had emerged, of which the main features were a landing in force on the South coast and a rising in the west country, which should launch two medium-sized but well-equipped armies towards London. There may also have been some plan for a stroke within the capital, but this is not clear. There were a number of soldiers 'in the know', such as Randall and Staunton, still in London, and furtive references were made to one Chamberlain, the Gentleman Porter of the Tower, who was alleged to be Dudley's 'assured friend'.[1] However, if there was such a plan, even the Commissioners failed to discover anything conclusive about it. Behind the whole conspiracy, of course, lay the unformulated but not altogether groundless hope that a great many discontented Lords and gentry would join the rising once it had made a good start. It was rumoured, without truth, that the Earl of Westmorland was 'privy', and claimed that ' . . . xxx knights and a grete many noblemen of Englande (who) . . . will make many menne in the field' were only waiting for the signal to rebel.[2] As with other conspiracies of the period, there were many reports of 'great men . . . close about the Queen's person' and Privy Councillors who would declare against the government. There was a shade of truth in such rumours, for many prominent men heartily disliked the royal policies, and few would have defended Mary in a last-ditch stand, but such men were adept at identifying the winning side. One of the conspirators boasted that with 300 men he would guarantee to ' . . . take the Quene from any house that she hath' because of the general disaffection of the Court and the Guard,[3] but he never ventured to make the attempt. Outside their own circle the conspirators relied upon propaganda to put their case and create a favourable atmosphere for their venture. One recorded statement by Ashton is typical of their approach:

[1] Confession of William Staunton, 10 April 1556. SP, Vol. VIII, no. 4.
[2] Statement by William Hinnes, 30 March 1556. SP, Vol. VII, no. 46.
[3] Confession of Thomas White, 30 March 1556. SP, Vol. VII, no. 47. The boast was alleged to have been made by Dethicke, who ' . . . thought that divers in the Queene's house of her gard and other . . . would at such point . . . rather help us than her.'

Mr Ashton (recalled Bedell) begane to discors of the ordar of Napoles, how that thayr nobility and gentelmen were browt to confusyon and the commons to slaveri, saying yf God were not marcyfull to us . . .it is lyke to come to the same passe if the kyng be here crownyd. . . .[1]

Similar arguments circulated freely in print, and made a considerable impact, but, as in 1554, it is probable that the intriguers greatly overestimated the ease of turning discontent into rebellion. The statement made by Bretville early in the proceedings reflected this easy optimism. 'If Dudley were to land with 1000 men, he would quickly have 20,000, and the best.'[2]

Dudley himself had learned the lessons of Wyatt's failure more thoroughly than most of his supporters. This is shown by his reliance upon arms rather than numbers, and his concern to obtain adequate money and trained leaders. It was this fact as much as the wide range and large number of his contacts which made his enterprise dangerous. He also had a shrewd eye for detail. We have seen that one of the stock arguments used against the coronation was that it would divert the succession from the order laid down in Henry VIII's will. Dudley therefore decided that when the rising began, the will should be publicly proclaimed. The posthumous approval of the King would give an aura of legality to the rebellion which might prove valuable in the kind of delicate situation with which Wyatt had been confronted. Henry Peckham was therefore entrusted with the duty of securing a copy of the will, 'for', as he was told, 'there is sufficient matter for our purpose'.[3]

As far as can be ascertained, no date was ever fixed for action to commence. Dudley would not act until he had an adequate force, and he realized that it might take several months to assemble one. Vague forecasts of 'a better world by Whitsun' suggest that the late spring or early summer was the period anticipated, but it seems that a general state of readiness rather

---

[1] Deposition by Bedell, 30 March 1556. SP, Vol. VII. no. 52.
[2] Bretville to Montmorency, n.d. Aff. Etr., Vol. IX, f. 660 (Harbison, p. 281).
[3] Declaration by Henry Peckham, 9 May 1556. SP, Vol. VIII, no. 52. There are many references to the will in different interrogatories and statements.

than a fixed date was the objective. However, long before that season arrived the government had dealt the whole enterprise a staggering blow. One of those involved in the exchequer plot, Thomas White, went to Cardinal Pole in the first week in March and revealed all that he knew.[1] The Council waited for the fruit to ripen a little, and then plucked it. On 18 March about 20 of the conspirators were arrested and sent to the Tower.[2] They had been aware of their danger for some time. Both Dudley and Ashton had left London in haste and secrecy; later it had been rumoured that two of Ashton's men had been taken, and had talked. Finally, about the beginning of March, Throgmorton had summoned his colleagues together, and pointed out that there were now so many involved in the conspiracy that there was serious danger of betrayal. He thereupon persuaded them to swear an oath of secrecy, so that if any one denounced the others, ' . . . they sholde revyle hym and stande together agaynst him.'[3] White was present at the taking of this oath, but whether he had already lodged his information or not is uncertain. In spite of Throgmorton's confidence, his precautions failed, for his associates were less stout-hearted than himself, and did not persist in their denials.

The conspiracy was not immediately defeated. The vanguard had been removed, but its ramifications among the gentry, especially in the west country, were still unsuspected; and the exiles were out of reach. However it was not long before the English side was sufficiently exposed to remove the leaders and terrorize the rest. Dudley and his associates in France continued to hope until the middle of the summer that some dramatic development in England would present them with an opportunity, but it never came. The loss of so many leaders, the prevailing atmosphere of fear and suspicion, and the actual failure to obtain the much-needed money, had temporarily cowed the opposition in England. Dudley had neither the

---

[1] Michieli to the Doge and Senate, 24 March 1556. *Cal. Ven.* Vol. VI, p. 384 and note.

[2] Machyn, p. 102.

[3] Confession of White. SP, Vol. VII, no. 37. Throgmorton consistently denied that any such oath was taken, but the testimony of Bedell agrees with White.

resources nor the confidence to act before the revelations daily emerging from the Tower between 18 March and the end of April had dismantled or paralysed his whole structure. In many ways a sounder scheme than Wyatt's, and coming at a more propitious time, Dudley's conspiracy thus achieved less. For this its *ad hoc* empirical character was partly to blame. In their determination to exploit the existing situation the 1556 conspirators neglected the asset upon which those of 1554 had chiefly relied; broadly based popular support. Dudley realized that his strength was chiefly among the gentry, and because Wyatt's attempt to 'carry the country' had failed, he did not essay it. As one of his followers remarked 'If everye gentleman wolde but take his owne servauntes, and so to make a power, the matter wolde be soner ended . . . for the commons were not to be trusted unto. . . .'[1] He therefore relied more heavily than Wyatt upon French assistance; and it was through the attempt to circumvent Henri's defection that the enterprise was brought to light. Each conspiracy broke at its weakest point, but Dudley was, if anything, the unluckier of the two.

IV

Events proved that the rebellion of 1554 was principally a 'gentleman's matter', and Dudley began where Wyatt had left off. Opposition to Mary had not been significantly reduced by defeat, and the events of the eighteen months separating Wyatt's execution from the fourth parliament of the reign had done nothing to allay fears or restore confidence. There was a significant continuity between the two crises; the objectives were the same, and the personnel overlapped. A statement attributed to Ashton shows how little the ideas of the leaders had changed: ' . . . a great meny of the western gentylemen (are) in a confederacy to send the Quenes Hygnes over to the Kynge and to make the Lady Elyzabeth Quene and to marry the Erll of Devonshyre to the sayed lady. . . .'[2] Reliance upon

---

[1] Indictment of Anthony Foster. *Cal. Pat.* Vol. III, p. 453.
[2] Deposition of Henry Peckham. SP, Vol. VIII, no. 52.

Elizabeth was inevitable, if only as a protection against the Stuart claim, but there was no justification for continued faith in Courtenay. Exiled and discredited it is hard to believe that he still 'held many hearts' as was claimed.[1] From his retreat in Venice, he hovered on the outskirts of the plot. Emissaries of the exiles visited him, trying to persuade him to go to France. His agent in England, John Walker, was deeply implicated. He tried to sell lands to the annual value of £200, and it was rumoured that the proceeds were to be used to finance the conspiracy.[2] From this it seems certain that he was aware to some extent of what was afoot, but misfortune had taught him caution, and there is no conclusive evidence of his implication. In June the Queen wrote to him, expressing her confidence that the calumnies were unfounded,[3] and if any hopes had been placed in him they were once again disappointed. No one expected Elizabeth to move, and she made no sign, but the lightning struck close nevertheless. Her woman, Catherine Ashley, and her Italian tutor, Baptiste Castiglione, were arrested and examined.[4] Nothing of importance was discovered, for both consistently denied all knowledge of the plot, but the former was removed from her post, and the proposal to send Elizabeth overseas was revived ' . . . urged . . . by the Queen in person.'[5] The idea was never implemented, because Philip intervened to prevent it, realizing the strength of Elizabeth's position in the popular imagination, and the danger which such a move would involve.

Over a hundred years ago John Bruce dismissed the Dudley conspiracy as a 'miserable and foolish plot', upon the ground that Dudley 'had no public character which justified him in putting himself forward in such a scheme'.[6] Bruce's observation was

---

[1] Notes from an alleged conversation between Throgmorton and Rossey. SP, Vol. VII, no. 63.

[2] Examination of William Hinnes, 28 March 1556. SP, Vol. VII, no. 39.

[3] Badoer to the Doge and Senate, 21 July 1556. *Cal. Ven.* Vol. VI, p. 539.

[4] Examinations of Baptiste and Mrs Ashley, 31 May and 9 May. SP, Vol. VIII, nos. 80, 54.

[5] Michieli to the Doge and Senate, 28 April 1556. *Cal. Ven.* Vol. VI, p. 423.

[6] *Letters and Papers of the Verney family*, edited for the Camden Society by John Bruce, 1852, pp. 63, 75.

more valid than his deduction, for Dudley was not himself aiming to raise a great rebellion in England. He realized that such a task could only be performed by local gentry with credit and influence in their neighbourhoods. Without the support of such men as Kingston, Courtenay and Uvedale, the danger from an invasion, even in some strength, would have been small. It was not so much 'the connection between the rebels in France and the refugees in Germany' which made the conspiracy 'one of the most far-reaching events of the Tudor period', as Miss Garrett described it,[1] but the alliance between the rebels in France and the disaffected gentry in England. In attempting to assess the real danger which it represented therefore, a number of considerations need to be borne in mind. The general context of discontent and weak government has already been examined; it remains to consider the personal influence of Dudley and those who accompanied him to France, the identity of those English gentry who were undeniably impli-cated, and the influence which they could reasonably be ex-pected to wield in such a situation.

Sir Henry Dudley[2] was the second son of John Sutton de Dudley, 'Lord Quondam', and the younger brother of Edmund Sutton, fourth Baron Dudley. His mother was Cecily, daughter of Thomas Grey, Marquis of Dorset, and his family contacts were thus widespread and distinguished, although not politi-cally of great potency. Under Northumberland he had natur-ally been in favour, and after serving for a time as Captain of the guard at Boulogne, in May 1551 he had been appointed to a similar post at Guisnes. During these early years of service he had made himself familiar with the French court, and it was probably for that reason that Northumberland chose him, upon Edward's death, for the vital task of soliciting immediate French assistance. When he returned his cousin was in the Tower, and there he speedily joined him. From then on his

---

[1] Garrett, p. 148.
[2] There is some doubt as to whether Dudley had been knighted. *DNB* Supple-ment claims that he was knighted on 11 October 1551, but in his various indict-ments he is described as 'armigerus'.

fortunes slumped. Although he secured his release from imprisonment by October 1553, and was generally recognized as a 'most valiant' soldier, he failed to secure a post. Northumberland's death had released both his brother and himself from the state of dependence into which their father's imbecility had led them, and the family estates were restored to Edmund in 1554, but Henry failed to profit by this. He had avoided implication with Wyatt, and seems to have been marked for some preferment, when the flight of his kinsmen the Staffords led to his dismissal in March 1554, and the ruin of his fortune. Perhaps he inherited his father's financial incompetence, but whatever the cause he spent the remainder of his life deeply in debt. He borrowed, or endeavoured to borrow, money from all his associates, continuously lamented his poverty, and showed no compunction in sponging upon such humble men as Staunton.[1] The common report at the time of his going to France, that he 'was fled for debt' was more than plausible, it was the truth,[2] although he was not mainly concerned to avoid his creditors. Nothing could be more improper than to represent Dudley as a disinterested patriot. His main concern was to employ his skill and knowledge for his own profit. He was quite prepared to make use of the patriotism of others, but his natural affinities were with those who hoped to profit materially by Mary's overthrow. This did not make him less dangerous as a conspirator, rather the reverse. He understood perfectly the elements of cupidity and political ambition which were strong in the opposition to Mary, and consequently knew how to shape attractive propositions, and stimulate useful fears. He was an adventurer, but a distinguished one with a great many contacts and the intangible power to inspire confidence, and even affection, in others.

[1] Confession of William Staunton, 10 April 1556. SP, Vol. VIII, no. 4.
[2] According to a report current among the conspirators, his departure was discussed at court, where his sister-in-law was one of Mary's personal attendants. The Queen was reported to have said that 'he neded not for det, for we have given him a $\frac{xx}{iiii}$ li by yere'. The story is probably apocryphal, for there is no trace of any such grant, and Dudley's demeanour does not suggest that he had received it (White's confession. SP, Vol. VII, no. 37).

From the point of view of the English opposition he was the ideal man to strike the first blow in an enterprise of this kind. A good soldier, with nothing to lose and everything to gain; supposed to possess the influence of long familiarity at the French court, and sufficiently discredited in England to be plausibly denounced if things went wrong.

After the collapse of the conspiracy he endeavoured to capitalize on his knowledge of the Pale, and the fact that his brother was Captain of Hammes. With the outbreak of war a silence descends upon his activities, which is not broken until June 1559. Sir Nicholas Throgmorton, then Ambassador in France, wrote in that month to Cecil: 'Harry Dudley begins to practise again for new credit . . .', and had approached Throgmorton with an offer to reveal French practices in Scotland.[1] In 1561 he was still in France, when Throgmorton reported dryly that his status in the French King's Privy Chamber had not prevented him from being thrown into the Chatelet for debt.[2] He seems to have returned to England early in 1563, significantly to a post in the household of his kinsman the Earl of Leicester, with whom he was in high favour.[3] In December 1563 he was granted an annuity of £150, by a Patent which describes him as 'the Queen's servant',[4] but nothing could cure his chronic improvidence. In March 1567 he was granted a year's protection from his creditors, which was renewed for two years in 1568,[5] and probably before that grace expired, he had died.

Dudley's chief confidant in England, and his companion in exile, was Christopher Ashton of Fifield in Berkshire, a man of somewhat similar stamp. His origins are unknown, but by 1537 he had become a gentleman usher of the Privy Chamber, and had married one Catherine, the widow of James Strangeways,

[1] Throgmorton to Cecil, 21 June 1559. *Cal. For.* Vol. III, p. 328. The Tremaynes and Cornwall had made similar approaches.
[2] Same to same, 26 November 1561. *Cal. For.* Vol. VI, p. 418.
[3] Guzman Da Silva to Philip, 27 June 1564. *Cal. Span.* Elizabeth, Vol. I, p. 364.
[4] *Cal. Pat.* Elizabeth, Vol. III, p. 188.
[5] *Cal. Pat.* Elizabeth, Vol IV (proof copy in P.R.O.), pp. 46, 246.

who had brought to him a number of manors in Berkshire.[1] In the spring of 1543 he appears briefly in the records of the Privy Council, being accused of 'exacting unlawful contributions' at the musters of that year, but with what result is not recorded.[2] Like Dudley, he seems to have been in perpetual financial difficulties, and actually to have been outlawed for debt at the time of his going to France. However, either as a result of piracy, or because he had sold his property in England, he told Dore in the summer of 1556 that he had ' . . . yt left a M crowneys or ii, the profyts whareof will be abull to fynd me . . .' and was consequently not dependent upon the French king's charity.[3] It is hard to believe that such a man should have kept a number of retainers, but so it was. Bedell was his servant, and the innkeeper at Southampton on the eve of his departure noticed suspiciously that his companions all treated him with deference, as servants to a master.[4] The only office he is known to have held is that of Captain of Douglas, and he was not a man of much weight in Berkshire, but among the adventurers and gentlemen servants who swarmed in London he seems to have been a man of influence. At least forty years of age at the time of the conspiracy, he was a generation senior to most of his associates, and was probably Dudley's father-in-law.[5] Dore asked him when they met in France ' . . . whether, in his old age he meant to brave the danger of the sea . . .' and since nothing certain is heard of him after 1557 it is reasonable to suppose that he died in France.

[1] *Cal. Pat.* Vol. I, p. 403. Grant of the reversion of these manors to Sir Thomas White. Ashton held them for 31 years from the death of his wife.

[2] *APC*, 26 April and 16 May 1543. Vol. I, pp. 120, 133.

[3] Examination of Martin Dore, 'March' 1556. SP, Vol. VII, no. 59. If Ashton had sold property in England, he still retained enough to be inventoried after his indictment. See below, p. 236.

[4] Confession of Bedell, 30 March 1556. SP, Vol. VII, no. 53. One of Ashton's companions was 'Reeve, his chamberlain'.

[5] Dudley's matrimonial status is uncertain. Ashton referred to him as his 'sonne', which suggests this relationship. Miss Garrett (op. cit. p. 149) assumed that he was married to a daughter of Lord Audely, but it appears from *Cal. Pat.*, Vol. III, p. 9, that 'Margaret . . . daughter of Thomas Audley, Lord Audley' was the wife of Lord Henry Dudley, Northumberland's son. King Henri, apparently thinking him to be unmarried, is alleged to have 'commended him in marriage to a rich widow'. *Cal. For.* Vol. II, p. 284.

His son, also named Christopher, fled and was indicted with him, but beyond the fact that ' . . . he was at the taking of the Spaniard'[1] there is no record of his activities or his fate.

Disregarding marginal cases, such as the Killigrews, the great majority of those who were associated with Dudley and Ashton in France conform to the same pattern. They were minor gentry who lived by their swords. The twin brothers Nicholas and Andrew Tremayne, the sons of Thomas Tremayne of Collacombe, were young men and their only previous appearance in the records was in connection with piracy. Presumably after the collapse of the rising they served in the French army, for they were still in France in 1559.[2] Shortly thereafter they must have returned to England, for by 1560 they were serving under Lord Grey on the Scottish border, where they were commended for valour and 'good service'.[3] Both were killed at the siege of Newhaven in 1563.[4] Robert Cornwall first appears in the royal service against Wyatt, but beyond the fact that he came from Essex nothing is known of his origins.[5] He took a servant with him to France, one Savage, who kept him in touch with affairs in England, but like the others he seems to have entered the French service by the end of 1556. He submitted to the new queen in 1559, and by August 1560 was commanding 200 men on the Scottish border.[6] Francis Horsey, Richard Ryth and Roger Reynolds were minor figures of the same kind, the last named being unwise enough to associate with Stafford, for which he was executed in 1557.[7] The most distinguished of this group was Edward Horsey, the elder son of Jasper Horsey of Exton. A young man at the time of his flight, he also entered

[1] Confession of Peter Killigrew, 21 August 1556. SP, Vol. IX, no. 26. Throgmorton interceded in 1561 for a Christopher Ashton, 'who would fain return to England', and whom he described as 'of good nature and proper service'. Probably the reference is to the younger Ashton, but there is no evidence that anything came of the recommendation. *Cal. For.* Vol. VI, p. 119.

[2] Throgmorton to Cecil, 21 June 1559. *Cal. For.* Vol. III, p. 328.

[3] Lord Grey to the Duke of Norfolk, 6 April 1560. *Cal. For.* Vol. IV, p. 510.

[4] Denys to Cecil, 18 July 1563. *Cal. For.* Vol. VIII, p. 459.

[5] Garrett, p. 128.

[6] Robert Cornwaylle to Cecil, 20 March 1559 and 2 August 1560. *Cal. For.* Vol. III, p. 180, and Vol. V, p. 209.

[7] Garrett, p. 271.

the French service and married, some time before 1559, a French Huguenot lady.[1] In July 1559 Throgmorton recommended him to Cecil, and was apparently already employing him as a spy. Cecil took the hint and employed him on a mission to his wife's co-religionists, advising him at the same time to sue for his pardon.[2] By 1563 he was considered of sufficient importance to be named with Oliver Manners, the brother of the Earl of Rutland, as one of the hostages for the surrender of Havre de Grace.[3] Thereafter he received several marks of royal favour, being appointed Captain of the Isle of Wight some time before 1568, and in 1573 a special envoy in France.[4] He died in 1582.

The general tone of the group was not affected by the small number of exceptions, but there were some: Andrew Pomeroy the engraver, and John Calton the London Goldsmith, who were sent over to operate the mint, and Richard Tremayne. Richard was the elder brother of Nicholas and Andrew; an ecclesiastic who had fled on Mary's accession to Louvain. In 1556 he returned to England as some kind of emissary for Dudley, the only protestant divine who can be shown to have been implicated, but his part was extremely shadowy. He was indicted, but made good his escape, probably to Germany, where he remained until 1559, when he returned to become Archdeacon of Chichester.[5]

Those exiles such as the Staffords and Brian Fitzwilliam who had been in France for some time by 1556 can only tentatively be included in this classification. They were gentlemen, and soldiers, and Fitzwilliam at least can be shown to have associated with Dudley after the conspiracy,[6] but there is no conclusive proof of their part in the plot itself. The original leader of the exiles, Carew, can be definitely excluded. He had

---

[1] Throgmorton to Cecil, 13 July 1559. *Cal. For.* Vol. III, p. 380.
[2] Edward Horsey to Cecil, 9 June 1562. *Cal. For.* Vol. VII, p. 90, et seq.
[3] *Cal. For.* Vol. VIII, p. 480.
[4] *DNB* and Garrett, p. 191.
[5] Garrett, p. 311. *Cal. Pat.* Elizabeth, Vol. I, p. 5, 7 October 1559.
[6] Wotton to the Queen, 20 October 1556. *Cal. For.* Vol. II, p. 267. This was in connection with Dudley's schemes against the Pale.

retired to Germany the previous year with the firm intention of making his peace with the English government, and there is some reason to suppose that he betrayed what he knew of the plot as part of the price of his pardon.[1] In France, as in England, a number of lesser figures appear dimly in the wings such as Thomas Gower and William Lant, but their presence adds nothing to our knowledge of the conspiracy, or of Dudley's principal associates.

In England the situation was much more complex. Firstly there were Dudley's agents, and his contacts among the 'captains' in London. Secondly there were the Exchequer plotters, some of whom were only dimly aware of the wider issue; and thirdly there were the substantial gentry in whom the main hope of the whole project resided. John Throgmorton, the leader of the enterprise in England after Dudley's departure, was the son of Sir Thomas Throgmorton of Coughton in Warwickshire, and hence the great-nephew of Sir Nicholas.[2] A man well placed for advancement, his career was given no chance to develop. There is a strong probability that he was implicated with Wyatt, and spent some time in France and Italy as a result. Returning to England, perhaps as a result of a pardon issued on 3 December 1554,[3] within a few months he had been caught up in the new conspiracy. There were a number of John Throgmortons in public life at this time, and the man of that name who sat in the parliament of 1555 was almost certainly not the conspirator.[4] A man of courage and ingenuity, he stayed at his post a little too long, and was arrested with the others on 18 March. About Bedell almost nothing is known. The testimony of Thomas White refers to him 'collecting the wool' of White and other merchants, and

[1] Garrett, pp. 104–5.
[2] Ibid. p. 305.
[3] *Cal Pat.* Vol. II, p. 195. This pardon was granted to 'John Torkmerton of Tortworth, alias of Gorseland co. Gloucester', who may, or may not, have been the same man.
[4] The Recorder of Warwick was a man with the same name, and it was almost certainly he who sat in Parliament.

using this as a cover for his treasonable activities.[1] Elsewhere he is referred to as 'Ashton's man', one high in his confidence who would be likely to 'know his master's mind'. After his execution a fulling mill which he had owned was granted by Patent to his widow, Elizabeth.[2] These meagre facts suggest that he was some sort of factor or agent employed by Ashton, in addition perhaps to being a small clothier on his own account. He owned a house at Beaconsfield, but spent much of his time travelling on business, legitimate and otherwise. In spite of being used as a recruiting agent, he seems to have had no military connections or experience.

Those 'gentlemen that be soldiers' who spent their time propping up the pillars in St Paul's were natural material for an enterprise of this kind. Such were the 'captains' who had promised Edward Randall that they would 'turn French' upon the spot if offered employment; Edward Turner, William Staunton, Powell, Leighton and others were of this kind. For the most part they are obscure figures about whom little can be discovered. Staunton had been involved with Wyatt, and had betrayed his fellow-exiles in return for pardon in the summer of 1554.[3] During the autumn he had returned to England, and in October his lands and goods were restored to him. It is possible that he came of a Nottinghamshire family, but he lived in London and was described as 'of London' in his indictment. Edward Turner, although called 'Gent.' was found upon indictment to possess no lands or goods,[4] and Powell and Leighton are only names. Randall himself was a slightly more substantial figure. A son of Avery Randall of Badlesmere, he had, as we have seen, by 1555 a considerable record of rebellion, espionage and double-dealing. Partly because of his own cleverness, and partly through Throgmorton's insistence that he was ' . . . the Kyng's servant and the Queen's hyghnes

---

[1] Deposition of White. SP, Vol. VII, no. 37. He is described in his indictment as 'clothier'.

[2] *Cal. Pat.* Vol. III, p. 452. 11 March 1557.

[3] See above, p. 109

[4] *Cal. Pat.* Vol. III, p. 465. He was granted an annuity of £40 for his services in September 1559. *Cal. Pat.* Eliz. Vol. I, p. 27.

trew subject',[1] he was never proceeded against for his part in this conspiracy. He seems to have remained in Philip's service until the end of the reign, and in 1560 appears as Esquire Sergeant Major under Lord Grey of Wilton on the Scottish border.[2] In June 1563 he was appointed Knight Marshal at Newhaven, and three years later went with the army to Ireland as 'Lieutenant of Ordonnance' and colonel of foot. On 12 November 1566 he was killed in battle.[3] John Danyell and Edward Lewkenor stand slightly apart from this group, because they were 'in service'. Danyell was a dependant of Lord Grey, and Lewkenor the Groom Porter of the Court, whose chief function seems to have been the supply of playing cards.[4] Danyell was a self-confessed fortune hunter, tempted by Dudley's offer of employment in France, but turning up his nose at the sum offered, and weighing it against his chances of marrying a wealthy widow for whom he was angling.[5] Neither had a subsequent career to reveal his potentialities, as Danyell was executed and Lewkenor died in prison.

In contrast, the small group of Exchequer plotters, Rossey, Dethicke, White and possibly Henry Smith, were all civilians. Rossey, a minor civil servant, is no more than a name. Smith was a London goldsmith, and is tentatively claimed by Miss Garrett to have gone overseas after his pardon in December 1556.[6] White is variously described as 'merchant' and 'gentleman', but beyond the fact that he was granted lands to the annual value of £27 in May 1557 'In consideration of his services in the late attempted conspiracy against the Crown by Dudley and his accomplices . . .' we know nothing of him.[7] To identify a Thomas White and a Henry Smith among the

---

[1] John Throgmorton's confession, 18 April 1556. SP, Vol. VIII, no. 14.
[2] Stow, *Annals* (ed. London, 1605), p. 1085.
[3] Ibid. p. 1118.
[4] Lewkenor is several times mentioned in the confessions of the conspirators, but the extent of his participation is uncertain. He was one of those involved with Alday and Hinnes in the plot to kill the Queen at the 'jeu de cannes' (Harbison, p. 198).
[5] Confession of Danyell, SP, Vol. VIII, no. 6.
[6] Garrett, p. 290.
[7] *Cal. Pat.* Vol. III, p. 485. 31 May 1557.

hundreds of others of those names who appear in the records would be an impossible task. Dethicke, on the other hand, in one of the numerous outpourings which he sent to the Council from the Tower, gave a complete account of his life from 1527 onwards.[1] He was a kinsman of Thomas Dethicke, Abbot of Thurgarton in Nottinghamshire, from whom he received an exhibition of £5 a year while studying at Balliol College, Oxford. He left Oxford with a bachelor's degree in 1528, so he must have been approaching fifty at the time of the conspiracy, one of the oldest involved. After 1528 he travelled in Germany for two years before entering one of the inns of court, which he left to become steward to Sir Richard Cawood. Thereafter he had served Sir Robert Southwell and Lord Grey. When Boulogne was returned to the French he had become Steward of the latter's household, but for some unstated reason had left or been dismissed, and was unemployed when the conspirators offered him a tempting means of restoring his fortunes. These men were little more than the tools of Throgmorton and Bedell, and had no hand in shaping the plot. Vital as their part was, they were kept largely in ignorance of the stakes for which their associates were playing.

From the point of view of the government those conspirators whom they had succeeded in arresting were important mainly because they might be used to flush bigger game. The known peril is always less fearful than the unknown, so Dudley and his followers in France, and their agents in the Tower, were less significant to the Council than those shadowy men of power who seemed to stand behind them. Suspicion hovered around all those who were known to be opposed to government policies, but some were specifically mentioned in the investigations, and others were actually proceeded against or saved themselves by flight. Thus it is possible to distinguish several degrees of involvement. In the first place there were those noted as 'vehemently suspect', or questioned in such a way as to imply suspicion.[2] In this category came the Earl of Oxford,

---

[1] Declaration of Dethicke, 9 May 1556. SP, Vol. VIII, no. 67.
[2] There are several lists of names 'vehemently suspect' among the depositions

Lord Grey, Sir John St Lowe, Sir Arthur Dennys, Sir Thomas Cawarden, Lord Thomas Howard and Sir Nicholas Pointz. Secondly there were those arrested and examined, but not actually proceeded against: Sir Nicholas Arnold, Sir John Chichester, Sir John Perrot and Sir Anthony Kingston (who was saved from process only by his death). Further, there was a group who were indicted, or fled, but were not actually punished: Sir Nicholas Throgmorton, Sir Ralph Bagnall, Sir William Courtenay, Sir John Pollard, Edmund and Francis Verney, Lord Bray, William West (calling himself Lord La Warre) and Anthony Foster. Finally there were the two who paid the full penalty, Henry Peckham and Richard Uvedale. Against Kingston, Peckham and Uvedale the evidence is conclusive. Throgmorton and Bagnall accused themselves by flight, although the latter does not seem to have been mentioned by any of the examinees until after his departure. Cawarden had been in trouble before, was indebted to the Crown to the extent of over £1,000, and was certainly one from whom the conspirators expected support.[1] Courtenay, Pollard, the Verneys, Bray, West and Foster were all at least aware of the plot before its discovery, and therefore guilty of misprision.[2] Their intentions cannot be accurately assessed, but they clearly bore the government no goodwill. The case against Arnold, Chichester and Perrot was purely circumstantial. All were known to be broadly sympathetic to the opposition. Arnold had been involved with Wyatt, and was on friendly terms with Ashton; Perrot had been in trouble for harbouring heretics, and Chichester was Sir William Courtenay's son-in-law. Lord Grey fell under suspicion because of the proven participation of at least one of his servants. The

and notes taken by the commissioners. SP, Vol. VII, nos. 23, 24, 25. A great many were questioned. See below, p. 230. Howard and Cawarden were arrested, but apparently soon released. *Cal. Ven.* Vol. VI, pp. 385–459.

[1] See above, p. 57. A precept to Cawarden to pay £1000 that he owed the Crown, dated 24 July 1555, is preserved among the Loseley MSS. *Seventh Report of the Historical MSS Commission,* App., p. 612.

[2] See below, p. 228, concerning their indictments. Bray and Edmund Verney had both been briefly in trouble for supporting Northumberland. *APC,* 25 July 1553, Vol. IV, p. 416.

case against Oxford, St Lowe, Dennys, Howard, and Pointz is too shadowy to be worth more than a passing mention.

It is possible that many sympathizers never appeared, but the only foundation upon which an estimate of the potential power of the rising can be based is those whose participation is beyond reasonable doubt. The last group can be discounted; so, less confidently, can Grey, Chichester, Arnold and Perrot. The assessment must rest upon the remainder.

Sir Anthony Kingston was the son of Sir William Kingston of Gloucestershire,[1] who had been Comptroller of the King's Household. In 1536 he had served with 1000 Gloucestershire men against the rebels in the north, and some time after 1535 had married the widow of Sir William Courtenay of Powderham, whose jointure included a number of manors in Devon. Thereafter he maintained connections in both Gloucestershire and Devon, being a member of Edward's Council in the Marches and Provost Marshal at the suppression of the western revolt of 1549, a duty which he discharged with ferocious enthusiasm. He sat for Gloucestershire in the parliaments of 1545, 1552-3 and 1555. His wealth was substantial without being spectacular, but the kind of leadership which he displayed in the Commons helped to make him a man of considerable influence in the west country. The rumours that he could raise 10,000 men and 'bring a great part of Wales at his back' were exaggerated, but it is not unfair to compare his position with that of Wyatt, and to add that it was probably less localized.

The other two west-country gentlemen chiefly involved, Sir William Courtenay and Sir John Pollard, were a curiously contrasted pair. The former was the son of Sir William Courtenay of Powderham, who had died in 1535, and was therefore Kingston's stepson. He had carefully avoided implication with Carew, and was by wealth and family connection one of the most influential gentlemen in the county. His only appearance at Westminster seems to have been in 1555;

[1] *DNB.*

at least two of his kinsmen were overseas apart from the Earl,[1] and the government had some reason to regard him with mistrust. Pollard, on the other hand, had raised himself from comparatively humble beginnings by the practice of law in the government service.[2] He became a Sergeant at Law in 1547, and was rewarded with a number of monastic properties in 1550. For a while he was Vice-President of the Council in the Marches, and sat in parliament for Oxfordshire in 1553–4, and Wiltshire in 1555, being Speaker for two years. Generally noted for his loyal tone, he had been one of the advocates of Philip's cause in 1554, and appears strangely in this context. As a civil servant and professional administrator it is not likely that his local influence was great, although, like Kingston, he owned property in both Devon and Gloucestershire.

Henry Peckham, the Verneys and Lord Bray form a single group, whose main centre of wealth and influence was Buckinghamshire. Edmund and Francis were the sons of Sir Ralph Verney,[3] who had died in 1546, leaving to the former lands valued at £330 a year. Both sat in the parliaments of 1552–3 and 1555. Neither enjoyed a public career of any prominence, however, as Edmund died in 1558, aged 30, and Francis, who was the fifth son, was overshadowed by the next heir, also named Edmund, who lived until 1599. They were typical of the restless younger gentry, and their impetuosity was greater than their influence. Lord John Bray was their maternal uncle, the grandson of Sir Reginald Bray,[4] the confidant and minister of Henry VII. The wealth of the Brays was very considerable and Lord John had begun his career most promisingly by marrying Anne, daughter of Francis Talbot, Earl of Shrewsbury. However, he quickly became estranged from his wife, whose conservative family disapproved of his political and religious opinions. Whether through

---

[1] His nephew Edward, and his brother John. Garrett, pp. 130–2.
[2] He was the son of Walter Pollard of Plymouth. *DNB*.
[3] The intricate relationships of this group are carefully explained by Bruce in his introduction to the *Verney Papers* (Camden Soc. 1852), pp. 59–74.
[4] Ibid. p. 52.

improvidence, or because of his known opposition to the regime, his fortunes seem to have suffered heavily by 1555.[1] The remark quoted in his indictment, that he should 'have his landes and debtes geven hym ageyne',[2] may signify some resumption of lands irregularly obtained, but more probably refers to sales enforced by extravagant tastes. Although Bray seems to have been a popular man, and to have had some personal following, his influence in the county was not as great as his family position might suggest. Like most of his kind, he and his nephews were soldiers by inclination, and later served with distinction at St Quentin. Henry Peckham was the younger son of Sir Edmund Peckham, and the brother-in-law of Bray's sister, Mary.[3] Sir Edmund had been in high favour under King Henry, to whom he had been cofferer of the House-hold, and had also been one of Mary's earliest and warmest supporters. His fortune, and his influence in Buckinghamshire were both great, but neither extended in any great measure to his younger son. Henry was a most active conspirator, but the claim that he could raise 'a great army of gentlemen' in his 'country' was wishful thinking.[4] He sat as Member of Parlia-ment for Chipping Wycombe, which was apparently the family borough, in each of Mary's parliaments down to 1555,[5] but his personal position was not a strong one. At first he had followed his father and brother in loyalty to the Queen, and in April 1554 had been awarded lands in Gloucestershire for his services against Wyatt.[6] The reason for his change of heart is not clear. It was alleged that the Queen had 'given (him) but one hundred marks a yere and taken away four',[7] but no

---

[1] Both Bray and Edmund Verney were arrested on 25 July 1553, but released ater the same day. APC, Vol. IV, p 416.
[2] Cal. Pat. Vol. III, p. 396.
[3] Verney Papers, p. 67.
[4] Notes out of depositions by White and Bedell, March 1556. SP, Vol. VII, no. 56.
[5] Return of Members of Parliament, Vol. I, pp. 383–95.
[6] Cal. Pat. Vol. I, p. 9.
[7] Declaration by Peckham. SP, Vol. VIII, no. 52. This may be connected with some lands 'that he purchased of my Lord Clinton that were the Duke of Norfolk's', mentioned in conversation with his brother. SP, Vol. VIII, no. 36.

details were given. Generalized discontent with his 'entertainment', and indebtedness were probably to blame.

The two fugitives, Sir Ralph Bagnall and Sir Nicholas Throgmorton, both had records of opposition to the regime. The latter was not released from the Tower until 18 January 1555, and was naturally one of the first suspected when the new conspiracy came to light. He was a courtier and man of affairs rather than a local magnate, as his subsequent career was to show, but his influence in Warwickshire was by no means negligible and his participation would certainly have added strength to a rising in the west. A younger son of Sir George Throgmorton, he came of an established county family, had sat in the parliament of 1552–3, and was to do so again in the first year of Elizabeth. Bagnall was also a courtier, who first appears as a rake in Edwardian London.[1] He was the son of a merchant in Newcastle under Lyme, and seems to have begun his career as a 'boon companion'. According to Strype, he alone of Mary's third parliament refused submission to the Pope, and consequently became a marked man. He had fled to the Continent before Dudley's plot was discovered, and although it is possible that he was a good soldier, his local influence in Staffordshire was negligible.

William West, who claimed the title of Lord La Warre, was little more than an adventurer.[2] Born in 1519, he was the nephew of Sir Thomas West, 8th Baron West and 9th Baron de la Warr. At some time before 1547 he had been adopted by his uncle as the heir to his titles, but by an Act of Parliament in 1547–8 he was disabled from all honours on the grounds that he had attempted to hasten his uncle's departure by poison. From then on he seems to have lived on his wits. After narrowly escaping the axe for his part in the conspiracy, he seems to have served in the war which broke out in the summer of 1557, and to have expressed voluble discontent at the inadequacy

---

[1] Garrett, p. 77. He was in favour under Elizabeth, and on 19 February 1560 eceived a grant of lands worth £73. 10s. 9d. annually for his services in Ireland. *Cal. Pat.* Elizabeth, Vol. I, p. 308.

[2] *DNB sub* Sir Thomas West. He was restored in blood in 1563.

of his reward.[1] Eventually he was to be restored in blood in 1563. In 1555, after his uncle's death, his fortunes would have been at their lowest ebb, which accounts for his participation in the conspiracy, but means that his part in a rising would have been insignificant.

The same applies to Anthony Foster. Foster's antecedents are obscure, but he seems to have been an adherent of the Dudley family. He sat in the parliament of 1555 for Nottinghamshire, but beyond the fact that he was indicted and subsequently pardoned for his part in the conspiracy, nothing more is known of him until he appears in the next reign as the steward and confidant of Robert Dudley, Earl of Leicester.[2] A man of the same name sat in the parliament of 1572 for Abingdon, but the identification is not certain.

Richard Uvedale was a man whose power lay in his office rather than his personal status, and it was reputed that he was 'sure' of the whole garrison of the Isle of Wight, and others to the number of over 1000 who would follow him in any enterprise.[3] He was also a local man, the son of Sir William Uvedale of Wickham, and so a member of a substantial Hampshire family.[4] As well as his normal residence at Chilling, he had another house at Chelsham in Surrey, and was a man of some wealth. As a soldier, a royal officer, and a man of local influence, he could probably have commanded some following in the county, especially if an invading force of any size had been in their midst. After Kingston, and possibly Courtenay, he was the most influential of the potential rebel leaders.

The fact that the conspirators' plans were never put to the test makes any attempt to estimate the danger which they represented extremely difficult. Given a few months and reasonable luck there was no reason why Dudley should not have invaded with a well-equipped and well-led force of two

---

[1] *APC*, 8 March 1558, Vol. VI, p. 280.
[2] *DNB sub* Robert Dudley, Earl of Leicester.
[3] Interrogatories drawn by White, 9 May 1556. SP, Vol. VIII, no. 62. It was also rumoured that Uvedale and his followers would collect all the armour in the county.
[4] *DNB*.

or three thousand mercenaries and English exiles. That some
sort of a rebellion would have supported him if he had done so
is certain. Uvedale was far too deeply committed to withdraw,
and unless the government had received ample prior notice of
the invader's landfall they would have obtained at least an
unopposed landing and a few hundred recruits. The possibility
of a west-country rising was genuine. Apart from a few active
leaders there was a great deal of general discontent which a
leader of Kingston's stamp could certainly have turned into
an insurrection of some kind. A man noted for his boldness, it
is unlikely that he would have allowed the opportunity to pass.
He was at least as well placed as Wyatt had been, and with the
support of Courtenay, Throgmorton, and possibly others such
as Arnold, could reasonably expect to make at least as good a
showing. The Buckinghamshire group was a much less promising proposition. Bray and the Verneys might conceivably have
succeeded in gathering a small force, but unless they could
have joined up with malcontents in London or East Anglia
they would not have presented much of a threat. London was
always an imponderable. There was probably a better chance
of a rising there in 1556 than in 1554, but Dudley was wise
enough not to count on it, even with his agents in the city. If
he won a victory in the south, or Kingston in the west, then the
capital might declare against the Queen, but otherwise it
would promise much and perform nothing.

The rebels hoped, and the government feared, that other
and more powerful men might also be stirred to action. Here
positive evidence is completely absent, and expectation rested
rather upon the general atmosphere of crisis than upon the
conspiracy in particular. Judging by what had happened
before, the danger lay rather in the magnates doing nothing
than rising in open rebellion. Had Dudley succeeded in making
as much headway as Wyatt, it is unlikely that he could have
been stopped in the same way, for the balance had swung
against the government since 1554. The situation in England
was more favourable to a determined minority *coup* in 1556
than at any time since the beginning of the reign. A conversa-

tion between Henry Peckham and his brother Sir Robert, which the latter related to the Commissioners,[1] shows that the issue was well understood by those most intimately involved:

I then said to hym (Sir Robert declared) that in myne opinione neithere Dudley nor Ashton were mene of any suche power or estimatione that althowgh there malice woulde provoke theym to enterprise anyethyng againste their allegiance, that anye feare was to be hadde of theyme that they were able to doo anye hurte. It is verye trew (said he), havynge respect to their owne powere onlye, and therefore . . . it is the more to be suspected there be other manere of personages that be confederate with theme.

The evidence concerning these confederates, although so imperfect, is sufficient to show that the danger was real and serious, and although the conspiracy failed, the government had little reason for satisfaction over its escape.

[1] SP, Vol. VIII, no. 46.

9

THE CONSEQUENCES OF DEFEAT

I

The arrests on 18 March were carefully planned, and must have taken place almost simultaneously in different parts of London. Machyn enumerates the prisoners as though they all arrived at the Tower in a single body:

[. . . divers gentlemen carried to the Tower by certain of the guard, viz John Throgmorton] Hare Peckam, master Bethell, master Tornur, master [Hygins master] Daneell, master Smyth marchand, master Henneage of the chapel, [George the] sherche of Graffend, master Hogys, master Spenser, and ii Rawlins and Rosey Keper of Star chambur, and master Dethycke and [divers] odur gentyll-men.[1]

Day by day thereafter fresh arrivals swelled the numbers in custody, some detected by independent investigations, others by the activity of the Commissioners at the Tower. The two starting-points were the exchequer plot which White had revealed, and the suspicious departures which had been detected from different points on the south coast. On 11 March the J.P.s of Hampshire interrogated William Draper, an inn-keeper from the village of Hythe, concerning a number of strangers who had visited his house on 1 March.[2] From his description of them, and their departure by boat, they would seem to have been followers of Ashton. From Draper the trail led to Stephen Rike, one of the sailors who had taken them off, to his employer John Peers, and to Richard Uvedale whose servant had conducted them.[3] At about the same time 'Brayce,

---

[1] Machyn, p. 102.
[2] SP, Vol. VII, no. 17.
[3] SP, Vol. VII, nos. 27, 31.

a Frenchman' and one Broune were sent up from Sussex to the
Tower 'vehemently suspected of High Treason'.[1] By the 23rd
Uvedale himself was in the Tower, and had made the first
of his many confessions concerning his association with the
conspirators.

On 24 March Michieli reported to his government as much
of the matter as he had been able to discover. According to
his somewhat garbled version the robbery of the exchequer
was to be carried out under the cover of arson, and the money
thus secured was to be shipped to the Isle of Wight, where the
standard of rebellion was to be raised. Many arrests had been
made, and although it was still not known how widespread or
dangerous the plot was, the Council were very worried.[2] That
same day Uvedale revealed conclusively that the secret departures of Dudley and his kind were part and parcel of the same
scheme, and the full extent of the conspiracy began for the
first time to be apparent.[3] On the 26th Thomas White penned
a long and somewhat inconsequential document which completed the basic outline by describing the proposed uprising in
the west, and the part which was to be played by Sir Anthony
Kingston.[4] There could no longer be any doubt of the seriousness of the situation, and it became a matter of urgency to
round up as many as possible of those implicated, lest they
should seek, as Wyatt had done, to get in their blow before
their strength was fully known. Mary wrote to Philip, explaining the situation, and at the end of the month Michieli reported
that she was 'much troubled, and appears little in public'.[5]

By this time the prisoners in the Tower, either under the
inducement of torture or through the more subtle persuasions
of alternate hope and fear, were pouring forth all manner of
details, relevant and irrelevant. William Hinnes, examined on

---

[1] *APC*, Vol. V, p. 246, 11 March 1556.

[2] Michieli to the Doge and Senate, 24 March 1556. *Cal. Ven.* Vol. VI, p. 383.

[3] SP, Vol. VII, no. 32. It seems to have been Uvedale's rapid confession, the news
of which was quickly spread around, which breached the morale of the other
prisoners. Throgmorton charitably attributed it to his bad health.

[4] SP, Vol. VII, no. 37.

[5] Michieli to the Doge and Senate, 30 March 1556. *Cal. Ven.* Vol. VI, p. 392.

28 March, recounted the original negotiations for the establishment of the mint in Normandy, and the hopes which the
plotters entertained of the Earl of Devon.[1] Two days later he
repeated a long and rambling conversation with Dethicke on
the same subject, by which he attempted to prove his virtuous
reluctance to become involved in such an enterprise.[2] It was
every man for himself in these examinations. Bedell accused
Staunton (who had been arrested on the 25th), White accused
Dethicke, Uvedale accused Bedell. This panic-stricken scramble
of accusation and counter-accusation has been often commented upon; it was pathetic, but quite understandable. With
one or two exceptions these men were agents and underlings;
most had either drifted into the plot, or had been tempted by
large-sounding offers. Only Throgmorton, Bedell and Uvedale
could be described as important conspirators, who might have
been inspired by loyalty or dedication to keep silent. Throgmorton resisted every pain and inducement, declaring that no
man should come to harm by his means, but his attempts to
instil a similar fortitude in the others failed completely.[3] The
gaolers seem to have allowed frequent communication between
the prisoners, which encouraged, and was probably designed to
encourage, the passing of fears and suspicions from one to the
other. A conversation between William Hinnes and an unnamed servant of Christopher Chudleigh illustrates this well:

I pray you, sayth Chidle's man, wher lieth Daniell; not nye us
saith Hinnes; can ye tell, sayth he, whether he hath confessed
anything or nott; sayd Hinnes he hath confest all that he knows,
wherefore if ye entend to have mercy, ye were best to tell all yt ye
know . . . ye more matter ye cane declare ye more mercy ye shall
fynd; sayth Chidle's man I have all redy denyed yt; saith Hinnes it
makes no matter so long as ye are not compelled by torment to
declare it; saith Chidle's man, I thanke you for your good counsell
I will do so. . . .[4]

---

[1] SP, Vol. VII, no. 39. At one point it was rumoured that the chief aim of the
conspiracy was to 'make the Lord Courtenay king'.
[2] SP, Vol. VII, no. 46. The impression now created by this document is that
Hinnes was an accomplished rogue.
[3] Declaration of Henry Peckham, 9 May. SP, Vol. VIII, no. 53.
[4] SP, Vol. VII, no. 43.

It was probably by such means that Hinnes earned his pardon. To men in such a predicament, who knew each other but slightly and had no real sense of loyalty or purpose to inspire them, the mere hint of a pardon would be sufficient to induce this kind of behaviour. They had no cause, of the kind which upheld many protestant prisoners 'suffering for the faith'. The mixture of grievances and ambitions from which their motives, like Dudley's own, were compounded, could not be expected to arouse a spirit of heroic martyrdom.

In some respects this volubility increased the Commissioners' labours. Some of the prisoners, particularly Bedell, Dethicke and Danyell produced a flood of trivial reminiscences, involving not only their fellow-prisoners but a large number of casual acquaintances. A prodigious amount of time seems to have been consumed interviewing people whose connection with the conspirators was entirely innocent. However, patience and discrimination resulted in steady progress. By the end of March between 25 and 30 people seem to have been in custody either in London or in the provinces. The exchequer plot had been laid bare, and the disclosures of Bedell had begun to reveal the intrigues of Bretville and the complicity of Noailles.[1] However, beyond the testimony of White, which had resulted in the arrest of Sir Anthony Kingston, and a single reference to Sir Nicholas Arnold, very little had been discovered about the complicity of the 'opposition' gentry which was so strongly suspected. The examinations of Kingston on 8 and 9 April revealed nothing beyond the fact that he was acquainted with Dudley and Ashton, which was known already. He admitted receiving a token from Ashton, but denied that it had any sinister implications, and disclaimed all knowledge of Throgmorton and his associates.[2] Conclusive evidence was very hard to come by, partly because no overt act had been committed, and partly because such transactions as had taken place were not known to the prisoners in the Tower. Only Danyell had much of interest to say, when he related the meetings of the

[1] SP, Vol. VII, no. 52.
[2] SP, Vol. VIII, nos. 2, 3.

opposition leaders at Arundel's before Christmas, and those gentlemen who had visited him upon his 'sickbed' in February.[1] William Bury, who seems to have been the 'Chidle's man' already noticed, admitted carrying letters from the Horseys in France to various people in England, including Sir William Courtenay and Sir John Butler, but he knew nothing of their contents.[2] Attempts were made to question such minor conspirators as Rossey on their knowledge of the suspects, but without significant results.

Meanwhile the trials had begun. Throgmorton and Uvedale were condemned on 21 April, and executed on the 28th. Their deaths were necessary for example's sake, and they were of no value to the investigators; the latter because he had told all he knew, and the former because he would tell nothing. The government used the trial to proclaim the fact that the connection with France was known, in the hope that opinion would thereby be swayed against the conspirators.[3] The outcome was unexpected, but not altogether unfortunate. Fear of the French had been completely submerged by fear of the Spaniards, and rumours that Philip was coming with an army to take the crown were widely circulated and believed.[4] This, together with the fact that the Queen desired to send her sister to Spain, added up in most minds to a conspiracy far more sinister than anything that Dudley or Throgmorton could conceive. The execution of Throgmorton and Uvedale was thus an occasion for sympathy rather than execration, and a number of the suspect gentry were unwise enough to express this sympathy openly, perhaps in the hope of influencing

---

[1] SP, Vol. VIII, nos. 6, 35. Not being 'a parliament man' himself, Danyell was not admitted to the deliberations of the group at Arundel's, and his description is therefore little more than a list of names.

[2] Examination of William Bury, 16–17 April 1556. SP, Vol. VIII, no. 12

[3] Henri II to Noailles, 7 May 1556. Aff. Etr. IX, f. 628 (Harbison, p. 291).

[4] Harbison, p. 289. William Crowe, a bricklayer, examined on 11 May expressed what was probably a widely held feeling when he had said 'If anyone would make a flag there would be 500, ye and more than 500 that would die in this quarrel that no stranger should have the crown.' SP, Vol. VIII, no. 70. Michieli to the Doge and Senate, 14 April. Cal. Ven. Vol. VI, p. 411.

opinion still further. Their action gave the government sufficient excuse to proceed against them, and on the 29th Courtenay, Perrot, Pollard, Arnold, Chichester and others were arrested.[1] By 5 May Sir Giles Strangeways and Lord Bray had joined them in custody, and the work of the commission entered a new phase.

Kingston had died on his way to London, about 15 April, but the security measures on the south coast were intensified rather than relaxed after these fresh arrests. Michieli reported on 21 April that armed ships were patrolling the Channel, and that the militia had been alerted in the southern counties.[2] It seemed at this stage that the government really meant business, and would not scruple to execute some of the more distinguished prisoners even if no conclusive proof of their guilt could be found. On 5 May Michieli wrote that their goods had been inventoried, which was a bad sign.[3] However, May advanced, and Staunton followed Throgmorton to the block, without any fresh discoveries being made. Either the investigators were chary of examining such men as Courtenay and Pollard, or else their depositions were suppressed, because none survive. Instead they continued to labour with Danyell, Dethicke and Rossey. On 23 April one of the inquisitors wrote a memorandum: ' . . . Danyell to be gently used and given some freedom'; he was to be allowed 'as if by accident' to communicate with some of his fellow-prisoners, but to be kept away from others.[4] The following day the wretched man penned two letters, protesting that he had told all he knew, and begging for relief. However, on 13 May another memorandum ran ' . . . Danyell, being yesterday removvyd to a worse lodging, begynneth this day to be more open and playne than he hath ben, wherebye we think he knoweth all . . . and wyll utter the same.'[5] By that time the investigators clearly felt that they were 'getting warm', for the same note continued

[1] Machyn, p. 104.
[2] Michieli to the Doge and Senate, 21 April 1556. *Cal. Ven.* Vol. VI, p. 417.
[3] Ibid. p. 440.
[4] SP, Vol. VIII, no. 26. Staunton was to be similarly treated.
[5] SP Vol. VIII, no. 72.

Then we callyd for Rossey, whereby we had intellygense of certayne conferens between Staunton and Dethycke touching matters off importance for concernyng of certayne persons seemyng to be of this conspiracye of whom hitherto we have nott had grette cawse of suspicyon. . . .

This may refer to the Verneys, who were arrested some time in May, or to William West, who was in prison by 2 June.[1] No fresh names of any importance appear among the examinees in the second half of May, so it is a hint which remains obscure. Danyell and Rossey were examined almost daily, Dethicke, White and some others less often, but apart from a single non-committal statement by Sir Nicholas Arnold, the more important prisoners are silent.

By the middle of May Bedell and Danyell had broken down completely, but instead of producing the expected revelations, this was manifested in abject pleas and mutual recriminations. At about the same time Sir Robert Peckham made a statement to the Commissioners, implying that his brother had joined the conspiracy as a spy, saying that his device should be kept secret from all but the Queen's 'old' councillors, ' . . . because Council matters are not kept as secret as they should be'.[2] It can hardly be an accident that Henry Peckham's surviving confessions were delivered just over a week later, on 9 May.[3] Peckham has been accused of 'infamous' conduct in reporting the conversations of his fellow-prisoners, and describing the proposed activities of Kingston. In fact he added very little to the overall picture, and of the three men chiefly implicated by his statements, Kingston and Throgmorton were dead, and Ashton in France.

The arrests which took place towards the end of May were virtually the last. According to Michieli they included Baptiste Castiglione and Catherine Ashley.[4] It was rumoured that a

---

[1] Michieli to the Doge and Senate, 2 June 1556. *Cal. Ven.* Vol. VI, p. 474.
[2] SP, Vol. VIII, no. 46. It was precisely these 'old' councillors, i.e. Mary's servants of long standing, who were conducting the investigations.
[3] SP, Vol. VIII, nos. 52, 53.
[4] Michieli to the Doge and Senate, 2 June 1556. *Cal. Ven.* Vol. VI, p. 474.

large store of seditious books and pamphlets had been found in the possession of the latter, but neither admitted anything incriminating, either against themselves or against their mistress. By July a virtual stalemate had been reached. Eight of the conspirators had been executed, and about 30 remained in prison on various grounds of suspicion, a handful of whom had been condemned. No one was prepared to intercede for the prisoners, for fear that they should themselves become involved, and the government shrank from the prospect of executing its enemies on the flimsy cases which had been established. Consequently they remained in prison, while the investigations petered out; a punishment in itself, as the treatment of Lord Bray testifies,[1] but one more calculated to create a sense of grievance than penitence. At the end of July a certain Leonard Marshall of Rye was arrested for complicity, and the minor disturbance created by Cleobury, the Suffolk schoolmaster, in the same month was also associated on very meagre evidence with Dudley and Ashton,[2] but neither reflected upon the main issue. New possibilities were created by the arrival in London on 8 August of Peter Killigrew and his followers, captured at sea a few days before. Killigrew was examined a number of times during August and September, but whereas he had plenty to say about Dudley, and the other Englishmen in France, his testimonies were irrelevant to the cases which the Council had in hand.[3] Indictments and trials continued in a desultory fashion until the end of November, but none of those tried after the beginning of June were actually executed. After a period of uncertainty, it was clear by the autumn that the government had decided to treat the conspiracy as an isolated episode, concentrating the blame upon the exiles and the French. Consequently they gave up trying to incriminate the

[1] *Verney Papers*, introduction, pp. 73–5.
[2] *APC*, Vol. V, p. 316, 29 July 1556. Cleobury attempted to proclaim Elizabeth Queen in the Suffolk village of Yaxley, having previously arranged to be supported with an armed force, but his accomplices did not arrive and he was arrested and executed. Strype, Vol. III, p. 336. Gage, *Antiquities of Hengrave*, London, 1822 p. 158.
[3] SP, Vol. IX, nos. 24, 25.

disaffected gentry, and thus made no real impression upon the leaders of hostile opinion.

However, one central figure did disappear from the opposition ranks. Although scarcely daring to proceed openly in such a hostile atmosphere, the government began at the trial of Throgmorton and Uvedale to indicate that it had grave doubts about the integrity of the French Ambassador. The Commissioners accompanied this by interrogating all suspects and prisoners as to their relations with him, and Michieli heard that the Council were debating the legality of proceeding against him as 'a plotter and contriver against the state and person of the sovereign with whom he resides'.[1] By the end of April rumours of these proceedings had reached Noailles, and he sent an urgent request for recall which left no doubt as to his nervousness. In the event the English government were not prepared to go to war for the sake of punishing him, but the gesture had served its purpose. So pressing were the circumstances that Henry appointed Noailles' youngest brother, Gilles, temporary agent in England, in order to let Antoine make an immediate getaway.[2] He took his leave on 25 May, and left on 4 June, still convinced of the desirability of the policy which Dudley's failure had discredited and his own peril almost brought to disaster.

II

The indictment and trial of the conspirators roughly corresponded with the end of their usefulness to the Commissioners. At one point the hard-pressed Throgmorton is reported to have enquired whether he could still be racked after sentence had been passed.[3] He was told that he could, but generally the trial and sentence indicated that there was no longer much hope of extracting information, although deferments and offers of

[1] Michieli to the Doge and Senate, 26 May 1556. *Cal. Ven.* Vol. VI, p. 460.
[2] Harbison, pp. 292–3.
[3] Statement by Henry Peckham. SP, Vol. VIII, no. 53.

pardon might still be used.[1] The first trials were those of Uvedale and Throgmorton, conducted before a special commission of Oyer and Terminer in Southwark on 21 April.[2] There was no doubt of their guilt, and both were condemned. Rossey was indicted on 24 April, and then on the 29th a True Bill was found in London against nineteen of the conspirators, including Dudley, the Ashtons, the Tremaynes, the Horseys, and a number of others in France.[3] Of this group only Bedell, Dethicke, Danyell, Peckham, Staunton, Turner and Thomas Hinnes were available to stand trial. The last named, although in custody, is rather mysteriously marked 'utlagatus' on the list, and was never tried, implying either that he escaped, or that there was some confusion of identity.[4] Peckham and Danyell were tried by Special Commission at the Guildhall on 7 May, and William Staunton similarly on the 12th.[5] On the 19th the arraignment of Bedell, Dethicke and Rossey was postponed on the Queen's orders, without any explanation.[6] Mary seems to have kept a personal watch upon the proceedings throughout, and her hand can be seen in a number of the letters sent to Sir Henry Bedingfield, the Lieutenant of the Tower, during this period. For instance on 2 April he was instructed that ' . . . the prisoners that remain . . . for the great cause of suspicion . . . ' were not to be admitted to the sacrament, and a series of letters between April and July allowed the wives of various prisoners to visit them.[7] The Queen was always suscep-

---

[1] Throgmorton was visited 3 or 4 days before his execution by Feckenham, the Dean of St Paul's, who warned him to prepare for death, but added that he could still hope for mercy if 'he gave good occasion for it'. Memorandum of 24 April. SP, Vol. VIII, no. 21.

[2] KB8/33. Appendix to the *Fourth Report of the Deputy Keeper of the Public Records*, p. 252. Both pleaded Not Guilty, but the Venire was awarded instanter, and the trials concluded the same day.

[3] Controllment Roll. KB29/189, r. 65d. A number of these had already been proclaimed traitors on 4 April. Machyn, p. 103.

[4] If Thomas Hinnes was really in prison there would have been no point in outlawing him; possibly the reference to his imprisonment is a mistake. William Hinnes was in prison and frequently examined.

[5] KB8/34. All three made unavailing pleas of Not Guilty.

[6] Bedingfield Papers, Cordell to Sir Henry Bedingfield. Appendix to the *Third Report of the Historical Manuscripts, Commission*, p. 238.

[7] Ibid. pp. 238-9.

tible to the pleas of a dutiful wife, as Lady Bray discovered to her advantage.

The deferred trial took place at Westminster on 2 June, and was the last of which the sentence was actually carried out. The arraignments which took place thereafter seem by comparison extraordinarily arbitrary. Francis and Edmund Verney were both indicted in London on 11 June and the wording of their indictments was identical.[1] Both were accused of being made privy to the conspiracy by Peckham, and agreeing to support it. Edmund had been the first informed, and Francis became involved through his means, yet only Francis was tried. He was arraigned at the Guildhall on 18 June in the company of Edward Turner, pleaded guilty and was condemned.[2] Edmund was respited on the Queen's orders on 30 June, and remained in prison without further process until the following April.[3] Sir Thomas Cawarden, against whom there was at least the makings of a case, was not indicted at all; nor were Arnold and Chichester, although both were kept in prison for several months. Pollard and Courtenay were not indicted until 4 November, and neither was tried. William West and Edward Lewkenor, however, both comparatively minor figures, were tried during June. They were indicted for being involved with Peckham in the procurement of the copy of Henry VIII's will, which Lewkenor was alleged to have delivered to West on 10 February.[4] Lewkenor was condemned at Guildhall on 15 June, and West, after unsuccessfully attempting to claim peerage, on the 30th.[5] The innocuous Henry Smith, who had been in prison since 18 March, but had contributed nothing to the inquiries, was indicted on 2 July, and tried as an afterthought on 21 November.[6] The only other person to stand trial for his share in the plot was Courtenay's agent, John Walker. He was accused of concealment, indicted on

[1] *Cal. Pat.* Vol. III, p. 539, and Vol. IV, p. 81.
[2] Ibid., and Machyn, p. 108.
[3] Bedingfield Papers, *HMC*, App., p. 238.
[4] West's Indictment, as set out in his pardon. *Cal. Pat.* Vol. III, p. 538.
[5] Ibid., and Machyn, pp. 108, 109.
[6] *Cal. Pat.* Vol. III, p. 530.

6 July and tried on 16 November.[1] Throughout he was treated purely as a private individual; his connection with the Earl was not mentioned, and no cognizance was taken of the suspicious transactions into which he had entered on his master's behalf.

The others indicted were Anthony Foster and Sir Ralph Bagnall, who were out of reach in France, Sylvestra Butler and Lord Bray. The last named, although it was several times hinted that very grave charges were pending against him, was eventually accused only of 'infraction of true obedience' by the uttering of false and contemptuous words.[2] Mrs Butler had been a familiar and confidant of the conspirators from an early stage, and her houses, both in London and Gloucestershire, had provided them with hospitality. She was alleged to have offered them all the assistance in her power, saying 'I would the King and Queen were in the sea in a bottomless vessel.' She was indicted in London on 27 June, and in Gloucester on 12 September.[3] Foster was indicted on 2 July for concealment, and Bagnall on 12 December for participation.[4] Several names are unexpectedly absent from this list. Peter Killigrew, pirate and confederate of Ashton, Edward Randall, William Bury, Roger Carter, Alday, and William Hinnes. Bury presents something of a problem. In the file of Ancient Indictments he appears to have been presented upon the same indictment as Mrs Butler, which would be logical, since she was supposed to have heard of the conspiracy from him.[5] This is confirmed by the Controllment Roll, where he is also noted as being first outlawed, then pardoned.[6] However he is known to have been imprisoned and examined in April; the only possible explanation is that he was released before the evidence upon which he was indicted became available. He may have gone to France, but there is no trace of him there, and his pardon does not appear in the

[1] Ibid, p. 402.
[2] Verney Papers, p. 75. Cal. Pat. Vol. III, p. 396.
[3] Cal. Pat. Vol. III, p. 400.
[4] Ibid. pp. 318, 453.
[5] KB9/589, f. 51.
[6] KB29/190, r. 66d.

Patent Roll. It would hardly be reasonable to accuse the King's Bench clerks of error, since references to him appear at least three times. The name of Christopher Perne also appears in the Controllment Roll, coupled with that of Foster, without any note of subsequent process,[1] and it is possible that he also went to France, although Miss Garrett found no trace of him. Randall was a prisoner for a short while, but apparently nothing was found against him. Carter and Alday disappear from view, and there is no direct evidence that the latter was ever caught. Hinnes, frequently examined and deeply implicated, must have purchased his immunity like White by turning Queen's evidence, unless he was mistakenly described as Thomas in the indictment mentioned above.

Collating all the sources of evidence, there are thirty-six recorded indictments for participation in Dudley's conspiracy. Of these, sixteen refer to men who were certainly out of the country, and two more to those who probably were. Of the remaining eighteen all were at one time or another in prison, and thirteen were tried. In addition a considerable number, somewhere between thirty and fifty, several of whom were substantially implicated, were arrested and examined without being proceeded against. The most notable fact about this official activity is the government's apparent reluctance to bring offenders to trial, and the resultant slowness of the proceedings. The only prisoners of any significance who were treated with the sort of despatch used against the rebel leaders of two years before were Throgmorton and Uvedale. This dilatoriness was not caused by a lack of urgency, for the Council showed the most acute anxiety, and had called the musters in all the southern counties by the middle of April.[2] Nor can it be entirely explained by the necessity to wring information out of the prisoners; it did not need a period of two months to persuade men like Bedell and Danyell to tell all they knew. When we also consider the suspicious silence of all the

---

[1] Ibid. Perne was one of the 'opposition' members of the fourth parliament, and had been imprisoned with Kingston in December 1555.
[2] Michieli to the Doge and Senate, 14 April 1556. *Cal. Ven.* Vol. VI, p. 411.

more substantial prisoners, except Uvedale, and the fact that none of those gentlemen arrested on 29 April were brought to trial, it becomes apparent that the explanation lies in the chronic weakness of the government. Even allowing for the fact that so many of the leaders were in France before the plot came to light, thirteen trials, two of them for misprision only, spread over a period of seven months from April to November, does not constitute a very heavy counter-attack against a conspiracy of such magnitude and peril.

III

This picture is reinforced by considering the consequences of the trials. Throgmorton and Uvedale were executed with exemplary despatch, a week after their convictions. The same is true of Staunton, who suffered on 19 May, and of the three who faced their judges on 2 June, Bedell, Dethicke, and Rossey.[1] Thereafter, however, the government's energy faltered. Danyell and Peckham, tried on 7 May, were not executed until 7 July,[2] and thereafter the executions ceased altogether. Turner, West and Verney, sentenced to death, were reprieved[3] and soon after released, while Walker and Smith, sentenced to life imprisonment, served no more than a few months.

When Wyatt's followers were hanged in London, there were some murmurings about the shedding of English blood for the sake of foreigners; when Dudley's accomplices suffered there were public demonstrations in their favour. It was as a result of the sympathy which they expressed with Throgmorton and Uvedale that Courtenay and the others were imprisoned. As Michieli observed, such demonstrations were 'very rare', but he added that the Queen was 'disillusioned with the results of clemency', and not to be moved.[4] Writing on 19 May, the

[1] KB8/34. Machyn, p. 107.
[2] Machyn, p. 109.
[3] Michieli to the Doge and Senate, 7 and 14 July 1556. *Cal. Ven.* Vol. VI, pp. 509, 525, Lewkenor was also of this group.
[4] Michieli to the Doge and Senate, 12 May 1556. *Cal. Ven.* Vol. VI, p. 447.

same observer painted a gloomy picture of mutual fear; arrests, trials and executions arising from the conspiracy; the continual sufferings of heretics, 'men and women, young and old', and the Queen remaining in seclusion, nursing her bitterness, and her grief at Philip's refusal to return.[1] On 9 June he reported that the general alarm had spread to Elizabeth's household with the arrest of her domestics, although no action was intended against the Princess herself.[2] By the middle of June Sir Thomas Pope had reluctantly taken over the post of Governor of her Household, and Mrs Ashley (then in prison) had been replaced.[3] By that time the proceedings against the prisoners had lost all their momentum. On 16 June Michieli reported that their despatch continued slowly; by 7 July he concluded that 'the affair of the conspiracy is now apparently at an end'.[4] William West was to have suffered with Peckham and Danyell on that day, but he was reprieved and a week later was still being deferred 'from day to day' with 'the other three' (Turner, Verney, and Lewkenor). This was done, the Venetian supposed, to give them a chance to save their souls, and make 'a Godly and Catholic end' as Peckham and Danyell had done.[5] It may have been for this reason that the latter two were so long deferred, although in the case of Peckham it is probable that interest was also at work. He was a man with 'a good record of service' having manned a gate against Wyatt, and his father's good service might also be taken into account.[6] A week after his trial there seemed to be a good chance that he would be spared, but on that at least the government stood firm.

There is very little evidence as to the fate of those numerous obscure individuals who disappeared into the Fleet or the Tower between March and July. One or two were sent down into the country 'to be ordered by law', but there is no indica-

[1] Same to same, 19 May, ibid. p. 454.
[2] Same to same, 9 June, ibid. p. 479.
[3] Same to same, 16 June, ibid. p. 484.
[4] Ibid. p. 510.
[5] Same to same, 14 July, ibid. p. 525.
[6] Same to same, 12 May, ibid. p. 447.

tion of the outcome.[1] Probably the great majority were released during the autumn. The more distinguished are naturally easier to trace. Perrot and Chichester were in prison less than a month, being released before the end of May.[2] Pollard, Courtenay and Arnold, after a few weeks of rigorous confinement, were gradually allowed more freedom, and were eventually freed in the early part of December.[3] Lord Bray remained in custody until the first week of April 1557, and ' . . . all the rest, save Edmund Verney', were released at the same time.[4] Edmund seems to have remained in prison about another month, but no mention is made of the actual date of his emergence. Edward Lewkenor died in prison on 6 September, and although he is marked in the Controllment Roll 'T & Susp.' the causes appear to have been natural.[5] In spite of the strictness with which he was at first treated, Peter Killigrew was also out of prison by the following summer, although 24 of his men were hanged, amost unnoticed at the beginning of September. They died, wrote Michieli, in a most godly manner 'which has marvellously edified the whole of Hampshire, and greatly rejoiced the Queen and all good men'.[6] The toll of a single pirate ship was three times that of one of the most serious conspiracies of the reign.

Appropriately enough one of the first men arrested was also the first to be pardoned. This was Henry Smith, whose pardon was enrolled only three weeks after his trial, on 15 December;[7] his goods were restored to him, and he seems to have lost no time in putting the channel between himself and any possible reconsideration of this clemency. Anthony Foster, who had not been tried, came next on 19 January 1557,[8] and thereafter

---

[1] For instance, one Henry Holloway, who was delivered to the Sheriff of Hampshire on 30 June. Council to Bedingfield. Bedingfield Papers, p. 238.
[2] Advis, 31 May 1556, Aff. Etr., IX, f. 645 (Harbison, p. 291).
[3] Advis, 15 December 1556, Aff. Etr., XIII, f. 122. (Harbison, p. 291).
[4] Thomas Edwards to the Earl of Rutland, 16 April 1557. HMC, Twelfth Report, Appendix IV, p. 68.
[5] KB29/190, r. 66d, Bedingfield Papers, p. 239.
[6] Michieli to the Doge and Senate, 15 September 1556. Cal. Ven. Vol. VI, p. 620.
[7] Cal. Pat. Vol. III, p. 530.
[8] Ibid. p. 453.

there was a pause of a month and a half before the more serious cases began to come under review. Sir William Courtenay was pardoned on 8 March 'for all treasons before 1 December last',[1] and William West on 10 April.[2] The same day the attainder of Francis Verney was reversed,[3] and on the 11th that of Edward Turner.[4] As we have seen, these men were released at about the same time, so presumably the whole situation was reconsidered almost exactly 12 months after the crisis had reached its height. On 6 May Sylvestra Butler and John Walker were pardoned,[5] the latter just a year after Sir John Mason had written to Courtenay that his release would be 'a matter of days'.[6] Bray's pardon was enrolled on 14 May, Killigrew's on 1 June, and Sir Ralph Bagnall's, in spite of his flight, on 28 June.[7] Bagnall had probably been negotiating with the government for some months, and had purchased forgiveness in the usual way. He seems to have returned to England before the outbreak of war, and by October 1557 was interrogating the French prisoners who had been taken with Stafford.[8] On 12 July Edmund Verney was pardoned, and finally, on 30 January 1558, Sir John Pollard.[9] There is no explanation for this long delay, except perhaps that Pollard had neglected to sue for it, not having been tried. Since he had died in August 1557 it must have been applied for by his heir and executors in the process of tidying up his affairs.

Most of those who had fled received no pardon. Many of them were in favour and in the royal service after 1559, but did not trouble to liquidate the indictments which stood against their names. Robert Cornwall received a pardon in March 1562, when he had been commanding the Queen's soldiers for two years.[10] Edward Horsey's was enrolled on 30 July 1565, by which time he had undertaken several respon-

[1] Ibid. p. 456.   [2] Ibid. p. 538.   [3] Ibid. p. 539.
[4] Ibid. p. 465.   [5] Ibid. pp. 400, 402.
[6] Sir John Mason to the Earl of Devon, 3 May 1556. SP, Vol. VIII, no. 48.
[7] Cal. Pat. Vol. III, p. 318.
[8] APC, Vol. VI, p. 181, October 1557.
[9] Cal. Pat. Vol. IV, p. 89.
[10] Cal. Pat. Elizabeth Vol. II, p. 333. See above, p. 204.

sible missions.[1] The general Pardon Roll of 1 Elizabeth contains some familiar names, but since the offences are not specified it is not easy to be sure of the identification. Christopher Chudleigh, Sir John Chichester, and a William Bery, described as 'citizen and draper of London' are enrolled. The first two are almost certainly the same men, although the pardon may not relate to the events of 1556, but the last may well not be that William Bury, 'yeoman', who was Chudleigh's servant. It seems clear that a pardon was a matter of personal taste if the party concerned had not been convicted. The most outstanding example of this is probably the case of Christopher Perne. Perne is recorded in the Controllment Roll as being indicted with Foster; he received no pardon, yet sat for Plympton in the Parliament of 1557/8.[2] About a third of the indictments presented for implication in this conspiracy were never cleared, either by punishment or pardon.

In contrast with the practice adopted after Wyatt's rising, there seems to have been no attempt made to compound with the prisoners for their pardons. The only man who was fined for his part in the plot was Edmund Verney. In the course of the investigations he was reminded that he still owed the Crown £100 for a fine which had been imposed upon him at the beginning of the reign for his share in Northumberland's conspiracy.[3] In the Trinity term 1557 he paid £1000 'for a fine imposed upon him for divers offences', which presumably included both episodes.[4] Sir John Chichester appears from time to time in the Exchequer records, but he was paying off his share in a joint obligation which had been entered into in June 1553.[5] Sir John Pollard also owed the Crown £143 upon a recognizance, but there is no evidence to connect this with his implication in Dudley's designs.[6] Neither the Exchequer records nor the Patent Rolls suggest that any consistent attempt

[1] *Cal. Pat.* Elizabeth, Vol. III, p. 319.
[2] *Return of Members of Parliament*, Vol. I, p. 396.
[3] Sir Robert Rochester to Sir Henry Bedingfield, n.d. Bedingfield Papers, p. 239.
[4] Receipt of the Exchequer. E405/241, f. 44.
[5] E159/334. Recognizances, r 4.
[6] E405/241 Various.

was made to mulct those offenders who escaped other punishment. The goods and chattels of all those who either fled or were indicted would have been inventoried and placed in the custody of the Sheriff, although the only actual record of this being done refers to the elder Ashton.[1] Because of the defeat of the government's measure in the parliament of 1555, this was all that could be done without a conviction. In the case of the thirteen who were convicted, all their property passed to the Crown. With a few small exceptions that of the eight who were executed was retained or re-granted, and that of the others returned. Lewkenor's lands were granted upon petition to his widow in February 1557.[2] On 28 November 1555 a grant was made to one Walter Lamedon ' . . . of all the goods, and chattels of Christopher Ashton . . . which came to the crown by reason of any indictment of Ashton for High Treason, or upon any outlawry promulgated against him for debt at the suit of John Aylworth or other. . . .'[3] This grant was made for £160, and refers only to moveables; the Crown's interest in Ashton's lands was similarly granted, but his lands could not be touched.

Thus although the proportion of those executed to those indicted was slightly higher in 1556 than in 1554, the benefit to the Crown was if anything less. No one had ventured to greet Wyatt's accomplices on their way to trial with tears and cries of goodwill, although they had later rejoiced at Throgmorton's acquittal. Noailles' policy had been discredited, and the French did not thereafter make any attempt to stir up rebellion in England, but the stalemate between the government and the domestic opposition continued unbroken. Another hole had been plugged in the leaky hull of Mary's regime, but it was no more seaworthy than it had been before. The Council was no longer torn by the violent feuds of Paget and Gardiner, but it was no nearer to a unified and constructive policy. One of the most significant features of the proceedings against the conspirators is the fact that the Queen could trust only a handful

[1] *APC*, Vol. V, p. 346, 31 August 1556.
[2] *Cal. Pat.* Vol. III, p. 451.
[3] Ibid. p. 549.

of her less able Councillors to conduct the investigations. Even so there is an unreal atmosphere about the mass of surviving documents, which contain so much painstaking triviality, and are silent on most of the important issues. Allowing for the persistent exaggerations of Mary's opponents, it is practically certain that there was more to the English side of this conspiracy than can now be proved from surviving evidence. Great secrecy, of which Michieli more than once complained,[1] surrounded the examinations. At one point it was rumoured and reported that nothing could be proved against Uvedale. The estimate which I have attempted to make is based upon the assumption that the degree of guilt of the various parties was more or less fairly reflected in the proceedings against them. This is a necessary assumption, but I am not convinced of its validity. The indictments are by no means reliable in the acts which they record, and it is very probable that the government showed a stern face towards its humble enemies as some compensation for not feeling strong enough to attack the greater. The absence of financial proceedings is particularly significant in this respect, and indicates the decline in the government's strength and confidence which had taken place since 1554. The exactions then made were uneven, and clearly subject to the pressures of influence. By 1556 that influence had apparently increased to the point where it could prevent them almost entirely. Peckham and Uvedale were executed, but their substantial associates escaped virtually unscathed. Once again the government's victory had failed to make any real impression.

[1] Michieli to the Doge and Senate. 7 April and 5 May 1556. *Cal. Ven.* Vol. VI, pp. 399, 440.

10

CONCLUSION

In March 1558 Simon Renard wrote a memorandum on the situation in England, which was virtually the epitaph of his own and his master's efforts.[1] It was certain, he wrote, that Elizabeth would succeed, and the main question was how long the ailing and despondent Queen would live. When she died it was very likely that the religious settlement would be overthrown, and that the French faction would triumph.

'It must not be forgotten that all the plots and disorders that have troubled England during the past four years have aimed at placing its government in Elizabeth's hands sooner than the course of nature would permit, as witness the actions of Peter Carew, the Duke of Suffolk, Courtenay, Dudley, (Bretville), Stafford and others . . . not to mention Wyatt.' The Princess was in the highest honour and regard, so that it was not only impossible to stand between her and the throne, but might not even be practicable to minimize the impact of her accession by marrying her to the Duke of Savoy. Renard believed that Elizabeth was supported, and had been supported from the beginning, by an organized and influential party which cared for her interests, and which had succeeded in bringing this situation about. It was these supporters who, led by Paget, had preserved her from danger after the collapse of Wyatt's rising. The same group had repeatedly thwarted in parliament the attempts by Gardiner and others to debar her from the succession. They had stood in the wings while their henchmen Dudley and Throgmorton had woven plots, and now stood to gain all the benefits which the upheavals of the reign had prevented Mary and her husband from enjoying.

[1] *Cal. Span.* Vol. XIII, p. 372.

By the time that he compiled these notes, it was two and a half years since Renard had been in England,[1] and his assessment was based largely upon what had happened before his departure. As always, he was quick to construe opposition into conspiracy, and quicker still to associate the French with both. These predilections marred what was otherwise a penetrating commentary. Elizabeth undoubtedly did enjoy much support, both popular and influential, from those who looked to her to reverse her sister's policies. As the daughter of Anne Boleyn she seemed to have been born the champion of the National Church, and the enemy of the Spanish connection. To the discontented gentry, and soldiers out of service, she was ' . . . a liberal dame, and nothing so unthankful as her sister'. The protestants, while the fires of Smithfield burned, 'longed for their Elizabeth'. Careful and enigmatic, she reaped all the benefits of Mary's mistakes, and thereby became the recipient of many incoherent loyalties. There is, however, very little evidence of the kind of purposeful organization which Renard conceived. Elizabeth was a lifelong opportunist, and those who managed her interests acted upon similar principles. The speed with which Cecil emerged from obscurity to high office at the beginning of her reign points to him as a leading figure among them, but his caution equalled her own. These men had the same general objective as the conspirators and rebels who plotted Mary's overthrow, but it is practically certain that they had no closer connection with them, and repudiated such methods as immoral—and unnecessary. It was the plotters, not Elizabeth's friends who compromised themselves by collaboration with the French. Noailles had little interest in the Princess, save as a means of breaking the Anglo-Imperial entente. The French candidate for the English throne was the young Queen of Scots, but it would have been impossible to have raised a party in her name. Renard's supposition that the triumph of Elizabeth would be synonymous with the victory of the French party was totally erroneous, and can only be ex-

[1] He had been recalled, in response to his own urgent request, after Philip's departure in August 1555.

plained by his preoccupation with European dynastic politics.

This preoccupation was shared by many others at the time, and since, a fact which has helped to obscure the real nature of the issues which were being contested. Many streams of controversy fed the muddy whirlpool of Mary's reign—catholic against protestant, ultramontane against nationalist, French against Spaniard—giving the impression that important international problems occupied the entire stage. In fact, although these problems were undeniably real, within England they were subordinate to the vital question of who was to rule. 'Whether the Crown belong to the Queen or to the realm, the Spaniards know not nor care not . . .' wrote John Bradford.[1] The Spanish alliance, when contracted by the marriage of a ruling Queen, was no mere matter of temporary alignments and short-lived wars, but carried the possibility that power would pass to an alien aristocracy as effectively as by military conquest. Philip was determined to rule in England, and married Mary for no other purpose, whatever limitations others may have subscribed to in his name. If he could do this with the aid of a party among his new subjects, so much the better. If not, he was quite prepared to use his own agents. Mary's enthusiastic participation in this scheme added doubt and confusion to the bitterness of the conflict. 'The Queen is a Spaniard at heart', ran the popular cry, 'and loves another realm better than this.' When she strove to effect Philip's coronation, and to pass the burdensome task of administration into his stronger hands,[2] her own position was compromised in an unprecedented fashion. 'The Queen may not lawfully disinherit the right heirs apparent', declared Bradford in a passage which would have been universally denounced as outrageous ten years before.[3] The nature and extent of the royal authority was subjected to

---

[1] *Copye of a letter* . . . ; Strype, Vol. III (2), p. 128.

[2] Mary's correspondence with the Emperor, particularly during the summer of 1556, makes it clear that she felt herself to be unequal to the task of keeping order in England, and believed it to be Philip's duty as her husband to relieve her of the responsibility.

[3] Strype, Vol. III (2), p. 129. Bradford's argument necessarily implies that where there was doubt as to the identity of the right heir (as through dubious legitimacy), the doubt could not properly be resolved by the ruler of the moment.

the indignity of an intense and critical scrutiny by those who were determined that it should not be used in the way Mary contemplated.

Efforts were therefore made to define and limit the powers of the Crown, but the concept of constitutional responsibility was unknown, and the arguments centred on the fundamental laws of the kingdom, rather than upon constitutional law. The question which had exercised the Commons in the autumn of 1553, when the treaty was under discussion, was not easy to answer: 'In the case the bonds should be broken between the husband and wife, either of them being princes in their own country, who shall sue the Bonds?'[1] If Mary chose to ignore the clauses in the marriage treaty which had been inserted to prevent her from giving away her own authority, what redress was to be had? If the Queen broke the fundamental law of the kingdom, what sanctions could be employed against her, and who could employ them? The only positive sanction known was rebellion, an evil against which English opinion had been assiduously educated for many years. 'He that nameth rebellion', ran the Homily of 1547, 'nameth not one only and singular sin, but the whole puddle and sink of sins against God and man. . . .' Rebellion was a grievous social evil, and a dangerously two-edged weapon, as Bradford hastened to point out. Having warned his readers against the Spaniards, he went on

I speake not this, as some Men would take yt, to move Dissension; for that were the best Way for the Spaniards to come to their Prey. Such a Tyme they look for; and such a Tyme, they say, some Nobleman hath promysed to provyde for them. I know not their Names, but let every Man therefore be trew to the Realm; and endeavor themselves to lyve and Love one another charitablye and quyetly; that ye go all one Waye, and so withstand all these thretened Counsaylls.[2]

The danger was a real one, but Bradford's remedy could hardly be called satisfactory. How could the country 'go all one way'

---

[1] See above, p. 18.
[2] Strype, Vol. III (2), p. 132.

to any purpose without some means of compelling the government to defer to its unanimity? The Homily was explicit. If the ruler should break any fundamental or Divine law, ' . . . then may I disobey with a good conscience, but I may not make any stir or rebellion . . . for if I do, I sin damnably.' To those driven by the fears and ambitions stirred up by Mary's actions, this was an intolerable situation, and produced a crisis of conscience which they could only solve by individual decisions, sometimes of great difficulty.

The rebellions and conspiracies against Mary failed, not because her actions commanded any large measure of support, but because the majority of influential men never ceased to hope that some less radical and dangerous means might be found of thwarting them. The bankruptcy of rebellion as a political weapon for the solution of this kind of domestic crisis was convincingly demonstrated. The shrewder and more far sighted could see that only chaos could result from a situation in which the sole means of redress against an irresponsible ruler was her replacement by someone more amenable. The complex and sophisticated administrative machine which had begun to evolve in the 1530's, the increasing power of commerce and finance, and the domestic demilitarization which had been undertaken by the Queen's father and grandfather all made such a crude constitutional counterpoise seem a grim anachronism. Increasing consciousness of this can be traced, not only in the failure of Wyatt and Dudley, but in the tactics of Elizabeth's more discreet allies, and in the remarkable development of parliamentary opposition.

In 1553 the Commons petitioned against the Spanish marriage, and members expressed grave doubts about the treaty, but it was accepted. In 1554 the parliament exacted a very high price for its endorsement of the reconciliation with Rome. In 1555 the Queen dared not even introduce the subject of Philip's coronation, and a measure to which she was committed was rejected. Both Mary and Gardiner wished to disinherit Elizabeth by Statute, but were dissuaded, partly by the real danger of defeat in the Commons, and partly by the way in which that danger was inflated by the Princess's friends. The parliamentary opposition was organized in October 1555 in a way never before recorded, and probably never attempted.[1] Michieli supplies the key to this transformation in his celebrated description of the composition of the House of Commons.[2] The change in composition was probably not as radical as the Venetian believed, but it was highly significant. The parliament traditionally embodied the consent of the realm, but since the beginning of its new importance in 1529 it had been far more susceptible to royal pressure than answerable to opinion in the country as a whole. The opposition leaders in 1553 were quick to despair of its effectiveness as a means of checking the royal will, but by 1555 their attitude was changing. Although parliament could exercise no positive influence upon the formation of policy, it could at least provide a national forum, and the opportunities which it offered for protest and obstruction relieved them to some extent from the excruciating dilemma of rebellion. As a result the Queen's opponents made their first serious attempt to wrest control of the parliament from the royal Councillors, and briefly succeeded. There was no question of the parliament employing sanctions against the Crown, but in the heat of the crisis a long step was taken towards the formation of a practice of constitutional opposition. It would be an anachronism to speak of a 'country party' in the 1550's, but the county gentry had undoubtedly begun by 1558 to use the House of Commons as a forum for their views, and a vehicle for their influence at the national level.

The structure of power in England was rooted in the counties, in the Commissions of the Peace, and in the gentlemen who served on them or aspired to serve on them. It was repeatedly demonstrated that those laws of which these gentlemen generally disapproved were virtually dead. 'It boots not how many laws be made,' wrote one commentator, 'for men see few or none put into effect. . . . ' This was equally true of

[1] Neale, *Elizabeth I and her Parliaments 1559–1581*, pp. 23–5.
[2] Michieli to the Doge and Senate, 18 November 1555. *Cal. Ven.* Vol. VI, p. 252.

Somerset's enclosure laws and of Mary's attempts to silence the voices of her enemies. In some areas it was also true of the statutes against heresy. No government could function efficiently without the co-operation of these local officials, and it was they who felt themselves to be most directly threatened by Mary's policies. Philip's determination 'to take a hand in the government', as Michieli euphemistically put it, might well mean the replacement of the diffuse local autonomy of the English counties by a more rigorous and centralized administration on the Spanish pattern. The danger that their tasks would be taken over by Alcades or similar officials seemed the more imminent because of the Queen's well-known distrust of her countrymen, and her preference for her husband's subjects. It is hardly surprising that they were willing to listen to voices which proclaimed that England was about to come ' . . . into the like servitude that Naples, Milan, and other the king's dominions be in. . . .'[1] Their ecclesiastical plunder was menaced by the Queen's notorious zeal, and their paths to preferment at court seemingly blocked by foreign favourites and advisers. Yet in spite of their many grievances, and their key position in society and administration, they had no means of reaching decisions among themselves, or of bringing their influence to bear upon the formation of policy. When they began to seek a remedy for these deficiencies by using the House of Commons, they brought to that institution an independence of mind and a political weight which it had never before possessed.

Wyatt's rising has been interpreted as a religious movement, similar to the Pilgrimage of Grace, and as a clash between the gentry and the commons, similar to that of Kett. In fact it was primarily a political movement, designed to bring about a change in the secular and international policy of the government. It was a 'gentleman's matter', and all the indications are that the commons participated as the instruments of their betters. In Leicester and Devon they followed the lead of the dominant party among the county gentry, and those parties

---

[1] Examination of John Bedell, March 1556. SP, Vol. VII, no. 52.

were led by the Earl of Huntingdon and Sir Thomas Dennis in the interests of the Crown. In Kent, where the gentry were more evenly divided, the active commons followed the more dynamic lead, which was given by Wyatt and his friends. The conspirators of 1556 were similarly in no doubt that the gentlemen in whom they reposed their trust would be able to ' . . . make many men in the field' from among their retainers and their local followings. The practice of maintenance was by no means dead, and the Patent Rolls abound with licences to prominent men to retain anything up to 200 servants in their livery. Apart from these bands themselves, the amount of local patronage which they imply conveys a strong impression of the influence of the gentlemen concerned in their own 'countries'. The excellent documentation of the Wyatt and Dudley conspiracies, particularly the former, enables us to see in some detail how this influence worked, and the motivation which lay behind its use. At the same time that the gentry were becoming aware of national issues, and anxious to make their voices heard at the highest level, they were preserving their hold upon local power and their authority over their poorer neighbours.

Elizabeth was undoubtedly aware of this, and strove throughout her reign to avoid colliding with the parliamentary gentry, and their military and adventurous younger sons. Her tact and wisdom removed most of the tensions which had caused her sister so much danger and anxiety. The crisis which had almost burst over Mary was preserved to confront James in the following century, by which time its elements had existed in England for over 50 years. Elizabeth was, in a sense, a 'gentleman's Queen'. She realized their strength, and recognized, even if she was not always prepared to satisfy, their ambitions. The Scottish, Irish and French wars of the early part of her reign gave suitable employment to most of those 'young heads' whose energies had found outlet in plotting against Mary. Edward Randall, Cuthbert Vaughn, Sir Peter Carew, the Horseys, Brian Fitzwilliam, the Tremaynes and many others appear among the military commanders of the early 1560's. Politically, as well as ecclesiastically, the new reign was a new regime. Mary, to whom sound religious principles were more important than ability, had employed scarcely anyone of capacity among her senior advisers after Gardiner's death. It was left to Elizabeth to command the loyalties of such men as Cecil. Renard's suspicions were probably correct, and there was a group among the nobility and minor councillors who protected the Princess's interests and looked to her, especially after 1556, as the rising sun. The conspirators constant hints of support in high places must have referred to them, but, like Elizabeth herself, they had no intention of associating themselves with movements which might fail, and therefore be treason. Harrington knew the problem at first hand when he wrote 'Treason doth never prosper. What's the reason? Why, if it prosper, none dare call it treason.'[1] After her accession it was these men, rather than the extremists who had brought her into peril, who filled the chief places of trust about Elizabeth's court. With the exception of Sir Nicholas Throgmorton and Henry Killigrew, none of those who had been in active opposition to her sister rose above a modest position in the new regime.[2] While not repudiating them, Elizabeth did not want it to be supposed that they had been her intimates and confidants. Apart from military service, their chief resort after 1558 was the household of the rising favourite, Robert Dudley. Cecil's list of Dudley's protégés, compiled as an argument against the Queen's proposal to marry him, reads like a roll call of the rebels and conspirators of the previous reign.

. . . he shall study nothing but to enhans his own particular Frends to welth, to offices, to lands: and to offend others. Sir (Henry) Sidney, Erl Warwick, Sir James Croft, Henry Dudley, Sir Fr. Jobson; Apelyard; Horssey; Leighton; Mollynex; Middle-

---

[1] John Harrington, *Epigrams*, Book iv, no. 5.

[2] A very large number of them, however, appear in the early parliaments of her reign. The returns for the first two parliaments contain the names of Sir Thomas Wrothe, William Winter, Sir Ralph Bagnall, Sir Thomas Cawarden, Sir William St Low, Christopher Perne, Sir John Chichester, Sir Gawain Carew, Sir Nicholas Arnold, Sir Nicholas Throgmorton, Sir James Croftes, Sir Edward Rogers, Leonard Dannet, William Gibbes and Sir John Perrot.

more; Colsill; Wyseman; Killigrew; John Dudley; ii Christmas; Fostar; Ellyss; Middleton.'[1]

Of these, at least half had been actively engaged in opposition to Mary. Robert himself had carefully kept out of trouble after his father's execution and his own imprisonment, but it is not unreasonable to suppose that he formed a point of contact between the hotter heads of the opposition and the Princess, or that this was anxiously mistrusted by her more moderate and powerful supporters.

Elizabeth inherited the high expectations of both the protestants and the secular gentry, and it was her peculiar triumph that she was able to disappoint both without alienating either. She was helped in this difficult task by another aspect of her inheritance—hatred and fear of Spain. Her subjects were prepared to accept many things that did not altogether please them in return for an assured escape from Spanish hegemony. One of the most lasting effects of Mary's unfortunate marriage was the Englishman's detestation of the Spaniard. There was far more to this hatred than a few seamen falling into the hands of the Inquisition; more even than the memory of the fires of Smithfield; there was fear based on the consciousness that England had once already had the narrowest escape from becoming part of the Habsburg Empire. All those, from the Queen down to the humblest adventurer, who had been associated with that escape benefited from the association. Most of all was this true of the parliamentary gentry, whose stubborn resistance to Philip's coronation and negligence in proceeding against Mary's enemies had finally wrecked the alliance and reduced the government to impotence. These gentlemen from 1558 onward became the backbone of English nationalism; the advocates of a national policy and a national church. Neither social upheaval nor changes at Westminster had substantially affected their power, for the centralization which had begun to transform the higher levels of the administration in the 1530's was still largely superficial. Detailed study

[1] George Adlard, *The Sutton Dudleys of England* (London, 1842), p. xv.

shows that local government was as personal as it had always been, and suffered from weaknesses which the central authority could do very little to cure. The exceptional amount of police work which fell to the local authorities during this period of crisis enables the historian to study them at work, and made the gentry themselves more aware of the vital role which they must play in the administration of national policies. They became more conscious of their powers of resistance, and more inclined to demand a voice in public affairs.

APPENDIX I
DISTRIBUTION OF RECORDED REBELS

Parish	No. of clergy and gentry	Others
Allington	1	1
Ash		1
Ashford		3
Aylesford	2	10
Badlesmere	1	
Bearsted		1
Bethersden		24
Birling		1
Bobbing		1
Borden		3
Boughton Malherbe	1	8
Boughton Monchelsea	2	3
Boxley	1	21
Brasted		12
Bredgar	1	
Brenchley		2
Bromley		1
Canterbury	1	4
Chalk		1
Charing		1
Chart Magna	2	12
Chart Parva	1	10
Chart Sutton	1	
Chiddingstone	1	
Chilham		1
Cobham	4	2
Cranbrook		14
Dartford		30
Detling		3
Ditton		1
Doddington	1	
East Farleigh		1
Egerton		7
Erith		2

Parish	No. of clergy and gentry	Others
Farningham		1
Faversham		1
Frindsbury		2
Frittenden		1
Gillingham		1
Gravesend		6
Greenwich		8
Hackington	2	1
Halden		1
Harrietsham		1
Hartley		1
Hartlip		1
Herne		2
Higham		2
Hinxhill	1	2
Hollingbourne		1
Horton Monarchorum	1	3
Hunton		4
Isle of Grain		1
Keston		1
Kingston	1	4
Langley		1
Leigh	1	1
Lenham	1	27
Maidstone	2	78
Malling		2
Milstead		2
Milton		11
Newington		4
Northfleet		2
Orpington		1
Pluckley	2	19
Rayham		4
Rochester		14
Rodmersham		1
St Margarets at Cliffe		1
St Mary Cray		1
St Paul's Cray		1
Sellinge		1
Sevenoaks		3
Sittingbourne		9
Smarden		32

Parish	No. of clergy and gentry	Others
Snodland		1
Southfleet	1	
Staple		1
Staplehurst		1
Stockbury		1
Stoke		1
Strood		6
Sundridge	2	16
Sutton Valence		2
Swanscombe		1
Thornham	1	
Tonbridge	2	11
Ulcombe		2
Upchurch		3
Waltham	1	
Welling		1
Wicheling	1	
Wickham	1	1
Willesborough		2
Wilmington		1
Woodchurch		1

WYATT'S RISING: (B) OTHER PLACES

Location	Clergy and gentry	Others
Bradgate (Leics.)		1
Brentford (Middx)		1
Deptford		1
Dulwich		1
Dunwich		1
Hackney		1
Halifax		1
Hamilton (Leics.)		1
Hatfield		5
Havant (Hants)		1
Lewes		4
London	15	61
Puddletown (Dorset)		1
Reading		3
Richmond		1
Southwark		37
Stoke Ferry		1
Thame (Oxon)		1
unidentified	2	67

SUFFOLK'S RISING

Location	Clergy and gentry	Others
Bradgate	6	
Coventry		3
Leicester		1
Loughborough	2	
Tilty (Essex)	1	
Woodcroft (Northants.)	1	

CAREW'S RISING

Mohun's Ottery	2	
Rewe	1	

APPENDIX II

FINES AND AMERCEMENTS RECORDED IN THE EXCHEQUER

(in order of record)

Note: Only those discharges specifically mentioned are recorded as such. In many cases where the amount of a fine is not stated, it was probably discharged in a single payment.

Name	Status	Amount due	Amount paid	Discharge
George Harper	Knt.	£1000		14/4/56*
Lady Willoughby	Widow of Anthony Knevett	£111/8/8	£20	
John Thorneton et al.	Yeoman	not stated		
Hugh Booth	Yeoman	£53	£60	7/11/55
Leonard Digges	Esq.	£49/17/8	£26/10	*
Thomas Pykes et al.	Husb.	£200	£24/18/10	13/2/55
John Warcoppe	Gent.	£40		10/11/56*
Gervase Maplesden	Butcher	£40		5/11/56
Edward Kingsnoth	Butcher	£60		10/11/56
Thomas Blundell	Mercer	£20		5/11/56
Clement Lutwyk	Yeoman	£26/13/4		29/10/56
William Smothing	Yeoman	£30		29/10/56
Peter Maplesden	Tailor	£133/6/8		16/11/56
William Tilden	Tailor	£100		29/10/56
Robert Merchant	Smith	£10		29/10/56
Alex. Fisher	Gent.	£40		16/11/56
Thomas Haslam et al.	Bricklayer	£10/13/4		29/10/56

* Indicates that process was originated in the upper Exchequer for the recovery of the debt.

Appendix II (contd.)—

Name	Status	Amount due	Amount paid	Discharge
John Barton	Butcher	£4	£3	10/11/56
Richard Tylman	Yeoman	£13/6/8		10/11/56
John Harris	Tailor	£30		3/11/56
William Smith et al.	Yeoman	£21/6/8		29/10/56
John Gosling et al.	Smith	£45/6/8		5/11/56
Humph. Dixon	Butcher	£40		13/10/56
John Fraye	Yeoman	£80		5/11/56*
David Willard	Yeoman	£66/13/4		10/11/56
William Browning	Gent.	£66/13/4		3/11/56
Thomas Bell	Butcher	£6/13/4		
Nicholas Butcher	Husb.	£133/6/8	£63/6/8	
William Cromer	Esq. }	£2666/13/4		
Robert Rudstone	Esq. }	+£500	£1637/6/8	2 Eliz. *
John Goldwell	Gent.	£66/13/4		30/10/59*
Thomas Culpepper	Gent.	£800	£266	*
William Isley	Knt.	£1000		29/5/60
Leonard Digges	(Iterum)	£241/13/4		7/5/58*
John Frankling	Gent.	£20		18/5/56
Henry Fane	Gent.	£266/13/4		25/10/57
Jane Wyatt	Widow of Sir Thomas Wyatt	£254/19/10		15/5/57
Thomas Milles	Gent.	n.s.		*
George Brooke	Lord Cobham	£452	£60	20/2/57

Name	Occupation			Date
Robert Piper	n.s.	£20		5/10/56
Thomas Godfrey	Innkeeper	n.s.	£5	
Clement Myllway	Yeoman	n.s.	£2	
John Standon	Yeoman	n.s.	£2	
Thomas Bourne	Gent.	n.s.	£2	
William Wingfield	Yeoman	n.s.	£5	
Thomas Plane	Yeoman	n.s.	£2	
John Stone	Tailor	n.s.	£1	
Roger Halford	Husb.	n.s.	£2	
John Godfrey	Mariner	n.s.	£1	
Henry Godfrey	Clothmaker	£26/13/4	£13/6/8	*
William Syming	Sadler	n.s.	£2	
John Spice	Glover	n.s.	£3/6/8	20/5/58
William Church	Tailor	n.s.	£6	*
John Levendale	Shearman	n.s.	£2/13/4	20/5/58
Richard Martyn	Tailor	n.s.	£2	20/5/58
Andrew Ockynfeld	Husb.	n.s.	£5	11/2/58
William Turner	Weaver	n.s.	£3/6/8	11/2/58
Jasper Loder	Minstrel	£3/6/8		20/5/58
Thomas Gylles	Carpenter	£1		15/2/58
Henry Glover	Labourer	£1		15/2/58
Edward Whatlowe	Tyler	£1		15/2/58
Thomas Crouch	Labourer	n.s.	£2	15/2/58
Robert Pell	Tailor	n.s.		

* Indicates that process was originated in the upper Exchequer for the recovery of the debt.

Appendix II (contd.)—

Name	Status	Amount due	Amount paid	Discharge
Henry Knock	Husb.	n.s.	£5	23/6/58
John Hunt	Weaver	n.s.	£4/6/8	29/6/58
Chris. Pollard	Shoemaker	n.s.	£2/13/4	20/5/58
John Pell	Clothier	n.s.	£6	13/5/58
Thomas Stonestreet	Clothmaker	£2		13/2/58
Gilbert Milles	Sawyer	n.s.		4/7/58*
Robert Knock	Husb.	£2/13/4	£4	20/5/58
John Tappenden	Labourer	£2		20/5/58
Peter Broadstreet	Miller	n.s.		21/5/58
William Hulse	Wheelwright	n.s.	£2	
Thomas Mapysden	Labourer	£2	£2/13/4	20/5/58
John Holnest	Labourer	£2		20/5/58
Lawrence Twysnod	Tailor	£2		20/5/58
Randolf Purcell	Clerk	£2		20/5/58
Henry Lodge	Butcher	£2		20/5/58
William Austen	Tailor	£2		20/5/58
William Jeffrey	Baker	n.s.		
John Lampnod	Labourer	n.s.	£2	
Thomas Laurence	Smith	n.s.	£2/13/4	20/4/59*
Nich. Selyard	Yeoman	n.s.	£2	20/4/59
Robert Crowe	Yeoman	n.s.	£5	20/4/59*
Oliver Maundry	Miller	n.s.	£5	20/4/59*
Thomas Foster	Husb.	n.s.	£2	

Richard Wood	Clothier	n.s.	£3/6/8
John Hawe	Tanner	n.s.	£1/13/4
Richard Gaston	Husb.	n.s.	£2

* Indicates that process was originated in the upper Exchequer for the recovery of the debt.

APPENDIX III

The Examination of Martin Dore
(SP, Vol. VII, no. 59)

Whatt was the fyrst occasyon of yor going into ffraunce and when yow went last over.

ffor whatt causes yow have remayned all this tyme in ffraunce.

How often tymes have yow hadd any talk or conference with Christofer Ashton Horses Tremaynes Dudley or any other of thatt companye and whatt hath byn theffect of the sayd talk or conference.

Whatt messages letters or tokens have yow hard or knowen to have byn sent from any the persons aforsayd to any within this realme, or from this realme to any of them.

How long remayned yow with Uvedale, att whatt tyme came yow fyrst to hym, uppon whatt occasion departed from hym, and whatt entertaynment hadd yow ther.

The fyrst occasyon of my goyng into france beyng the v or vi wycke after mycellmas was for that I (agreed) with Udall and ondman as conserneyng ondmans commysyon that he had granteyd of the emperor and farder for the transporteyng of wareys of my own and other marchants of lymington by yermothe.

After my aryvall yn france . . . I sharchyd the parteys in france for sum fraught vessell thatt myght have beyn a good pryse. thys I spendeyd the teyme for xiiii or xvi days. I returneyd agayn unto newhavyn and for that I sawe no good to be don for that present I sent my barcke unto the ile of wyghte agayn. After y remayneyd thare in france sharchyng the havens agayn the space of iii wyckes, then seyng no good to be don and drawyn towards crysmas, and for that I had never beyn at pareys y went thether whareas I remayneyd unteyll yt was vi or vii dayes before ester . . . and by cause of the dayley rumour of pese and warre beyng the heynderance of my purpose, and after the conclusyon of the pese the tyme drawyng towards ester (sic) y cam from parys unto deipe,[1] thynkeyng to have passeyd over into ynglond, whare I hard report that the passing (into) ynglond was layd that noman myght com over into france, nor from france into ynglon but that he was stayed and (sent) unto the consell, for that thare ware sarteyn gentelmen of ynglon in

[1] Dieppe.

trobull as Uvedall and frogmorton and sarteyn others, the whyche causeyd me to stay untell a more quyet teyme, and for that y supposeyd my remayneyng in france after that teyme myght have beyn an occaseyon of trobull y imageneyd whyche way I myght devyse to serfe the queynse heyghenys whareby I myght the better be abull to answer for my beyng yn france after that teme, wharefore y thowght yt good to worcke sum keynd of meaneys to (disparage) henry dudley and the fraynche men, so that the rest of the ingleysh-men myght have an evel opeyneyon in them.

Wharefore an viii days after ester y cam unto nuhaven[1] whareas y found asten franseys horsey and peter kelegrew. Ashedon and franseys declareyd unto me that they had resevyd iiii C crownes a peyce of the frayche kyng and shuld have iiii C crownes penseyon by the yere, after the end of whyche converseyseyon y calleyd ashedon and franseys horsey ageyn unto home y declareyd that henry dudley as I supposeyd was both a prowde man, not wyse and a leyer, and that the franche men ware (ungrateful) and untrue men that wold promys myche and dow notheyng and yf they deyd show aney plesure they wold loke to reseve x tymes as myche a gayne and to conclud that they ware the worst natur(ed) men levyng as henrey keylleygrew had showyd me before. They mad andswer agayn as conserneyng dudley they had provyd yt tru all redey for he showyd us that thare was x M pound at the waterseyd sente by the franche keyng before owre areyvale, the which sayd they aprovyd to be most untru and as conserneyng the franche men by cause of yowre report we wyll requere dudley immedeytly by letter that we may be ansereyd with expedeyceyon whyle that we have sum money lefte to helpe owre selfes withall, otherwyse we wyll detarmeyn sum other remedey whyle that owre money dothe last. After that I askeyd them what there pracketeys wase and what they shuld do they ansereyd agayn they knewe not but they ware comandyd from the keyng by master bartefeyld[2] to resort unto bartefeylds sisters howse and there to remayne untell they hard farder of the keyngs plesure. Thus y departyd from them for that teyme towardeys pareys whareas I remayned iiii days dureyng the whyche teyme y persuadeyd with nycolas tremayne conserneyng dudley and the franche men as y had done with ashedon and horssey whareupon he declared unto me that dudley was myche offendeyd with hym at heys fyrst commeyng over for that he shuld go abowt and practeys with owt heys consent meneyng yt as he seyd by the Robbeyng of the excheker unto whome tremayne ansereyd agayn that he wase to fare of beyng in france to

---

[1] Newhaven (i.e. Le Havre).
[2] Jean Bretville.

17*

be made prevey unto shyche thynges as ware don in Inglon howbeyt
sayde he yf yt had com to pase yt was determyneyd that yt shuld have
beyn brot into france and that yow shuld have had the ordereyng
thare of, with the whyche answere tremayne sayd that dudley was
well contenteyd, but then tremayne sayd unto me yf yt had com to
pas indeyd dudley shuld have had leyteyl to do tharewith. Then I
askeyd heym whether Uvedall was prevy unto that practeys he
ansereyd me that he was not, and as conserneyng dudley dureyng the
iiii days that y remayned in pareys y was ii teymys in hys companey
with henrey kylleygrue and nycolas tremayne and had con-
verceyaseyon with hym but on of the teymes thefeyckte whareof
after heys salutaseyon wase howe that ashedon horssey and the
keleygrews dyd. Y ansereyd well and had them comendeyd unto
hym, he demandeyd me how long y had remayneyd in france, y
showyd hym, he demandeyd me agayn how long y ment to remayne
in france y sayd I knew not my selfe. Thys was the chefeyst effeyckte
of owre talcke for he ys a man with whom y have had leytell
aquentense, and for that I perseveyd so many gentellmen of inglon
to resorte together y thowght yt not good to tarry long in pareys
wharefore y went agayn unto Nuhaven whareas y fownd franseys
horssey and peter keyleygrew who ware determeyneyd to travell
towardeys cane[1] whose companey y keypte and at owre comeyng
unto cane we met thare edward horssey with home y practeysseyd to
(disparage) dudley and the franchemen as y had don with the rest
before and at the last the horseys beyng determyneyd to go unto
bertefeylds sisters howse in Normandey whareas they ware com-
mandeyd by the Kyng to tarrey untell the hard farder of the kyngs
plesure y departeyd from them beyng a vi or vii wekeys after ester
towardeys nance[2] in bryttayn upon the reyver of low whare y
remayneyd about x or xi wekeys to understand the trafeyckes that
ware useyd thare and what good was to be don in them and farder
for that yt was a place whare a man mycht leve good chepe after the
whyche terme y returneyd agayn towardeys breyttanyne (sic) for
that y hard saye that on of the keleygrews was drowneyd and the
other takeyn. And to under Stand the truthe thareof and farder to
under Stand as well as y coud what ashedon the horsseys and the
rest of the genteyl men determyned to do and what shuld have beyn
there meneyng and after that to have resorteyd unto my lord
imbassedur and to have declareyd the hole unto hym and thareapon
to have deseyeryd heys favorabull letters over with me the whyche
yf he wold have refuseyd to have don y determeyneyd to have gone

---

[1] Caen.
[2] Nantes, on the Loire.

unto napuls in Italy unto champneys a frynd of myne and thare to have serveyd for a terme. And as y came from nance into normandey y hard that the keleygrews ware at the hoge[1] whereas asheton the horsseys the tremaynes and others ware also and that the keleygrews had beyn thare iiii or v weyckes, unto the which place y resorteyd also determyneyng in my selfe as nere as y coud to understand there hole pretence and then to have sort to have hendered yt as myche as y myght. So that at my comeyng thether the tusday at neyght the Wansday in the morneyng y communeyd with ashedon in demandeyng hem whether he ment in heys old ayge to seycke the favor of the se and what heys pretense wase, he answereyd me agayn that he was veray glad of my comeyng for that y wyll be bold to breycke my mynd unto yow and to have yowre adveyse declareyng that the keleygrews and the rest of the gentellmen hathe a viage in hand and what thare pretence ys y do not yt thoroley knowe, but they say unto jersey and they thyngke thoroley to have my companey and y have sort as myche as y cane to have them together that we myght thoroley comeyn of the matter but y can not yt breyng yt to pase for y promys yow sayd he thys ys a enterpreys not to be rashley takeyn in hand for thar be many matters to be comeyneyd of, sayng yf we shuld thus depart withowt the franche keyngs leafe in so myche as we have resevyd hys money and promysseyd hem serves we must nowys have hys dysplesure, and then loseyng thys contry whether shuld we resort y knowe not, wharefore sayd he y wyll tell yow secretley deseireyng yow to keype yt unto yowreselfe y mene not to take thys jurney in hand for yt ys to paynfull for me and yf the fraynche keyng withdrawe heys intertaynment sayd he yt as long a y may have the leyberte of hys contrey y care not for y have yt left a M crowneys or ii the profyts whareof wyll be abull to fynd me, and a man or ii apon the whyche determynaseyon y commendeyd hem verey myche yn saying that yt was wysly determyneyd of hym and as for that he had sayd unto me yt shuld be as secret as thowghe yt ware yn hymselfe. Whareupon the nexte daye erley yn the morneyng he departeyd so that after hys departeyng the hole companey ware in dowte of hys meneyng and that he wold com nomore. After thys y bracke with edward horssey that y dowteyd myche that ashedon wold not go thys journey that was determyneyd as y supposeyd by cause of sarteyn words that y hard hym report in declareyng how he dowteyd to depart withowt the franche kyngs faver and the rest of the comynycaseyon that he had with me, in persuadeyng farder with hym that yf ashedon shuld not go thys jurney yt was verey dowtfull what he shuld mene thare by and that the jurney wase not to be

---

[1] La Hogue, or Hougue, in the Cotentin Peninsula.

takeyn yn hand for that he myght yf he wente unonestley to worke them myche trobull, whareapon he was thoroley determyneyd not to go the jurney withowt that ashedon went with theym and then was franseys horssey determyneyd to do as hys brother edward deyd whareapon thare grew halfe a contenseyon betwyxte the tremaynes and the horsseys so that the tremaynes sayd that they wold go with the keleygrews for that they had promyssed them althowghe the rest wold not. Whareapon on of the tremayns cam unto me persuadeyng me to contynue the jurney with them and that yt shuld be a teyme well spent and that myche profeyt myght come thareof yn sayng farder that or yt ware long he hopeyd that on shuld com into france that shuld make them all glad in declareyng secretly unto me that the vedam[1] had sent unto my lord cortney that yf yt shuld plese hym to come into france he wold provyd for hym xxx M crowneys and aney other theyng that he had besed shuld be at hys commandement. Treymayne sayd that my lord cortney sent the vidame word agayn that he thankeyd hym myche deseyreyng hem to continue hys fryndshyp towards hem but my lord cortney sayd that yt was not for hym to enter aney keyngs realme apon aney subgets promys. Tremayne showyd me farder that they had wonne goer[2] to be of there companey. He had declareyd unto them that he was sent over by the quenes heyghnys and the consell to be a spey amongeyst them to have under Standeyd ther doyngs and so to have made sertyfycat. As conserneyng tremayns request to go with them that jurney, y answereyd hem agayn that yf y persevyd that the companey dedd agre within them selfes and that y myght perseve aney lykelode of good sucseyse in the jurney y wold go with them. Then after thys the horsseys came unto me and sayd we have persevyd yowre wordeys to be tru bothe of dudley and also of the fraychemen for dudley hathe resevyd a dereyckte answere of the franche kyng that he wyll (meddle) no farder with the inglyshemen and farder thare hathe beyne a proclymacyon in normandy whareas we lay that no ynglysheman shuld remayne in that contry so that (we are) drevyn of forse to depart that contry. Then y persuadeyd with them that y thowght yt best for them to go into italy whyle there money deyd last and to seycke to serfe thare and yn so doyng y sayd y wold keype them companey, thys y sort to spend the teme amongeyst them untell y myght se the uttermost of there (intention) and then to have resorteyd unto my lord imbassadour to have made report of the hole and to have requesteyd hys faverabull letters. Thys in spendeyng the time amongst them beyng at deyner with them a shypebord the sunday

---

[1] François de Vendôme, Vidame of Chartres.
[2] Gower. Probably Thomas Gower, at one time treasurer of Berwick.

after my comyng thether was takeyn by the quenes heyghtness shyps and so brot into inglon.

As conserneyng letters or tokeyns sent by them into ynglon or from ynglon unto them y have knowne of none for y have not remayneyd myche amongest them as yt dothe apere by my declaracion of my doings.

My fyrst comyng unto Uvedall wase about the begynnyng of lent was twelfemoneythes and y remayned at yermothe untyll my goyng over into france the which was v or vi wyckes after mycaylmas last past the occasion of my departeyng was for the ajoineyng with hym and ondman in ondmans commysion whyche was the occasion of my comyng over into france. My entertaynment was xx markys by the ere and to go and com as y thowght good.

The namys of the gentelmen that ware in pareys at my beyng there

henrey dudley	I have beyn in dudleys companey at on time ii days
Sr rafe bagnole	in ashedons at ii sondrey times vi days
cornwale	in the tremaynes at ii sundrie times viii days
nycolas tremayne	in the horsses companey at iii sundrey times xii or xiiii days.
chydle	
colbe	
Wrothe	

Clearly the date tentatively assigned to this document in the SP (March) is much too early. The chronology of Dore's movements after Easter is not very clear, but the conversations which he relates seem to have taken place on a number of occasions between mid-March and the end of June. The rumour of the Killigrews' disaster to which he refers seems to have been a false alarm, several weeks before their real discomfiture. Dore's reliability is not above question, but his mention of the proposed trip to Jersey, and Henri's temporary reaction against the exiles are convincing. The manner of his own capture is obscure. It is almost certain that he was not with the Killigrews, and he may have been apprehended by sheer chance, although the escape of his dining companions is also puzzling. The probable date of his examination is July, and the fact that no action was taken against him suggests that his suspicious behaviour was not taken very seriously. The main interest of his rather rambling self-justification lies in the picture which it presents of the exiles' position in France after the collapse of their main 'practyse'. The clear implication that the exchequer plot was independent of Dudley's main intrigue is not supported by any other evidence, and it seems probable that in the irritation of disappointment the other exiles were simply belittling Dudley and all that he had attempted to do. This is supported by some remarks in Killigrew's examination (SP, Vol. IX, no. 25) which show that the exiled gentry were profoundly disillusioned with Dudley and his schemes during June and July 1556. Francis Horsey is reported as saying that ' . . . he lamentyd mowche hys cas, & hys brothers & all the reste of the gentillmens yt were yn those pts, & tolde me that they were all bownde to curse Dudley for that he hadde browght them to theyre utter undowyng. . . .'

APPENDIX IV

Names of those arrested, indicted, or examined for their part in the Dudley conspiracy.

Name	Date of arrest	Date of indictment	First examination	Trial	Execution or pardon
Sir Nicholas Arnold	29 April	—	6 May	—	—
Catherine Ashley	—	—	9 March (May?)	—	—
Christopher Ashton (Sen.)	*	29 April	—	—	—
Christopher Ashton (Jun.)	*	29 April	—	—	—
Sir Ralph Bagnall	*	12 Dec.	—	—	†28 June '57
Balcriffe	—	—	March	—	—
John Bedell	18 March	20 April	26 March	2 June	9 June
Blacklock	—	—	April	—	—
Brace	11 March	—	—	—	—
Lord Bray	May	Oct.	—	Nov.	—
Jean Bretville	*	29 April	—	—	—
Brown	11 March	—	—	—	—
William Bury	—	27 June (?)	16 April	—	†14 May '57
Catherine Butler	—	—	20 March	—	—
Sylvestra Butler	—	27 June	—	—	—
John Calton	*	29 April	—	—	†6 May '57
Roger Carter	13 April	—	13 May	—	—
Sir Thomas Cawarden	March	—	—	—	—

* Fled overseas   † Pardoned   All dates 1556 unless otherwise stated

Appendix IV (contd.)—

Name	Date of arrest	Date of indictment	First examination	Trial	Execution or pardon
Sir John Chichester	29 April	—	—	—	—
Robert (alias Edward) Cornwall	*	29 April	—	—	†4 March '62
Sir William Courtenay	29 April	4 Nov.	—	—	8 March '57
John Dale	*	29 April	—	—	—
John Danyell	18 March	29 April	11 April	7 May	7 July
John Dethicke	18 March	29 April	18 April	2 June	9 June
Martin Dore	—	—	March (May?)	—	—
William Draper	—	—	11 March	—	—
Henry Dudley	*	29 April	—	—	19 Jan. '57
Anthony Foster	*	2 July	—	—	—
William Hammond	*	(Proclaimed 4 April)	—	—	—
Thomas Hinnes	18 March	29 April	27 March	—	—
William Hinnes	—	—	—	—	—
Edward Horsey	*	29 April	—	—	30 July '65
Francis Horsey	*	29 April	—	—	—
Peter Killigrew	8 Aug.	—	26 Sept.	—	—
Sir Anthony Kingston	March	—	8 April	—	May '57
Edward Lewkenor	—	June	—	—	Died April
Fernando Lygons	March	—	23 April	—	Died Sept.
Leonard Marshall	29 July	—	30 July	15 June	—
Meverell	*	(Proclaimed 4 April)	—	—	—

Henry Peckham	18 March	29 April	9 May	7 May	7 July
John Peers	—	—	16 March	—	—
John Perrot	29 April	—	—	—	—
Sir John Pollard	29 April	4 Nov.	—	—	†30 Jan. '58
Edward Randall	March (?)	—	—	—	—
Rawlins (2)	18 March	29 April	—	—	—
Roger Reynolds	*	—	—	—	—
Stephen Rike	—	24 April	—	2 June	—
William Rossey	18 March	—	16 March	—	9 June
Sir John St Lowe	—	—	30 March	—	—
Henry Smith	18 March	2 July	31 May	21 Nov.	†15 Dec.
William Staunton	25 March	29 April	March	12 May	19 May
John Throgmorton	18 March	18 April	31 March	21 April	28 April
Nicholas Tremayne	*	29 April	—	—	—
Richard Tremayne	*	29 April	—	—	—
Edward Turner	—	29 April	23 March	18 June	†11 April '57
Richard Uvedale	March	18 April	—	21 April	28 April
Edmund Verney	—	11 June	—	—	†12 July '57
Francis Verney	—	11 June	—	18 June	†10 April '57
John Walker	March	6 July	—	16 Nov.	†6 May '57
William West	May	27 June	—	30 June	†10 April '57
Thomas White	March	—	30 March	—	—

* Fled overseas   † Pardoned   All dates 1556 unless otherwise stated

A blank (—) simply indicates lack of information; thus Lewkenor, who was tried in June, was clearly arrested, but no date is known.

A SELECT BIBLIOGRAPHY

Of sources and secondary works

MANUSCRIPT SOURCES

In the Public Record Office

King's Bench   Placita Coram Rege, Michaelmas Term 1553 to Michaelmas 1558.
Controllment Rolls 1553/4—1558/9.
Files of Ancient Indictments 1553–8.
Baga de Secretis, Pouches 26, 28, 29, 30, 32, 34.

Exchequer   Brevia Recepta January 1555/6—January 1557/8.
Receipt Rolls, Michaelmas Term 1554—Easter Term 1560.
Memoranda Rolls of the King's Remembrancer 1553/4—1558/9.

State Papers   Domestic, Mary. Vols. 1–4, 7, 13. Addenda Vol. 8.

In the British Museum

The Wyatt MSS. Loan Collection 15, deposited by the Earl of Romney.
(A MSS book, compiled in the eighteenth century, with a numbered contents list).

In the London Guildhall

Letter Books of the Court of Aldermen. Journal of the Common Council.

PRINTED SOURCES

Bendlowes, William; *Les Reports de G.B. des divers pleadings et cases en le Court del Common-bank etc.*, London (1689).

Brown, Rawdon; *Calendar of State Papers, Venetian,* by Rawdon Brown and others, London (1864–98).

Bruce, John; *Letters and Papers of the Verney Family*, Camden Society, lvi (1853).

Calendar of the Patent Rolls, Philip and Mary, London (1936–39). Elizabeth, London (commenced 1938).

Cobbett, William; *A complete collection of State Trials*, by William Cobbett, T. B. Howell and others, London (1816–98).

Dasent, J. R.; *Acts of the Privy Council*, London (1890–1907).

Hamilton, W. D. (ed.); *A Chronicle of England*, by Charles Wriothesley, Camden Society, New Series, xi (1875, 1877).

Luders, A.; *Statutes of the Realm*, by A. Luders and others, London, (1810–28).

Muller, J. A.; *Letters of Stephen Gardiner*, Cambridge (1933).

Nichols, J. G.; *The Greyfriars Chronicle of London*, Camden Society, liii (1852).

The Diary of Henry Machyn, Camden Society, xlii (1848).

The Chronicle of Queen Jane, and of two years of Queen Mary, Camden Society, xlviii (1850).

Rawlinson MS, B 102, ff. 83–5. *English Historical Review*, Vol. xxxviii (1923).

Reports of the Historical Manuscripts Commission, Appendices to various reports.

Returns of Members of Parliament; Parliamentary papers 1878, lxii, pts. i-iii.

Steele, Robert; *Tudor and Stuart Proclamations*, Oxford (1910).

Turnbull, W.; *Calendar of State Papers, Foreign*, London (1861).

Tyler, Royall; *Calendar of State Papers, Spanish*, by Royall Tyler and others, London (1862–1954).

Vertot, R. A. de; *Ambassades de Messieurs de Noailles en Angleterre*, by R. A. de Vertot and C. Villaret, Leyden (1763).

Whatmore, L. E.; *Archdeacon Harpesfield's Visitation*, 1557, by L. E. Whatmore and W. Sharp, Catholic Record Society, xlv-xlvi (1950–51).

CONTEMPORARY PRINTED WORKS

Bradford, John; *The copye of a letter sent by J. Bradforthe to the erles of Arundel, Darbie, Shrewsbury and Penbroke*, London (?) (1556).

Griffiths, J.; *An exhortation concerning good order and obedience* reprinted from the edition of 1547 in *Homilies appointed to be read in churches*, by J. Griffiths, Oxford (1859).

Goodman, Christopher; *How superior powers ought to be obeyed of their subjects*, J. Crispin, Geneva (1558).

Huggarde, Miles; *The displaying of the Protestantes*, R. Cayley, London (1556).

Ponet, John; *A shorte treatise of politike power*, Strasburg (1556).
Proctor, John; *The Historie of Wyate's rebellion*, London (1554). Reprinted by E. Arber in *An English Garner*, London (1877–96), Vol. VIII.

SECONDARY WORKS

Allen, J. W.; *A history of political thought in the sixteenth century*, London (1928).
Archaeologia Cantiana.
Baumer, F. L.; *The Early Tudor theory of kingship*, New Haven (1940).
Cruden, R. P.; *The history of Gravesend and the port of London*, London (1843).
Dodds, M. H. and Ruth; *The Pilgrimage of Grace, 1536–7, and the Exeter conspiracy, 1538*, Cambridge (1915).
Dugdale, William; *The Antiquities of Warwickshire*, edited by William Thomas, London (1730).
Economic History Review. Articles and contributions by R. H. Tawney, Lawrence Stone and H. R. Trevor-Roper concerning the 'rise of the gentry', 1941–1954.
Elton, G. R.; *The Tudor Revolution in Government*, Cambridge (1953).
Foxe, John; *Acts and Monuments of the English Martyrs*, edited by S. R. Cattley and George Townsend, London (1837–41).
Garrett, C. H.; *The Marian Exiles*, Cambridge (1938).
Harbison, E. H.; *Rival Ambassadors at the Court of Queen Mary*, Princeton (1940).
Hasted, Edward; *A history and topographical survey of the county of Kent*, Canterbury (1778–99).
Holinshed, Raphael; *Chronicles*, edited by Henry Ellis, London (1807–8).
Muller, J. A.; *Stephen Gardiner and the Tudor reaction*, New York (1926).
Neale, Sir John; *Elizabeth I and her parliaments 1559–1581*, London (1953); and *Queen Elizabeth*, London (1934).
Nichols, John; *History of the antiquities of the county of Leicester*, London (1795–1815).
Pollard, A. F.; *The history of England from the accession of Edward VI to the death of Elizabeth*, London (1913).
Pollard, A. W. and Redgrave, G. R.; *A short title catalogue of books printed in England, Scotland and Ireland, and of English books printed abroad, 1475–1640*, Bibliographical Society (1926).
Prescott, H. F. M.; *Mary Tudor*, London (1953).
Read, Conyers; *Mr. Secretary Cecil and Queen Elizabeth*, London (1955).

Rezneck, Samuel; 'The trial of treason in Tudor England', in *Essays in honor of C. H. McIlwain*, Cambridge (Mass.) (1936).

Rose-Troup, Frances; *The Western rebellion of 1549*, London (1913).

Russel, F. W.; *Kett's rebellion in Norfolk*, London (1859).

Shaaber, M. A.; *Some forerunners of the newspaper in England, 1476–1622*, Philadelphia (1929).

Stephen, Leslie, and Lee, Sidney; *Dictionary of National Biography*, London (1885–1903).

Stow, John; *The Annals of England*, London (1592).

Strype, John; *Ecclesiastical Memorials*, London (1721).

Tawney, R. H.; *The agrarian problem in the sixteenth century*, London (1912).

Tytler, P. F.; *England under the reigns of Edward VI and Mary*, London (1839).

Weisner, Louis; *La jeunesse d'Elizabeth d'Angleterre*, Paris (1878).

Zeeveld, W. G.; *Foundations of Tudor policy*, Cambridge (Mass.) (1948).

INDEX

Names of other places are to be found in Appendix I (pp. 249–52) and of other people in Appendix II (pp. 253–57) and Appendix IV (pp. 265–67).